THE STRANGE CASE

OF

ROBERT LOUIS STEVENSON

Malcolm Elwin has also written:

THE FIRST ROMANTICS
THE LIFE OF LLEWELYN POWYS
SAVAGE LANDOR
OLD GODS FALLING
DE QUINCEY (Great Lives)
VICTORIAN WALLFLOWERS
THACKERAY: A Personality
CHARLES READE: A Biography

ROBERT LOUIS STEVENSON

Aged thirty-five. From the portrait by John Singer Sargent
Reproduced by kind permission of the Taft Museum, Cincinnati, Ohio

The Strange Case

of

ROBERT LOUIS STEVENSON

by

MALCOLM ELWIN

MACDONALD : LONDON

First published 1950

Published by
Macdonald & Co. (Publishers) Ltd.,
43 Ludgate Hill
Made and printed in Great Britain by
Purnell and Sons, Ltd., Paulton
(Somerset) and London

PREFACE

BY WAY OF DEDICATION

to Louis Marlow

Dear Louis,

At various times between the ages of thirteen and thirty, I read all Stevenson's novels and stories, except *Prince Otto* and, I think, one or two of his less successful efforts, like *The Dynamiter* and *The Story of a Lie*. In the winter of 1937–38, when preparing my study of popular Late-Victorian and Edwardian literature, *Old Gods Falling*, I re-read all of them—even *The Black Arrow*, which alone defied the enthusiasm of an enjoyable journey through the twenty volumes of the Pentland Edition last winter. As you know from that study, I have scant respect in general for George Moore's integrity as critic or as artist, but I was impressed by the flash of shrewd discernment that enabled him to assert, so long ago as 1888, in *Confessions of a Young Man*, 'If any man living in this end of the century needed freedom of expression for the distinct development of his genius, that man is R. L. Stevenson'.

The truth of this statement becomes astonishingly apparent in reading Stevenson's fiction. He is a master of narrative, with an unerring sense of the essential, enabling ruthless rejection of the temptation to digressive embellishment; he is evidently fascinated, not only by the analysis of character—as in *Jekyll and Hyde*, in Herrick of *The Ebb-Tide*, in Dodd of *The Wrecker*—but also in the play of character upon character, as with Alan Breck and David in *Kidnapped*, with the brothers in *The Master of Ballantrae*, with Dodd and Pinkerton, with father and son in *Weir of Hermiston*. Yet, except inconclusively in *Prince Otto* and rather tiresomely and trivially in *Catriona*, he never admits sex into the conflict of his characters. As he confessed, 'I usually get out of it by not having any women in it at all', but *The Master of Ballantrae* might have been one of

v

the world's masterpieces in romantic tragedy if he had allowed Alison Durie to act according to character and the demands of his design.

Stevenson was too complete an artist not to recognise the limitations self-imposed upon his fiction, and it seemed to me that no other novelist, except Thackeray, had suffered more restively under the censorship of what Charles Reade called the 'prurient prudery' of popular taste, dictated by worship of the 'old gods', respectability and humbug. Ample evidence supporting this impression appeared from an examination of Stevenson's *Letters to His Family and Friends*, though, as Henry James wrote to Sidney Colvin on publication of the first edition, the reader has a 'sense of omissions and truncations—one *smells* the things unprinted.' Yet none of Stevenson's earlier biographers attempted any explanation; all were content with lip-service to the legend successfully established by Stevenson's widow through her two principal satellites—Stevenson's old friend, Sidney Colvin, as editor of his *Letters*, and Stevenson's cousin, Graham Balfour, who wrote the official biography, published in 1901, under the direction of Fanny Stevenson and Colvin.

Stevenson's death in Samoa in 1894, at the age of forty-four, supplied a sensation for the reading public in the golden age of moneyed materialism, which delighted in sentimentality as relief from the tedium of routine respectability. It had been interesting to reflect that a celebrated romantic novelist had been driven by tubercular disease to seek health, as adventurously as any hero of his own romances, from residence in a remote island of the South Seas. His sudden end, at an age when he had been expected to produce the crowning achievements of his career, impressed as a tragedy for literature —an impression fortified by the timely publication of two unfinished works, the lively historical romance of *St. Ives* being completed with due, if somewhat perfunctory, competence and reverence by Sir Arthur Quiller-Couch, while the fragment of *Weir of Hermiston* was justly assessed as the making of a masterpiece.

The custodians of his reputation recognised that the maintenance of his royalties might depend upon an endorsement of the popular impression of Stevenson by the eagerly awaited biography and edition of his letters. Since his death, all the writers of reminiscences, like Andrew Lang and Edmund Gosse, had paid tribute to his gallantry and his personal charm; it seemed necessary that nothing should be admitted to disturb the popular conception of a *beau chevalier* of letters. Graham Balfour was presented with a difficult task, which he performed with a strategic skill worthy of one destined to a distinguished career in the public service.

The only child of respectable, God-fearing parents, Stevenson was shown to have progressed from a sheltered childhood to dutiful studies at the university with a view to entering his father's profession of engineering. His father was naturally afflicted with disappointment when his only son renounced the security of the engineering profession for the precarious pursuit of his literary gift, but a society still based upon the rewards of individual endeavour could applaud the courage of a decision eventually leading to eminence. The happiness of a home life otherwise 'harmonious' was threatened by youthful tendencies to free-thinking in religion and politics, but the extent of these tendencies was presumably exaggerated by Stevenson's father, a high Tory and a devout churchman; Stevenson himself stated, in 'Crabbed Age and Youth', that 'all opinions, properly so called, are stages on the road to truth,' and his biographer was able to show that he committed no very revolutionary indiscretion beyond the pardonable extravagances of youth. He affected eccentricities of manner and dress, induced by a partiality for the bohemianism of the painters' settlements at Fontainebleau; but he was saved from worse excesses by the wise influence of a lady who afterwards married his friend Colvin and became a courted literary hostess. At twenty-nine, this gallant, charming, irrepressible, if somewhat irresponsible, romantic effected the most romantic gesture of his life in crossing half the world to California to win a wife from a broken marriage. Though wounded by his want of consideration, his parents behaved nobly, bestowing forgiveness and an income sufficient for supporting a wife, and their generosity was fittingly rewarded by finding that their irresponsible son had chosen a middle-aged woman of character and respectability, whose correct deportment would curb any indecorous inclinations in the future. Providence justly rewarded his recklessness with a decline in health condemning him to an invalid existence, but recompensed him with the tender devotion of a steadfast wife, whose watchful nursing enabled his survival to produce the works that entertained the world.

Such was the legend. One of his oldest friends, W. E. Henley, raised a solitary voice in protest that 'this Seraph in Chocolate' was not the 'old, riotous, intrepid, scornful Stevenson' who had sometimes shared the struggling journalist's poor lodgings before he 'trained it "across the plains" and ended for the time being as a married man and a Silverado squatter'. But Henley was an unsuccessful man of letters, subsisting with the aid of a civil list pension, who was known to have quarrelled with Stevenson after his rise to fame; and Henry James expressed the general view in regarding his outburst as 'rather a striking and lurid—and so far interesting case—of long discomfortable jealousy and ranklement turned at last to posthumous (as it were!)malignity.'

The legend survived Henley's attack. But its failure to supply any adequate indication of the directions of Stevenson's artistic development produced an effect upon you, Louis—and upon others of your generation, like our friend, John Cowper Powys—inspiring suspicion that there was 'something spurious' about Stevenson. It is surprising that the seeds of suspicion lay scattered so long before sprouting into the argued analysis of Mr. Frank Swinnerton's *R. L. Stevenson: A Critical Study* in 1914. Yet even then—a decade before 'debunking' became the fashion in biography—Mr. Swinnerton spoke too soon, for, when his book was reprinted ten years later, he referred ruefully to the 'extraordinary indignation' excited by his criticism.

After Fanny Stevenson's death in February 1914, a quantity of Stevenson's 'literary remains' were sold by auction in New York. Evidence appeared that Balfour had suppressed facts in such a bowdlerised version of Stevenson's youth as Stevenson himself had foreseen that Colvin might have written. In an unpublished letter to Henley, written in 1881 after reading Colvin's monograph on Landor, Stevenson wrote: 'As you say, his life of R.L.S. will be a joke. "Chapter 2, Youth in Edinburgh" is like to be a masterpiece of the genteel evasion.'

Yet the legend lingered, though decayed and down-at-heel. Some years after J. A. Steuart—in his *Robert Louis Stevenson: Man and Writer*, 2 vols., 1924—had investigated the facts of Stevenson's youth, the feminine author of a brief biography remarked briskly of his early 'love-affairs': 'it seems a waste of time to speculate on the possible details, for Stevenson never denied that he did have affairs, nor do any of the particular incidents seem to have made a lasting impression on his life or work.' The 'details' include the emotional effects upon Stevenson's character; if she chose to ignore them, this lady was evidently wasting her time and that of her readers. Steuart's revelations of Stevenson's troubled youth effectively refuted Mr. Swinnerton's most cogent charge against his quality as an essayist—if, as the legend related, Stevenson had passed from a sheltered childhood, through only the usual vagaries of adolescence, to his character as a gifted, charming, and industrious invalid, how could he have acquired the experience to probe the problems of life in *Virginibus Puerisque*?

Though comprising only two chapters in a survey of a period, my study of Stevenson in *Old Gods Falling* attempted a critical account of his life and work in the light of all published material; its second part advanced the theory, derived from an examination of his letters and his novels, that his art as a novelist seriously suffered from the limitation on freedom of expression imposed by popular taste, and that his wife's restrictive influence rendered his marriage the controlling factor in his literary career, as well as in his later life. The critics, in general, remained unconvinced. 'To say that Stevenson suffered frustration rather than resort to the subterfuges of convention,' wrote one English reviewer, 'is surely putting too great a strain upon our credulity'. Discussing in three columns 'the upshot' of my 'young and lively book', the *New York Times* had scant patience with the chapters on Stevenson; deriding the suggestion that 'Stevenson's marriage ruined his health and his art', the reviewer added with almost spinsterish venom, 'I think it is time to admit that men, even when they are writers, marry where their inclination is, and that wives should not be blamed for uncovering their deficiencies.'

I think the idea of your novel, *The Devil in Crystal*—in which the hero is enabled to live part of his life over again, repeating the same situations with the same people—would have appealed to Stevenson. Particularly he would have appreciated the scene where the hero, afflicted with sudden panic at the prospect of 'going through all that again' with one of the women in his life, escapes into a lavatory to avoid meeting her for dinner. If Stevenson could have lived over his life again and returned once more from his inland voyage for that first glimpse of Fanny Osbourne 'in the lamplight through the open window' at Grez, surely, instead of entering by the window, he would have slipped away, silently and unseen, under cover of the night!

At the time of *Old Gods Falling*, my conception of Fanny's part in Stevenson's life was largely speculative, suggested by occasional remarks in Stevenson's letters and substantiated by deductions from hints in his letters and Fanny's. I was then unaware that his original letters to Mrs. Sitwell and to Henley were available for inspection at the National Library of Scotland. Last year, when I was re-reading Stevenson in preparation for writing an introduction to the Macdonald Illustrated Classics edition of his essays, I realised that, though there had since appeared several studies of Stevenson, none had added to the information available when I was writing on the subject twelve years ago. My edition of the essays was to appear in celebration of the centenary of his birth; surely a true and fully documented biography was long overdue. I set to work on investigating the possibilities, and the result is here.

In the course of my work I have accumulated many debts of gratitude. I am deeply indebted to the enthusiasm and assiduity of Mr. R. B. Childs, of the University of Nevada and Oriel College, Oxford, in making copies for me of countless unpublished letters of Stevenson's. I am indebted to the National Library of Scotland and their Keeper of Manuscripts, Mr. W. Park, for their courtesy and consideration in placing at my disposal Stevenson's letters to Mrs. Sitwell and to Henley. I tender my grateful thanks for various acts of kind and generous assistance to Mrs. Muriel Mirylees, of Stevenson Memorial House, Edinburgh; to Mr. Harold Downs and Mr. Harold G. B. Wood, of the Robert Louis Stevenson Club, London; to Mr. Frank Otto, of the Savile Club, and to Mr. Douglas W. Bryant, the Director of Libraries at the United States Information Service. To my friends, Eric Harvey and W. F. Parrish, I am indebted for an unfailing fund of patient consideration and wise counsel during this book's preparation.

To the Society of Authors, as literary representatives of the Estate of the late Robert Louis Stevenson, I am deeply indebted for generous permission to use copyright material for quotation. To my predecessors among Stevenson's biographers, I have already indicated my inevitable debt to the official *Life of Robert Louis Stevenson*, by Sir Graham Balfour, 2 vols., 1901, and to *Robert Louis Stevenson: Man and Writer*, by J. A. Steuart, 2 vols., 1924; of the many other biographical and critical studies of Stevenson, besides the short studies by Frank Swinnerton and G. K. Chesterton, I would mention, for reference by students, the *Life of Robert Louis Stevenson*, by Rosaline Masson, 1923. To the late Sir Sidney Colvin, every student of Stevenson must record a debt of gratitude. His task, as editor of Stevenson's *Letters*, was fraught with pitfalls. Doubtless he suffered many qualms of conscience from such criticism as Henry James's about 'omissions and truncations'; he added many more letters when he published the four-volume edition of Stevenson's *Letters* in 1911; still more when, in the year of his wife's death, he edited the five volumes in the Tusitala Edition, 1924. I have used the Tusitala Edition of the *Letters*, though, for general reading purposes, I prefer the well-printed, if ill-edited, Pentland Edition of 1906, and the Skerryvore Edition of 1924, which contains the prefatory notes and introductions by Fanny Stevenson and Lloyd Osbourne.

To you, Louis, I offer the dedication of this book, partly as a mark of our friendship and partly in gratitude for the immense assistance you generously gave to me when I was writing the *Life* of your old friend, Llewelyn Powys. But I also feel that it is appropriate for you to be thus associated with this attempt to present a true biography of Stevenson, firstly, because you were confessedly prejudiced against his work by the apparent falsity of the legend associated with his name, and secondly because, like Stevenson, you have always professed and practised a passionately fastidious care for the art of writing. If this book enables you, and other readers, to enjoy more fully the varied works of one of the most graceful writers in English, it will have amply achieved its purpose.

Your affectionate friend,

MALCOLM ELWIN.

Vention Sands,
North Devon,
August 1950.

CONTENTS

xiii

CONTENTS

ILLUSTRATIONS

CHAPTER ONE

BACKGROUND AND BOYHOOD

'Any view of Burns would be misleading which passed over in silence the influences of his home and his father.'—*Some Aspects of Robert Burns.*

IN EDINBURGH, towards the end of the eighteenth century, lived a merchant-burgess named Thomas Smith. A shipowner and underwriter, he also owned a manufactory, one department of which was devoted to oil lamps. His father—also a shipowner in a small way—had been drowned at sea, and memory of that tragedy may have suggested to the son the value of his oil lamps for use in lighthouses. He succeeded in impressing the authorities with his idea, and, having designed a method of oil-lighting to supersede the primitive fires used as beacons, he was appointed engineer to the Board of Northern Lighthouses.

This was in 1786. Though only thirty-three, Smith was a widower with five children. Seeking a wife who would play a mother's part to his young family and also grace his increasing prosperity and improved position in life, he chose wisely. About his own age, Jean Stevenson had as a girl made a romantic marriage with the heir to a handsome estate in the West Indies, but her husband, at twenty-two, had died of fever while pursuing a defaulting manager in the Caribbean. Jean Stevenson was left with an infant son; in the years of her struggle with poverty she found consolation in piety and cherished the hope that her son might become a minister. In marrying Smith she could feel gratitude for being restored to the comforts of her youth and satisfaction in finding a stepfather for her son at an age when he most needed a man's guidance.

Robert Stevenson was in his fifteenth year at the time of his mother's second marriage. A boy who had never known a father's authority might have resented its usurpation by a stepfather; he might have felt hostility towards the man who had ousted him from monopoly of his mother's affections. But Thomas Smith was an enthusiast; having earned his appointment by the success of an invention, he was full of zeal for innovation and improvement, and he infected his stepson with his enthusiasm. As Robert's grandson was to write just over a century later, in *Records of a Family of Engineers*:

'The engineer of to-day is confronted with a library of acquired results; tables and formulæ to the value of folios full have been calculated and recorded; and the student finds everywhere in front of him the footprints of the pioneers. In the eighteenth century the field was largely unexplored; the engineer must read with his own eyes the face of nature; he arose a volunteer, from the workshop or the mill, to undertake works which were at once inventions and adventures. It was not a science then—it was a living art; and it visibly grew under the eyes and between the hands of its practitioners.'

Probably his mother's ambition that he should become a minister had never much appealed to Robert. Eagerly he embraced the adventurous career opened to him by his stepfather, spending his summers on expeditions for the erection of lighthouses on remote and rocky islets, his winters in the necessary studies at the university. At nineteen he was superintending the building of a lighthouse on an islet in the Firth of Clyde, absorbed in the work which remained the passion of his life.

'The seas into which his labours carried the new engineer were still scarce charted, the coasts still dark; his way on shore was often far beyond the convenience of any road; the isles in which he must sojourn were still partly savage. He must toss much in boats; he must often adventure on horseback by the dubious bridletrack through unfrequented wildernesses; he must sometimes plant his lighthouse in the very camp of wreckers; and he was continually enforced to the vicissitudes of outdoor life. The joy of my grandfather in this career was strong as the love of woman. It lasted him through youth and manhood, it burned strong in age, and at the approach of death his last yearning was to renew these loved experiences. What he felt himself he continued to attribute to all around him. And to this supposed sentiment in others I find him continually, almost pathetically, appealing; often in vain.'

With fellow-feeling his grandson recognised in Robert Stevenson the romantic artist, doomed to loneliness in companionship with aspirations beyond the power of others to appreciate.

Having romance enough in his work, he sought none in a wife.

'By an extraordinary arrangement, in which it is hard not to suspect the managing hand of a mother, Jean Smith became the wife of Robert Stevenson. Mrs. Smith had failed in her design to make her son a minister, and she saw him daily more immersed in business and worldly ambition. One thing remained that she might do: she might secure for him a godly wife, that great means of sanctification; and she had two under her hand, trained by herself, her dear friends and daughters both in law and love—Jean and Janet.'

He was twenty-seven, she twenty; for twelve years they had lived as brother and sister. But the girl must have grown up accustomed to regard with awe and admiration the young man who returned from adventurous absences full of romantic stories of unbelievable endeavour and endurance, while he, seeing nothing of gentlewomen outside his home circle, found in his mother's favoured stepdaughter all the desiderata of fragrant femininity.

The elder Jean had not brought up her namesake to be an accomplished housewife. Stories of how his grandfather sawed savagely at roasts overcooked beyond edibility, while his wife watched anxiously with deprecatory excuses from the other end of the table, suggested to their grandson his description of similar scenes at the Justice Clerk's table in *Weir of Hermiston*. But apart from contrition for her shortcomings in housewifery, Robert Stevenson's wife felt none of Mrs. Weir's timid inferiority; in matters spiritual she was the senior partner. Writing home enthusiastically of difficulties adventurously overcome in pursuit of ambitious projects, the man of action would add, like a guilty schoolboy, the anxious assurance that he had been 'in time for afternoon church'; while he prosecuted unbridled his aspirations abroad, on the domestic hearth he deferred to the edicts of his spouse's piety.

As their children grew up, neither parent permitted criticism of the other. The mother might purse her lips in disapproval of their father's worldliness, and the father might shake his head with lifted glance in open exasperation over matters of household mismanagement, but these were inter-marital privileges which their children could not presume to share. In this loyalty was a mutual understanding inspiring a confidence that commanded respect; the sons followed their father's example in unquestioning deference to their mother's dominion of their upbringing, while they learned to admire and respect his self-discipline in returning from adventurous triumphs to contentment in the narrow social circle of their mother's pious gossips. And in the uncritical acceptance of circumstances required of them they laid the foundation of a similar self-discipline.

Brought up thus much as their father had been brought up, the sons naturally inclined to escape like him from prim home comforts into a hard life of rough adventure. Robert Stevenson intended that only one of his sons should enter his own profession, but three—David, Alan, and Thomas—followed in his footsteps even to succeeding him together or in turn, as engineer to the Board of Northern Lights. David wrote his father's biography though Robert's grandson edited in his unfinished *Records* the journal kept during the four years of his greatest achievement— the building of the lighthouse on the Bell, or Inchcape, Rock. Thomas, the youngest son, was just thirty when, in 1848, he married Margaret Isabella, the nineteen-year-old daughter of the Rev. Lewis Balfour, a descendant of the Balfours of Pilrig. Two years later—a few months after the death of Robert Stevenson at the age of seventy-eight—Thomas Stevenson's only child was born at 8 Howard Place, Edinburgh, on 13th November 1850. Baptised according to Scots custom in his father's house, the child was given the names of both his grandfathers, together with the surname of his mother's family— Robert Lewis Balfour Stevenson.

In Edinburgh at Stevenson's birth De Quincey and 'Christopher North' were still living, and Francis Jeffrey but just dead. It was the most conservative city in the country; when Thackeray visited it in 1851, there was little alteration from the days when the stormy entry of *Blackwood's Magazine* had disturbed its serenity, when 'Christopher North' had successfully contested his election to the university chair of moral philosophy, when Scott and Raeburn were familiar figures in Princes Street, and North and Tickler and the Ettrick Shepherd forgathered for their 'Noctes' at Ambrose's Hotel. Thackeray found 'a vast amount of toryism and donnishness everywhere', and though he met only the cream of literate society, which thronged his lectures on *The English Humourists*, Edinburgh still proudly sustained its reputation as the Athens of the North. Its upper class was professional and academic—professors, doctors, lawyers, clergymen—the class which in the old days had formed the middle quality between the aristocracy and the masses, but which received promotion to the upper class from the new middle classes created by industrialism. Gentility was their god before respectability was substituted by those lacking pedigrees beyond grandparents; they practised the gospel of humbug with the same zeal as their late-Victorian successors, but with the additional spice of snobbery, impelling an attitude of unwilling condescension to all in trade or short of antecedents.

To this society Thomas Stevenson belonged—for, though Thomas Smith had been a tradesman, Robert Stevenson had raised to professional status the standing of engineer to the Board of Northern Lights; a member of the Institute of Civil Engineers, he had been elected a fellow of the Royal Society of Edinburgh, as well as of the London Geological and Astronomical Societies. Thomas Stevenson was the son of a distinguished citizen of Edinburgh; already a partner in his father's firm at the time of his marriage, he chose a wife well suited to his station in the daughter of a minister descended from an ancient family of Lowland lairds. His professional achievements are enumerated in the obituary notice written by his son and reprinted in *Memories and Portraits*:

'He served under his brother Alan in the building of Skerryvore, the noblest of all extant deep-sea lights; and, in conjunction with his brother David, he added two—the Chickens and Dhu Heartach —to that small number of man's extreme outposts in the ocean. Of shore lights, the two brothers last named erected no fewer than twenty-seven; of beacons, about twenty-five. Many harbours were successfully carried out. . . . In the improvement of rivers the brothers were likewise in a large way of practice over both England and Scotland, nor had any British engineer anything approaching their experience.'

Like his father and grandfather, he was an inventor, and the revolving light for lighthouses was his innovation.

'New apparatus for lights in new situations was continually being designed with the same unwearied search after perfection, the same nice ingenuity of means; and though the holophotal revolving light perhaps still remains his most elegant contrivance, it is difficult to give it the palm over the much later condensing system, with its thousand possible modifications. The number and the value of these improvements entitle their author to the name of one of mankind's benefactors.'

A studious meteorologist, he devised a louvre-boarded screen for instruments which was adopted for popular production. Holding a government appointment, he regarded his inventions as part of his official duty and never applied for a patent; hence, as his son said, 'my father's instruments enter anonymously into a hundred light-rooms, and are passed anonymously over in a hundred reports, where the least considerable patent would stand out and tell its author's story'. It was fitting that such a record of distinguished service should be rewarded in his last years with election to the presidency of the Royal Society of Edinburgh, two of whose members, Professors William Swan and P. G. Tait, were counsellors and collaborators in his inventions and the closest of his friends.

Little over two years after his son's birth, Thomas Stevenson moved from Howard Place to a larger house, more befitting his increasing dignity and prosperity, in Inverleith Terrace, vacated by the Edinburgh professor of English literature, W. E. Aytoun, the son-in law-of 'Christopher North'. Here he resided little more than four years, for on 6th February 1857 Mrs. Stevenson noted in her dairy that 'Lou is still so feverish that we are alarmed', and though Dr. Christison declared 'it is nothing but bronchitis' and 'he should soon be better', he pronounced that 'this house is bad for him it is so cold from being an end house'. So, in the spring of that year, the Stevensons moved to 17 Heriot Row, one of a stately block of houses filled with sunlight from facing south across spacious open gardens, which remained the Edinburgh home of Robert Louis Stevenson till his father's death just thirty years later.

From his mother Stevenson inherited a tendency to weakness of the lungs. Till middle age his mother was always delicate and ailing; his maternal grandfather had been threatened in his youth by consumption—in the essay on 'The Manse', Stevenson wrote, 'He sought health in his youth in the Isle of Wight, and I have sought it in both hemispheres; but whereas he found it and kept it, I am still on the quest.' Colds and coughing denied him the sound sleep of the healthy child, and, like most imaginative children, he suffered in wakefulness from night fears, as he describes in 'A Chapter on Dreams':

'He was from a child an ardent and uncomfortable dreamer. When he had a touch of fever at night, and the room swelled and shrank, and his clothes, hanging on a nail, now loomed up instant to the bigness of a church, and now drew away into a horror of infinite distance and infinite littleness, the poor soul was very well aware of what must follow, and struggled hard against the approaches of that slumber which was the beginning of sorrows. But his struggles were in vain; sooner or later the night-hag would have him by the throat, and pluck him, strangling and screaming, from his sleep. His dreams were at times commonplace enough, at times very strange: at times they were almost formless, he would be haunted, for instance, by nothing more definite than a certain hue of brown, which he did not mind in the least while he was awake, but feared and loathed while he was dreaming; at times, again, they took on every detail of circumstance, as when once he supposed he must swallow the populous world, and awoke screaming with the horror of the thought. The two chief troubles of his very narrow existence—the practical and everyday trouble of school tasks and the ultimate and airy one of hell and judgment—were often confounded together into one appalling nightmare. He seemed to stand before the Great White Throne; he was called on, poor little devil, to recite some form of words, on which his destiny

23

depended; his tongue stuck, his memory was blank, hell gaped for him; and he would awake, clinging to the curtain-rod with his knees to his chin.'

When, as a child in the nursery, he woke up crying, he was sometimes soothed by his father. Thomas Stevenson's taste for romantic adventure was not entirely satisfied by his travels and voyages as an engineer; in bed at night he sent himself to sleep by imagining stories about 'ships, roadside inns, robbers, old sailors, and commercial travellers before the era of steam'. Adapting this device to soothe his son, he would 'feign conversations with guards or coachmen or innkeepers, until I was gradually quieted and brought to myself'.

'In the child's world of dim sensation,' wrote Stevenson in his essay on 'Child's Play', '"making believe" is the gist of his whole life.' In his autobiography John Cowper Powys remarks that few people understand how imaginative a child's life is, because 'when we grow up we ourselves forget'. Stevenson was one of the few; he always remembered vividly the scenes and feelings of his childhood, which he recalls in many essays. It has been suggested that he wrote so much in reminiscence of childhood because later unhappiness induced nostalgia. But all personal experience provided grist for Stevenson's creative mill, and after he had dedicated his life to literature, every memorable experience marked a milestone in the itinerary of his artistic development; if he reverted much to his earliest years, it was because throughout his life he retained, unimpaired by the prosaic demands of practical considerations, the same romantic and poetic habit of imagination that revelled unrestrained in childhood, and he recognised the buds whence sprang the branches of his maturity.

His romantic instinct was fostered and developed by his bonny Scots nurse, Alison Cunningham, known as 'Cummy'—a type of the faithful family retainer belonging to the days when girls went into service at fourteen and stayed in the same place all their lives, becoming in time an essential element of the household, like Smither in *The Forsyte Saga* and Maggie and Amy in *The Old Wives' Tale*. She became Stevenson's guardian when he was eighteen months old, having successfully supervised his cousin, Walter Blaikie, till his graduation from the nursery; long after he had ceased to need her ministrations, she remained with the Stevensons as housekeeper and privileged companion. Sprung from Covenanting stock, Cummy was a rigid Calvinist, with visions of the hell whither the wicked were damned luridly painted by a picturesque imagination, which, readily susceptible to supersition, enlivened such stories of bogles, witches, and warlocks, as inspire an imaginative boy with a haunting terror of the dark. 'A woman in a thousand, clean, capable, notable; once a moorland Helen, and still comely as a blood horse and healthy as the hill wind.' An idealised portrait of Cummy, Kirstie Elliott is thus described in *Weir of Hermiston*.

'Her feeling partook of the loyalty of a clanswoman, the hero-worship of a maiden aunt, and the idolatry due to a god. No matter what he had asked her, ridiculous or tragic, she would have done it and joyed to do it. . . . Like so many people of her class, she was a brave narrator; her place was on the hearth-rug and she made it a rostrum, miming her stories as she told them, fitting them with vital detail, spinning them out with endless " quo' he's " and " quo' she's," her voice sinking into a whisper over the supernatural or the horrific; until she would suddenly spring up in affected surprise, and pointing to the clock, "Mercy, Mr. Archie!" she would say, "whatten a time o' night is this of it! God forgive me for a daft wife!"'

If Cummy's stories fevered his night-fears, her manner of telling them awakened Stevenson's literary sense. In one of his last essays, 'Rosa quo Locorum', he applauds 'the ear of my old nurse', who read 'the works of others as a poet would scarce dare to read his own; gloating on the rhythm, dwelling with delight on assonances and alliterations'. Thus early he learned to love the beauty of words, unconsciously tuning his ear to the melody and rhythm that makes unfailing music of his prose.

The Bible and the works of the Rev. Robert Murray M'Cheyne were Cummy's favourite reading; when she read aloud from *Cassell's Family Paper*, she would lay it aside if she suspected that a decorous 'tale for family reading' was 'going to turn out a regular novel'. Her Calvinistic zeal inspired her charge to play at preaching in his nursery, improvising a pulpit with a stool and a chair. Cards were a device of the devil, and when Stevenson's parents indulged in an occasional game of whist, their son devoutly prayed that their delinquency might be pardoned. His first literary composition was a 'History of Moses', dictated to his mother at the age of six. To Cummy's Calvinism he owed his 'Covenanting childhood', as he often called it; though he developed a tolerance and breadth of vision in striking contrast with the narrowness of contemporary convention, he derived from his upbringing the didactic tendency apparent in his essays, in the morality of much of his fiction, in such compositions as the unfinished *Lay Morals* and prayers for use in his Samoan household, and the tender susceptibility of conscience which dominated his character and career.

In Cummy's company he first pressed his nose to the window of the stationer's shop described in 'A Penny Plain and Twopence Coloured' of *Memories and Portraits*, greedily gazing at the toy theatre laid out inside, 'with a "forest set", a "combat", and a few "robbers carousing" in the slides; and below and about, dearer tenfold to me! the play themselves, those budgets of romance, lay tumbled one upon another'. For Stevenson the paper covers of Skelt's Juvenile Drama were the gates of such a romantic world as a later generation found in W. T. Stead's 'Books for the Bairns', but none of the thousands to whom Stead furnished the first foods for imaginative illusion have paid to him such just and grateful tribute as Stevenson to Skelt.

'What am I? what are life, art, letters, the world, but what my Skelt has made them? He stamped himself upon my immaturity. The world was plain before I knew him, a poor penny world; but soon it was all coloured with romance. If I go to the theatre to see a good old melodrama, 'tis but Skelt a little faded. If I visit a bold scene in nature, Skelt would have been bolder; there had been certainly a castle on that mountain, and the hollow tree—that set-piece—I seem to miss it in the foreground. Indeed, out of this cut-and-dry, dull, swaggering, obtrusive and infantile art, I seem to have learned the very spirit of my life's enjoyment; met there the shadows of the characters I was to read about and love in a late future; got the romance of *Der Freischütz* long ere I was to hear of Weber or the mighty Formes; acquired a gallery of scenes and characters with which, in the silent theatre of the brain, I might enact all novels and romances; and took from these rude cuts an enduring and transforming pleasure.'

Doubtless the desire to read Skelt for himself stimulated Stevenson to learn to read; Cummy was an exceptional personality, but she must have sometimes resorted to the trick, common among her kind, of using her power to secure obedience—'if you don't do as you're told, like a good boy, I won't read Skelt!'

He was late in learning to read, for delicate health much interrupted his schooling. His frequent periods of convalescence were spent under the care of his Aunt Jane Balfour at Colinton Manse, of which he wrote lovingly in 'The Manse', in 'Child's Play', and in an early unpublished essay quoted in Balfour's biography. This 'great and roomy house', overlooking the churchyard, where 'after nightfall "spunkies" might be seen to dance, at least by children', was recalled as the house of Hermiston; in its fine old garden, 'cut into provinces by a great hedge of beech', Stevenson and his cousins played at Red Indians or hide-and-seek. 'Out of my reminiscences of life in the dear place, all the morbid and painful elements have disappeared,' he wrote: 'That was my golden age.' Accused by William Archer of singing the light of life and skirting its shadows, he confessed, 'you are very right about my voluntary aversion from the painful sides of life. My childhood was in reality a very mixed experience, full of fever, nightmare, insomnia, painful days and interminable nights; and I can speak with less authority of gardens than of that other "land of counterpane". But to what end should we renew these sorrows?'

At six he started at a small school near his home, to which he was doubtless daily escorted by Cummy; then he attended a preparatory school from which, when he was not absent through illness, he made a practice of playing truant. He was about eight before he learned to read, and he enjoyed at Colinton, as he tells in 'Rosa quo Locorum', his first taste of the pleasures of literature. With his cousin Henrietta Traquair (who figures in his *Letters* as Mrs. Milne) he had been playing throughout a warm summer's day:

'then came the evening with a great flash of colour and a heavenly sweetness in the air. Somehow my playmate had vanished, or is out of the story, as the sagas say, but I was sent into the village on an errand; and, taking a book of fairy tales, went down alone through a fir-wood, reading as I walked. How often since then has it befallen me to be happy even so; but that was the first time: the shock of that pleasure I have never since forgot, and if my mind serves me to the last, I never shall, for it was then that I knew I loved reading.'

The book that effected this revelation was none of the world's masterpieces, but 'a work rather gruesome and bloody for a child, but very picturesque, called *Paul Blake*'. This, with *Robinson Crusoe* and 'the books of that cheerful, ingenious, romantic soul, Mayne Reid', produced upon him 'the three strongest impressions' among boys' books. But a single shelf of Christmas and birthday presents provides no more than the door-step from which the adventurer among books starts upon his travels. Every volume is a potential trove of pleasure; every binding wears an air of romantic mystery, inviting search for the secrets between its covers. There are frequent disappointments. We soon learn that fine feathers do not always dress the best birds—that dullness often dwells in gilt-tooled calf, while an experience ever memorable unexpectedly lurks between loose shabby covers. Sometimes we venture too impertinently, to meet austere rebuff where afterwards our more mature approach is warmly welcomed. Stevenson tells in 'Rosa quo Locorum' how 'time and again' the early part of *Rob Roy* 'choked me off'; how, 'lying on the floor one summer evening', he struck with sudden delight upon the first scene with Andrew Fairservice, and read on, snatching gleams of sunlight between skipping the clouds, till he found he was no longer grasping the thread of the story; how 'years elapsed before I consciously met Diana and her father among the hills, or saw Rashleigh dying in the chair'.

His reminiscences of boyhood mostly recall his reading or his early efforts to write. His 'voluntary aversion from the painful sides of life' imposed almost total silence about his schooldays. At eleven he went to Edinburgh Academy for eighteen months of unprofitable misery; he was lazy at lessons, played no games, recoiled from fisticuffs and horse-play, and received the derisive label of a 'softie'. In 1863 he spent one term at an English boarding school—Spring Grove, Isleworth, Middlesex—which enabled his comparison between English and Scottish schoolboys in 'The Foreigner at Home'.

'The boy of the South seems more wholesome, but less thoughtful; he gives himself to games as to a business, striving to excel, but is not readily transported by imagination; the type remains with me as cleaner in mind and body, more active, fonder of eating, endowed with a lesser and a less romantic sense of life and of the future, and more immersed in present circumstances. And certainly, for one thing, English boys are younger for their age. Sabbath observance makes a series of grim, and perhaps serviceable, pauses in the tenor of Scottish boyhood—days of great stillness and solitude for the rebellious mind, when in the dearth of books and play, and in the intervals of studying the Shorter Catechism, the intellect and senses pray upon and test each other.'

Comparative release from the tyranny of Sunday observance did not compensate the terrors of football—'mightily exercised about the presence of the ball', he 'had to spirit himself up, whenever he came to play, with an elaborate story of enchantment, and take the missile as a sort of talisman bandied about in conflict between two Arabian nations'. The earliest of his published letters was written from this school when his parents were leaving to spend the winter at Mentone:

'My dear papa, you told me to tell you whenever I was miserable. I do not feel well, and I wish to get home. Do take me with you.'

The appeal succeeded, and he went a second time to the Riviera, the land he learned to love the best before he visited the South Seas. He had been with his parents at Mentone in the previous winter, travelling on through Italy as far as Naples, and returning home by way of the Rhine. But he drew little for his writings from childish impressions of this journey, apart from the setting of the story of *Will o' the Mill* in the neighbourhood of the Brenner Pass.

On his return from Mentone in May 1864, he entered the Edinburgh seminary of Mr. Robert Thomson, where one of his earliest biographers, H. Bellyse Baildon, was a fellow-pupil. Mr. Thomson was evidently a 'crammer', one of those patiently enduring experts who specialise in difficult or backward boys, for Baildon relates that his pupils numbered no 'more than a dozen boys, ranging in ages from nine or ten to fourteen or fifteen, and our intellectual calibre varied fully as much as our years'. Baildon became a university don and reintroduced himself as a correspondent during the last years of Stevenson's life; he claims to have been his intimate at Thomson's, but clearly appears hard pressed for recollections of their companionship. There was no reason why Stevenson should have been more popular at Thomson's than at his previous schools. The average boy, like the average man, measures his fellow with the yardstick of material success. A lazy and erratic student, Stevenson cannot have found favour with his tutor, so his intellectual attainments commanded no respect from his fellow-pupils, and he lacked the athletic prowess that supplies a passport to popularity. Baildon admits that his appearance was unprepossessing: 'in body he was assuredly badly set up', his limbs 'long, lean, and spidery, and his chest flat, so as almost to suggest some malnutrition, such sharp corners did his joints make under his clothes'.

But the attributes that did not invite admiration failed also to excite envy or dislike. His oddities could be tolerated with amusement. He was sufficiently friendly with Baildon to retain a lively impression of his home at Murrayfield, which he described as the house where the hero finds the body in *The Misadventures of John Nicholson*. He found associates to join him in the exploits remembered in 'The Lantern-Bearers'. After his grandfather's death the visits to Colinton were replaced by summer holidays further afield, and at North Berwick the boys slipped out after dark, a bull's-eye lantern buckled to the waist on a cricket belt under an overcoat, to assemble in the belly of a fishing-boat or in a hollow of the sand-dunes —the same dunes that supplied the setting of *The Pavilion on the Links*. Their talk was mostly 'silly and indecent' as they squatted in discomfort, 'very cold, spat upon by flurries of rain, and drearily surrounded'. The romance lay, not in the companionship, but in the solitary clandestine journey to the meetings—'the essence of this bliss was to walk by yourself in the black night; the slide shut; the top-coat buttoned; not a ray escaping, whether to conduct your footsteps or to make your glory public: a mere pillar of darkness in the dark; and all the while, deep down in the privacy of your fool's heart, to know you had a bull's-eye at your belt, and to exult and sing over the knowledge'. The same delight in stealing out after dark led him to join—as his mother noted in her diary—'a number of boys who went about playing tricks on all the neighbours on Springhill, tapping on their windows after nightfall'. There was no malice in the mischief; the excitement of stealthy approach to windows with shafts of light at the edges of the blinds, the danger of detection, and the possibility of pursuit, satisfied a spirit of adventure.

He was an accepted leader in such exploits, others being impressed by the imagination with which he dramatised an otherwise commonplace adventure, his eloquence fortified by the picturesque resources of his reading. As he relates in 'A Gossip on Romance', the romantic spirit 'in the bright, troubled period of boyhood' required a story to 'repeat itself in a thousand coloured pictures to the eye'.

'Eloquence and thought, character and conversation, were but obstacles to brush aside as we dug blithely after a certain sort of incident, like a pig for truffles. For my part, I liked a story to begin with an old wayside inn where, "towards the close of the year 17——", several gentlemen in three-cocked hats were playing bowls. A friend of mine preferred the Malabar coast in a storm, with a ship beating to windward, and a scowling fellow of Herculean proportions striding along the beach; he, to be sure, was a pirate. This was further afield than my home-keeping fancy loved to travel, and designed altogether for a larger canvas than the tales that I affected. Give me a highwayman and I was full to the brim; a Jacobite would do, but the highwayman was my favourite dish. I can still hear that merry clatter of the hoofs along the moonlit lane; night and the coming of day are still related in my mind with the doings of John Rann or Jerry Abershaw; and the words "post-chaise", the "great North Road", "ostler", and "nag" still sound in my ears like poetry.'

He never lost this zest for romance. At the end of his life he enjoyed 'exquisite pleasure' in Stanley Weyman's cloak-and-sword story, *A Gentleman of France*, and was tempted away from the heavier labour of *Weir of Hermiston* to set a post-chaise rattling up the Great North Road in *St. Ives*. 'Certain illustrated dessert plates in a hotel at Nice,' seen during the winter visit of 1863–64, inspired his first reading of Dumas 'in one of those pirated editions that swarmed at that time out of Brussels.' But he confesses in 'A Gossip on a Novel of Dumas's' that, at this first reading of *Le Vicomte de Bragelonne*, he 'understood but little of the merits of the book'. His devotion to Dumas began with his second reading of the *Vicomte* during his university days.

In his schooldays 'penny dreadfuls' were his favourite reading, and his first efforts in writing followed their pattern. 'As soon as I was able to write,' he says, 'I became a good friend to the paper-makers.' His history of Moses had been followed by other dictated stories; the first written in his own hand were 'bungling adaptations from Mayne Reid'. Charging a reading fee of a penny to those who would pay it, he compiled manuscript magazines, one of which, dated 1863, contained a ghost story and a thriller—set, like *The Pavilion on the Links*, against the background of the North Berwick beach—called 'The Wreckers'. This taste for what he called 'crawlers' inspired an interest in the story of Deacon Brodie who, like Charles Peace of later date, carried on business as a burglar by night, long protected from suspicion by his reputation in the light of day for rectitude of conduct. Baildon remembered that Stevenson wrote a play about Brodie while still at Thomson's.

From 'crawlers' he was led by Colinton associations and Scott to stories of the Covenanters. He was fascinated by the figure of Hackston of Rathillet, motionless on horseback, his cloak about his mouth, an aloof spectator at the murder of Archbishop Sharp; at fifteen he filled 'reams upon reams' of paper with a romance called *Rathillet*. The same period of history inspired a second novel, describing the Pentland rebellion of 1666. Impressed by its literary competence and historical knowledge, his father asked him to rewrite this narrative as history, omitting the fiction, and paid for the

R.L.S. and his Father

printing of the revised version. Written in the month of his sixteenth birthday, *The Pentland Rising: A Page of History* is an essay of about seven thousand words, divided into five chapters. For such an effort, an undergraduate of nineteen or twenty might win his tutor's compliments, perhaps a small college prize, and certainly credit for a neat style in narrative. In a boy of sixteen it was a remarkable achievement, in which Thomas Stevenson felt just paternal pride; Edmund Gosse, visiting the Stevensons fifteen years later, saw a little pile of the slim green pamphlets in the study at Heriot Row, and was invited to 'take one'.

This encouragement was intended only to mark parental approval of scholastic diligence. His father had no thought of allowing his son to depend on literature for a precarious livelihood. As an only son, he was naturally destined by his father to sustain the family's professional tradition, and when, in the autumn of 1867, his crammer successfully contrived his entry into Edinburgh University, Stevenson attended the engineering class.

CHAPTER TWO

EXPERIMENT OF YOUTH

'Youth is wholly experimental.'—*Letter to a Young Gentleman Who Proposes to Embrace the Career of Art.*

'ALL THROUGH my boyhood and youth I was known and pointed out for the pattern of an idler; and yet I was always busy on my own private end, which was to learn to write. I kept always two books in my pocket, one to read, one to write in. As I walked, my mind was busy fitting what I saw with appropriate words; when I sat by the roadside, I would either read, or a pencil and a penny version-book would be in my hand, to note down the features of the scene or commemorate some halting stanzas. Thus I lived with words. And what I thus wrote was for no ulterior use, it was written consciously for practice. It was not so much that I wished to be an author (though I wished that too) as that I had vowed that I would learn to write.'

Following this opening to the essay on 'A College Magazine' in *Memories and Portraits*, Stevenson proceeds to describe his early methods of learning to write. He discarded the keeping of diaries as 'a school of posturing and melancholy self-deception', but wrote down descriptions of places he visited and reported conversations from memory. This practice, he found, taught him only 'the lower and less intellectual elements of the art, the choice of the essential note and the right word'. Like all beginners, he lacked any critical standards; nor had he any mentor of literary experience. His early discovered delight in reading led him in the right direction.

'Whenever I read a book or passage that particularly pleased me, in which a thing was said or an effect rendered with propriety, in which there was either some conspicuous force or some happy distinction in the style, I must sit down at once and set myself to ape that quality. . . . I have thus played the sedulous ape to Hazlitt, to Lamb, to Wordsworth, to Sir Thomas Browne, to Defoe, to Haw-thorne, to Montaigne, to Baudelaire, and to Obermann.'

This much-quoted confession has been sometimes cited as the basis of a charge that Stevenson was an artificial—not a natural —writer. 'Style is the man,' says the well-worn platitude, and the man must be himself artificial if his style is derivative. In 'Truth of Intercourse' Stevenson forestalled this criticism: 'The difficulty of literature is not to write, but to write what you mean; not to affect your reader, but to affect him pre-cisely as you wish.' He added: 'Anybody, it is supposed, can say what he means; and in spite of their notorious experience to the contrary, people so continue to suppose.' Justly in-structed that preservation of integrity is the highest quality of character, but ignorant that integrity cannot exist before the components of character have been co-ordinated by self-discipline, opinionated youth persists in repeating the banalities of inexperience with fond belief in their originality. The un-disciplined egoist—as Oscar Wilde said of George Moore— conducts his education in public; at the age of forty or so, having loudly insisted on being himself in the years when he should have been learning, the late James Agate was sedulously aping the manner of Hazlitt in his dramatic criticisms for the old *Saturday Review*.

Stevenson was not primarily concerned with expressing his ego on paper; what he wrote was 'for no ulterior use' but 'was written consciously for practice'. He was at this stage inspired less by the need for self-expression than by the desire to acquire the art of expressing himself well. Soon he was to recognise that 'what Whitman has to say is another affair from how he says it', but during these years of learning to write he studied masters of style rather for their manner than their matter. One of the most gifted of his modern admirers, Mr. Compton Mackenzie, has expressed surprise at 'Stevenson's eagerness to submit his work to his friends for their advice and the amount of time he wasted, as I should think, in announcing before-hand what he was going to write, where he was in a book he was writing, and what he felt about the work in progress'. He thinks 'it is true to say that Stevenson remained to the end the

35

passionate amateur'. If 'amateur' is interpreted as 'virtuoso', it may be true, for Stevenson never allowed himself to be tempted by his popularity into loose or careless writing, and remained to the end as painstakingly fastidious in the art of expression as during his early years of experiment. Prose was his instrument, as the piano was Paderewski's, the violin Joachim's, and he took the same pains in practice and performance. His letters to Henry James show the recognised master regarding himself as still a student; in the last year of his life he admonished Baildon for his 'licence with grammar'.

Mr. Frank Swinnerton remarks upon the 'bitter comment' excited by the essay 'On Some Technical Elements of Style in Literature' from those critics who followed William Archer in accusing Stevenson of being more concerned with manner than with matter in his essays. Mr. Swinnerton is the sharpest of Stevenson's adverse critics because he is the most shrewd; he abjures the absurdity of assuming that this essay described Stevenson's methods of composition in maturity on the obvious grounds that he was 'a prolific writer, and would never have afforded the time to be a mere hanger-on of words'. Stevenson wrote 'On Some Technical Elements of Style', as he wrote most of his later essays, to record the lessons of his own literary apprenticeship for the benefit of similar aspirants. For their benefit he describes the methods of analysing a writer's style that he himself practised when playing the sedulous ape to his chosen masters. From studying the choice of words—'the lower and less intellectual elements of the art' because merely the bricks and mortar, the builder's materials—he proceeded to the web, 'at once sensuous and logical, an elegant and pregnant texture', into which the words were woven. In studying the methods of weaving the web, he fell to analysing the anatomy of phrasing, the combinations of vowels and consonants devised to satisfy the senses of sound and sight.

He cites examples from Shakespeare, Milton, and Coleridge, none of whom he names among the masters imitated in youth. Certainly he must have applied his methods of analysis to Thackeray. 'At the age of thirteen,' he writes, 'I had tried to do justice to the inhabitants of the famous city of Peebles in the style of "The Book of Snobs".' His memory was at fault in recalling his age, for it was during his fifteenth year that he spent a holiday at Peebles with his cousins, Bob Stevenson and his sister Katherine. At thirteen he was still concerned with schoolboy 'crawlers'; the date of his stay at Peebles shows that Thackeray was among the first of the masters to whom he played the ape—the significance of which in regard to his later development seems to have escaped most of his biographers and critics.

The confession that he had studied the mechanics of style in literature was shocking to those who, preserving in shameful secrecy memories of their own anxious labours in learning to write, preferred style to be considered a product of divine inspiration, and their attitude to the revelation reflects that of Stevenson's college contemporaries to the practice—such an occupation was the mark of a smug and a prig. Stevenson made friends no more easily at college than at school. In *Weir of Hermiston*, asked if he is a friend of Archie Weir's, Frank Innes replies 'with his usual flippancy and more than his usual insight: "I know Weir, but I never met Archie"', and the comment follows:

'No one had met Archie, a malady most incident to only sons. He flew his private signal, and none heeded it; it seemed he was abroad in a world from which the very hope of intimacy was banished; and he looked round about him on the concourse of his fellow-students, and forward to the trivial days and acquaintances that were to come, without hope or interest.'

As W. E. Henley was to protest after his death, few ever came to know Stevenson intimately; they knew Stevenson but never met Louis. As an only child, he had at home developed the habit of sedulously guarding his private occupations from unsympathetic elders, and feeling himself 'abroad' in a world without sympathy, he extended his reserve. Conscious of loneliness, he did not retreat into timid seclusion, resigning himself to being a pariah, like De Quincey. Finding that he was regarded with contempt or derision as an oddity, he acted the part expected of him. 'No better histrion ever lived,' wrote Henley, one of the few who knew him well. The school softie became at the university the eccentric bounder. Always he wore his hair long, as a precaution against taking cold; under an antiquated straw hat, 'his long, lank hair fell straggling to his shoulders, giving him the look of a quack or a gipsy'. His habitual dress consisted of a shabby black velvet jacket, duck trousers, a loose collar, 'and' (says a fellow-student quoted by J. A. Steuart) 'a tie that might be a strip torn from a cast-away carpet'. It was said that 'there must be a family trunk full of old clothes which he was wearing out'. His figure accentuated the eccentricity of his dress, for he was 'a slithering, loose flail of a fellow, all joints, elbows, and exposed spindleshanks, his trousers being generally a foot too short in the leg . . . so like a scarecrow that one almost expected him to creak in the wind'.

To his fellow-students 'his airs were even more ridiculous than his clothes'. 'He was always posing, always . . . showing off,' and they all 'just laughed at him, dubbing him crank and humbug'. Derision excited defiance in self-defence, and 'the more we jeered and gibed the more he posed'. He affected 'an offensive, provocative attitude of sneering', omitted no opportunity of intimating that he regarded the university teaching as 'an elaborate and stupid joke, fit only for asses', and irritated his critics by 'the smile of disdain on his queer, foreign-looking face'. Some dismissed him as a mere poseur, 'so consumed with conceit that he could not even walk properly, but must for ever go mincing and posing like a dancing-master'. Others saw him as 'a bundle of affectations . . . suggesting a touch of insanity'. All agreed that he was an oddity and a bounder. And he seemed the more outrageous on account of the impeccable respectability of his social standing. If his origin had been obscure, he might have been dismissed with contemptuous tolerance, but there could be no excuse for the son of the highly respected and respectable Thomas Stevenson, the grandson of the reverend and well-descended Lewis Balfour.

In 'Some College Memories' Stevenson confesses that he denied himself many opportunities by 'acting upon an extensive and highly rational system of truantry, which cost me a great deal of trouble to put in exercise'. He tells how, though he could not remember 'to have been present in the Greek class above a dozen times', he applied at the end of a term for a certificate of attendance to the presiding professor, J. S. Blackie, who remarked, as he obligingly signed the necessary document, that he did not know his face. Blackie was justly celebrated as a scholar and an educationist, but he may not have possessed the rare talent of imparting his intellectual treasures through the medium of lectures. Apparently Edinburgh University employed in Stevenson's day an abundance of interesting lecturers no greater than other universities in later times, and Stevenson's lively mind did not suffer boredom gladly. 'In class, when it pleased him to attend,' wrote a contemporary, 'he was the worst-behaved man of my acquaintance.' He was not noisy; his method of barracking was impertinent comment, in the art of which his alert perception and agile imagination—qualities which later made him a delightful companion—must have rendered him a formidable antagonist. If he respected a professor too much to bait him, as he respected Fleeming Jenkin and apparently Blackie, he stayed away from his lectures.

Jenkin, the professor of engineering, was a young don only seventeen years older than Stevenson; he became one of his earliest friends, and after his death Stevenson wrote a memoir to be prefixed to a collection of his writings. Perhaps because it was his habit to extend such civilities to students of his special subject, perhaps because Stevenson evinced interest in his hobby of amateur theatricals, Jenkin several times asked him to his house during the first months of his studentship, and Stevenson felt reluctant to repay his courtesy by his usual bad behaviour in class. Remarking that Jenkin had such 'fibre in him that order always existed in his class-room', Stevenson writes:

'I do not remember that he ever addressed me in language; at the least sign of unrest his eye would fall on me and I was quelled. Such a feat is comparatively easy in a small class; but I have misbehaved in smaller classes and under eyes more Olympian than Fleeming Jenkin's. He was simply a man from whose reproof one shrank; in manner the least buckramed of mankind, he had, in serious moments, an extreme dignity of goodness. So it was that he obtained a power over the most insubordinate of students, but a power of which I was myself unconscious. I was inclined to regard any professor as a joke, and Fleeming as a particularly good joke, perhaps the broadest in the vast pleasantry of my curriculum. I was not able to follow his lectures; I somehow dared not misconduct myself, as was my customary solace; and I refrained from attending. This brought me at the end of the session into a relation with my contemned professor that completely opened my eyes. During the year, bad student as I was, he had shown a certain leaning to my society; I had been to his house, he had asked me to take a humble part in his theatricals; I was a master in the art of extracting a certificate even at the cannon's mouth; and I was under no apprehension. But when I approached Fleeming I found myself in another world; he would have naught of me. "It is quite useless for *you* to come to me, Mr. Stevenson. There may be doubtful cases, there is no doubt about yours. You have simply *not* attended my class." The document was necessary to me for family considerations; and presently I stooped to such pleadings and rose to such adjurations as make my ears burn to remember. He was quite unmoved; he had no pity for me.—"You are no fool," said he, "and you chose your own course." I showed him that he had misconceived his duty, that certificates were things of form, attendance a matter of taste. Two things, he replied, had been required for graduation: a certain competency proved in the final trials, and a certain period of genuine training proved by certificate; if he did as I desired, not less than if he gave me hints for an examination, he was aiding me to steal a degree. "You see, Mr. Stevenson, these are the laws and I am here to apply them," said he. I could not say but that this view was tenable, though it was new to me; I changed my attack: it was only for my father's eye that I required his signature, it need never go to the Senatus, I had already certificates enough to justify my year's attendance. "Bring them to me; I cannot take your word for that," said he. "Then I will consider." The next day I came charged with my certificates, a humble assortment. And when he had satisfied himself, "Remember," said he, "that I can promise nothing, but I will try to find a form of words." He did find one, and I am still ashamed when I think of his shame in giving me that paper. He made no reproach in speech, but his manner was the more eloquent; it told me plainly what a dirty business we were on; and I went from his presence, with my certificate indeed in my possession, but with no answerable sense of triumph. That was the bitter beginning of my love for Fleeming; I never thought lightly of him afterwards.'

Jenkin could have chosen no surer method of humbling Stevenson, for a chiding conscience, inculcated during his 'Covenanting childhood' under Cummy, was always lurking to curb and admonish his impulses. The correct and upright Dr. Jekyll is represented as feeling horror and loathing for his baser self in Mr. Hyde, and the allegory of that famous story was suggested as much by Stevenson's own conflict of conscience as by his reflections on the repression imposed by the rigid conventions of Victorian society.

The deception of his father, necessitated by indulging the Hyde of his inclination, was bitterly regretted by the Jekyll of his conscience. He felt love, as well as admiration for his father. To the end of his life he remembered him in the prime of his manhood, 'running down the sands into the sea near North Berwick, myself—*aetat.* 11—somewhat horrified at finding him so beautiful when stripped!' Physically thin and delicate himself, he admired his father's burly robustness, and recognised that his athletic deficiencies must have been a source of disappointment in an only son. He admired his father's rectitude of character, his kindliness and goodness, his passionate absorption in his life's chosen work.

So in childhood and boyhood he sought sincerely to please his father. Written originally as a story to suit his own delight in romance, his adaptation of *The Pentland Rising* as an historical essay is evidence of effort to use his talent in a form calculated to earn his father's approval. In adolescence he still dallied with the notion of fulfilling his father's hopes of him, while compromising with his inclinations. But his sharpening perceptions showed him the unbridgeable vastness of the gulf between his father's intellectual outlook and his own.

'On Tweedside, or by Lyne or Manor, we have spent together whole afternoons; to me, at the time, extremely wearisome; to him, as I am now sorry to think, bitterly mortifying. The river was to me a pretty and various spectacle; I could not see—I could not be made to see—it otherwise. To my father it was a chequer-board of lively forces, which he traced from pool to shallow with minute appreciation and enduring interest. "That bank was being undercut," he might say; "why? Suppose you were to put a groin out here, would not the *filum fluminus* be cast abruptly off across the channel? and where would it impinge upon the other shore? and what would be the result? Or suppose you were to blast that boulder, what would happen? Follow it—use the eyes God has given you—can you not see that a great deal of land would be reclaimed upon this side?" It was to me like school in holidays; but to him, until I had worn him out with my invincible triviality, delight.'

Thomas Stevenson was not insensible to poetry and romance in landscape; he had his father's and grandfather's romantic approach to his craft and a measure of imagination inevitable in the Celtic strain emphasised by his son. But conscience demanded as a duty that he should instruct his son, whose fanciful tendency seemed indeed 'invincible triviality'. Youth is rash and cruel in critical judgment, and instinctively resorts to perversity in self-defence. Stevenson would have been superhuman if he had not inclined to criticise his father's insistence on practical considerations as indicating a want of poetic feeling and romantic susceptibility—if he had not exaggerated his own attitude on sensing it to be the object of disapproval.

Later in life he grievously lamented his failure to appreciate his father. In *The Wrecker* the sailor Nares, regretting his quarrels with his dead father, remarks: 'I guess we're all beasts,' and Loudon Dodd replies: 'All sons are, I guess . . . I have the same trouble on my conscience.' In some 'Reflections and Remarks on Human Life'—apparently notes for projected essays during the *Virginibus Puerisque* period of 1876–78 —he wrote:

'The love of parents for their children is, of all natural affections, the most ill-starred. It is not a love for the person, since it begins before the person has come into the world, and founds on an imaginary character and looks. Thus it is foredoomed to disappointment; and because the parent either looks for too much, or at least for something inappropriate, at his offspring's hands, it is too often insufficiently repaid. The natural bond, besides, is stronger from parent to child than from child to parent; and it is the side which confers benefits, not which receives them, that thinks most of a relation. . . . What do we owe to our parents? No

man can *owe* love; none can *owe* obedience. We owe, I think,
chiefly pity; for we are the pledge of their dear and joyful union,
we have been the solicitude of their days and the anxiety of their
nights, we have made them, though by no will of ours, to carry
the burthen of our sins, sorrows, and physical infirmities; and too
many of us grow up at length to disappoint the purpose of their
lives and requite their care and piety with cruel pangs. . . . It is the
particular cross of parents that when the child grows up and becomes
himself instead of that pale ideal they had preconceived, they must
accuse their own harshness or indulgence for this natural result.
They have all been like the duck and hatched swan's eggs, or the
other way about; yet they tell themselves with miserable penitence
that the blame lies with them; and had they sat more closely, the
swan would have been a duck, and home-keeping, in spite of
all.'

Undoubtedly Thomas Stevenson blamed himself for any
deficiencies detected in his son, for his conscience had been
coached by his pious mother to be a monitor as stern as Stevenson's by Cummy.

'He was a man of a somewhat antique strain: with a blended
sternness and softness that was wholly Scottish and at first somewhat bewildering; with a profound essential melancholy of disposition and (what often accompanies it) the most humorous
geniality in company; shrewd and childish: passionately attached,
passionately prejudiced; a man of many extremes, many faults of
temper, and no very stable foothold for himself among life's
troubles.'

He had 'a morbid sense of his own unworthiness', and 'cases of
conscience were sometimes grievous to him'. His only son was
his most abiding case of conscience; every blemish in Stevenson's
character, every declension from perfection, comprised a matter
for parental reproach. Stevenson was evidently thinking of his
father's 'blended sternness and softness' in reproof when
Loudon Dodd in *The Wrecker* says of his father:

'You can see for yourself how vain it was to argue with my
father. The despair that seized upon me after such an interview
was, besides, embittered by remorse; for I was at times petulant,

43

but he invariably gentle; and I was fighting, after all, for my own liberty and pleasure, he singly for what he thought to be my good. And all the time he never despaired. "There is good stuff in you, Loudon," he would say; "there is the right stuff in you. Blood will tell, and you will come right in time. I am not afraid my boy will ever disgrace me; I am only vexed he should sometimes talk nonsense." And then he would pat my shoulder or my hand with a kind of motherly way he had, very affecting in a man so strong and beautiful.'

However accurately he afterwards appreciated his father's attitude, at the time Stevenson's reaction was antagonistic. Sensitively conscious of being always under a critical microscope, he was instinctively on the defensive, sullen, resentful, evasive. Like Archie Weir:

'He made no attempt whatsoever to understand the man with whom he dined and breakfasted. Parsimony of pain, glut of pleasure, these are the two alternating ends of youth; and Archie was of the parsimonious. The wind blew cold out of a certain quarter—he turned his back upon it; stayed as little as was possible in his father's presence; and when there, averted his eyes as much as was decent from his father's face.'

Such evasion inflicted a grievous wound upon the father's tender conscience, since he was bound to brood upon his failure to win his son's confidence. The sorrow and yearning in his eyes afflicted Stevenson with self-reproach; he felt remorse, but his shrinking from the pain of it caused him to avoid his father's company more then ever.

For three and a half years after entering the university, Stevenson unwilling conformed with his father's plans for his future. Instead of family holidays he spent his long vacations in pursuit of practical professional experience. The summer of 1868 was divided between such unwelcoming resorts as Anstruther in Fife and Wick on the bleak coast of Caithness, of which he recalled his impressions just twenty years later in an essay for *Scribner's Magazine* on 'The Education of an Engineer'. To Anstruther, he says, he went 'to glean engineering experience from the building of the breakwater'.

Experiment of Youth

'What I gleaned, I am sure I do not know; but indeed I had already my own private determination to be an author; I loved the art of words and the appearances of life; and *travellers*, and *headers*, and *rubble*, and *polished ashlar*, and *pierres perdues*, and even the thrilling question of the *string-course*, interested me only (if they interested me at all) as properties for some possible romance or as words to add to my vocabulary. To grow a little catholic is the compensation of years; youth is one-eyed; and in those days, though I haunted the breakwater by day, and even loved the place for the sake of the sunshine, the thrilling seaside air, the wash of waves on the sea-face, the green glimmer of the divers' helmets far below, and the musical chinking of the masons, my one genuine preoccupation lay elsewhere, and my only industry was in the hours when I was not on duty. I lodged with a certain Bailie Brown, a carpenter by trade; and there, as soon as dinner was despatched, in a chamber scented with dry rose-leaves, drew in my chair to the table and proceeded to pour forth literature, at such a speed, and with such intimations of early death and immortality, as I now look back upon with wonder. Then it was that I wrote "Voces Fidelium", a series of dramatic monologues in verse; then that I indited the bulk of a covenanting novel—like so many others, never finished. Late I sat into the night, toiling (as I thought) under the very dart of death, toiling to leave a memory behind me.'

At this time, when—as he remarks in one of his earlier published letters—his delicate health cost his parents 'an enormous —nay, elephantine—sum of money for drugs and physician's fees', he saw himself in moods of self-pity as a second Keats —or rather, as a second Robert Fergusson, who died likewise untimely—and derived most of his poetic inspiration from the illusion. With youth's self-absorption and thoughtless disregard for inflicting distress of mind, he evidently neglected no opportunity of impressing this conception of himself upon his fond mother, to whom he wrote from Anstruther:

'I am utterly sick of this grey, grim, sea-beaten hole. I have a little cold in my head, which makes my eyes sore; and you can't tell how utterly sick I am, and how anxious to get back among trees and flowers and something less meaningless than this bleak fertility.'

45

With his father his strategy was more subtle; he spoke flippantly of his physical ailments—after a 'severe attack of gripes' from drinking 'chilly table beer', he had to buy green ginger 'for the benefit of my stomach, like St. Paul'—and posed as persevering in pursuit of his father's wishes despite all physical and intellectual incompatibilities.

'It is awful how slowly I draw, and how ill: I am not nearly done with the travellers, and have not thought of the jennies yet. When I'm drawing, I find out something I have not measured, or having measured, have not noted, or, having noted, cannot find; and so I have to trudge to the pier again, ere I can go farther with my noble design.'

He found Wick even worse than Anstruther, though, when recording recollections of the place in one of his earliest essays, 'On the Enjoyment of Unpleasant Places', he affected a philosophy little comforting to his feelings at the time. 'Wick in itself possesses no beauty,' he told his mother; 'bare, grey shores, grim grey houses, grim grey sea; not even the gleam of red tiles; not even the greenness of a tree.' Commenting in the essay on the barren 'nakedness of the North,' he says, 'the earth seemed to know that it was naked, and was ashamed and cold.'

At Wick he read the poetry of Herbert, 'a clever and a devout cove, but in places awfully twaddley', and *The Moonstone*, then just published. Stevenson's critics have rarely recognised his debt to Wilkie Collins, but then few modern critics have appreciated the importance of Collins in the development of the novel. After Dickens's death in 1870, Collins was a close second to Charles Reade as the leading popular novelist; like Reade, he drew away from the discursive vastness of Dickens and Thackeray to practise an economy excluding everything that did not contribute directly to his main plot and characters, and he competes with Poe's importance in the ancestry of the modern 'thriller'. Stevenson studied his methods of construction—the device of introducing autobiographical narratives by different characters, as in the *Strange Case of Dr. Jekyll and Mr. Hyde*, derives from Collins—and a letter to Henley defends *The Pavilion on the Links* as 'carpentry, of course, but not bad at that;

and who else can carpenter in England, now that Wilkie Collins is played out?'

The summer of 1869 he spent on a lighthouse steamer in the Orkneys and Shetlands. His letters during this trip were omitted by Colvin from *Letters to His Family and Friends* as lacking interest, but he recalled the pleasures of the voyages when Henley objected to his introduction of boat-cloaks in *The Merry Men*:

'The proudest moments of my life have been passed in the stern-sheets of a boat with that romantic garment over my shoulders. This, without prejudice to one glorious day when standing upon some water stairs at Lerwick I signalled with my pocket-handkerchief for a boat to come ashore for me.'

In 1870 he went for his summer vacation to the Western Isles, where, on the steamer between Portree and the mainland, he first met Edmund Gosse. Gosse afterwards professed to have been 'instantly attracted' and to have remembered Stevenson as 'tall, preternaturally lean, with longish hair, and as restless and questing as a spaniel'. But the description suits just as well the Stevenson whom Gosse met again some years later; though he recalled this early meeting in *Critical Kit-Kats* after Stevenson's death as 'a delightful memory', even its embellishment as good 'copy' revealed that their conversation was limited to a casual remark on an alteration in the course of their boat. In a letter to his mother Stevenson says nothing of Gosse but much of a pretty girl on the boat and of the Scottish painter, Sam Bough. When Bough died eight years later, Stevenson wrote a brief obituary notice, which, besides being a graceful model in that sort of journalism, displays perspicacity in judgment of character astonishing in a writer so young.

'He affected rude and levelling manners; his geniality was formidable, above all for those whom he considered too fine for their company; and he delivered jests from the shoulder like buffets. He loved to put himself in opposition, to make startling, and even brutal speeches, and trample proprieties under foot. But this, although it troubled the amenities of his relations, was no more than a husk, an outer man, partly of habit, partly of affectation; and inside the burr there was a man of warm feelings, notable powers of mind, and much culture, which was none the less genuine because it was not of the same character, not altogether concerned in the same fields of knowledge, as that training which usually appropriates the name. Perhaps he was a little disappointed with himself, and partly because he loathed fustian, partly because he did not succeed in living consistently up to the better and more beautiful qualities of his nature, he did himself injustice in the world, and paraded his worst qualities with something like a swagger.'

The first man of artistic distinction he had met outside academic circles, Bough naturally impressed Stevenson.

Gosse relates that Stevenson put off from the steamer 'to visit some remote lighthouse of the Hebrides', and it was doubtless to make his stay at Earraid, whence he wrote to his mother. His impressions of Earraid, gleaned during pleasant days of 'sea-bathing and sun-burning', produced a rich harvest in the setting of *The Merry Men* and a chapter of *Kidnapped*, besides the 'Memoirs of an Islet' in *Memories and Portraits*. Writing to James Payn from Samoa in the year before his death, he remembered how, 'when the Franco-Prussian war began, and I was in Eilean Earraid, far enough from the sound of the loudest cannonade, I could *hear* the shots fired, and I felt the pang in my breast of a man struck. It was sometimes so distressing, so instant, that I lay in the heather on the top of the island, with my face hid, kicking my heels for agony'. In 'Memoirs of an Islet' he further describes these symptoms of imaginative sensibility:

'In that year cannon were roaring for days together on French battlefields; and I would sit in my isle (I call it mine, after the use of lovers) and think upon the war, and the loudness of these far-away battles, and the pain of the men's wounds, and the weariness of their marching. And I would think too of that other war which is as old as mankind, and is indeed the life of man: the unsparing war, the grinding slavery of competition; the toil of seventy years, dear-bought bread, precarious honour, the perils and pitfalls, and the poor rewards. It was a long look forward; the future summoned me as with trumpet calls, it warned me back as with a voice of weeping and beseeching; and I thrilled and trembled on the brink of life, like a childish bather on the beach.'

Stevenson's Mother in 1854

The normal university student who unquestioningly concentrates upon the prescribed academic curriculum as the indispensable prelude to a good degree, itself the indispensable passport to a professional career, is the chrysalis from which emerges the successful, law-abiding citizen who complainingly pays the taxes demanded by the ever-increasing expenses of the civilised state. He is the backbone of democracy—as, indeed, he is very pleased to boast; but the brains develop from those who, declining to conform with authority's decrees, find time 'to stand and stare' and think for themselves. There is no doubt as to which course is the more conducive to ease, and Stevenson at this time began to suffer the pains of reflection. In *Lay Morals*, a projected work of popular philosophy which was never finished, he afterwards reconstructed in rapid outline his adolescent state of mind as 'a few pages out of a young man's life'.

'He was a friend of mine; a young man like others; generous, flighty, as variable as youth itself, but always with some high notions and on the search for higher thoughts of life. I should tell you at once that he thoroughly agrees with the eighth commandment. But he got hold of some unsettling works, the New Testament among others, and this loosened his views of life and led him into many perplexities. As he was the son of a man in a certain position, and well off, my friend had enjoyed from the first the advantages of education, nay, he had been kept alive through a sickly childhood by constant watchfulness, comforts, and change of air; for all of which he was indebted to his father's wealth.

'At college he met other lads more diligent than himself, who followed the plough in summer-time to pay their college fees in winter; and this inequality struck him with some force. He was at that age of a conversible temper, and insatiably curious in the aspects of life; and he spent much of his time scraping acquaintance with all classes of man- and woman-kind. In this way he came upon many depressed ambitions, and many intelligences stunted for want of opportunity; and this also struck him. He began to perceive that life was a handicap upon strange, wrong-sided principles; and not, as he had been told, a fair and equal race. He began to tremble that he himself had been unjustly favoured, when he saw all the avenues of wealth, and power, and comfort closed against so many of his superiors and equals, and held unwearyingly open before so idle, so desultory, and so dissolute a being as himself. . . . *If one of these could take his place*, he thought; and the thought tore away a bandage from his eyes. He was eaten by the shame of his discoveries, and despised himself as an unworthy favourite and a creature of the back-stairs of Fortune. He could no longer see without confusion one of these brave young fellows battling up-hill against adversity. Had he not filched that fellow's birthright? At best was he not coldly profiting by the injustice of society, and greedily devouring stolen goods? The money, indeed, belonged to his father, who had worked, and thought, and given up his liberty to earn it; but by what justice could the money belong to my friend, who had, as yet, done nothing but help to squander it?'

A prig? In youth priggishness is adolescence taking itself too seriously; in maturity it results from arrested development or repression. The Puritans were mainly prigs, and Stevenson was the child of his ancestry and upbringing; he had a Covenanter's conscience. He might have consoled himself with the example of Coleridge's patron, Tom Wedgwood, who regarded his inherited wealth as a trust to be used for the benefit of mankind. Or, as he says:

'A more sturdy honesty, joined to a more even and impartial temperament, would have drawn from these considerations a new force of industry, that this equivocal position might be brought as swiftly as possible to an end, and some good services to mankind justify the appropriation of expense. It was not so with my friend, who was only unsettled and discouraged, and filled full of that trumpeting anger with which young men regard injustices in the first blush of youth; although in a few years they will tamely acquiesce in their existence, and knowingly profit by their complications. Yet all this while he suffered many indignant pangs.'

Such pangs were inexplicable to his father, who, having accepted an education from his own father and worked hard to acquit himself with professional distinction, asked only that his son should do likewise. Besides the New Testament, the reading of Herbert Spencer and Walt Whitman produced an unsettling influence on Stevenson. Both were writers whose reputations were then established only among progressive intellectuals. Thomas Stevenson was 'a strong Conservative, or, as he preferred to call himself, a Tory', staunch in the creed of Christopher North and *Blackwood's Magazine*. To him, Spencer, like Mill and Darwin, must have seemed a purveyor of new-fangled ideas extremely dangerous to inflammable youth, while Whitman was a wild American revolutionary whose peculiar poetry had been recently publicised in England by William Michael Rossetti, a member of that notorious artistic clique, the Pre-Raphaelite Brotherhood. With determined self-discipline he attempted to argue patiently with his son, and strove to hide the wounds inflicted by 'trumpeting anger'. At the end he would make a pathetic gesture of conciliation, like Loudon Dodd's father—'I am not afraid my boy will ever disgrace me; I am only vexed he should sometimes talk nonsense'. Nonsense indeed it must have seemed to him, but so to describe youth's newly-discovered convictions is to excite resentment and antagonism.

He was even more vexed when he heard that his son was expounding his 'nonsense' in public. On 16th February 1869 Stevenson was elected a member of the university's Speculative Society, described in the essay, 'A College Magazine'. A year later, in March 1870, he opened a debate—like Archie Weir in *Weir of Hermiston*—advocating the abolition of capital punishment. Though implying no such personal affront to his father as Archie's to 'the hanging judge', the advocacy of such revolutionary reform was equally galling to Thomas Stevenson's Toryism.

His activities at the 'Spec.' led to the foundation of a 'mysterious' society called the 'L.J.R.', which held its meetings at a public house in Advocates' Close. According to his own description in 'Crabbed Age and Youth', he was at this time 'a red-hot Socialist', and the aims of the society—besides the general principles of liberty of thought and freedom from prejudice—included abolition of the House of Lords. Among the society's members were the three earliest of his intimate friends, Bob Stevenson, Charles Baxter, and James Walter Ferrier.

Of his cousin Bob there is little information outside Stevenson's writings and Henley's *in memoriam* essay on 'A Critic of Art' in *Views and Reviews*. He is the cousin of 'Child's Play', with whom Stevenson played games of imagination over their breakfast porridge; he is Spring-Heel'd Jack of 'Talk and Talkers'; he is the Young Man with the Cream Tarts in *New Arabian Nights* and figures fleetingly in *The Wrecker* as the elder of the Stennis brothers, that 'pair of hare-brained Scots'. Born in 1847, the son of Thomas Stevenson's elder brother Alan, Robert Alan Mowbray Stevenson was educated at Windermere School and Sidney Sussex College, Cambridge. On leaving Cambridge he apparently spent some time at Edinburgh before going to Paris to study painting, and of this time Stevenson wrote in a fragment of autobiography drafted at San Francisco in 1880, and published in the Balfour biography, that 'the mere return of Bob changed at once and for ever the course of my life. . . . I was at last able to breathe'.

Like Hazlitt before him, Bob Stevenson bravely faced the bitter discovery that he had no genius for painting and found his vocation as a critic of art. At his death in 1900 his work as a critic was praised—highly by Henley, less generously by other contemporaries—but it remains for a discerning editor to recover his scattered papers with a view to a representative selection that may establish his claim to be remembered as a writer. But he was of those, like Landor's friend Francis Hare and Thackeray's 'bright, broken Maginn', who lavished their genius in conversation and left no abiding memorial commensurate with their stature. Henley—whose shrewd discernment as a critic, despite his prejudices, still awaits adequate appreciation—considered him 'a far rarer spirit, a far more soaring and more personal genius than I found in his famous cousin'.

'Had you met him by chance, and been privileged to hear him discourse on his prime subject, you must inevitably have thought him a prince among artists: so full of reasoned inspiration were his conclusions, so luminous his statements, so far-reaching and suggestive his illustrations. You could not have helped yourself; yet in the end you must have wept to find yourself mistaken. For mistaken you must certainly have been: the truth being that this wonderful and delightful creature, though he might have stood for the Ideal Artist, had never an art complete in all his fascinating and unique endowment. Contained in him were the beginnings of all the arts that be; but they were inarticulate, and as it were incapable of self-assertion.'

To Stevenson he came as the first boon companion he had ever known, armed with the prestige of three years' seniority in age and proportionately superior knowledge of the world. In his description of his cousin as 'the very best talker' he had met, Stevenson shows how his talk helped to stimulate his own judgment and elucidate his problems.

'He doubles like the serpent, changes and flashes like the shaken kaleidoscope, transmigrates bodily into the views of others, and so, in the twinkling of an eye and with a heady rapture, turns questions inside out and flings them empty before you on the ground, like a triumphant conjurer. It is my common practice when a piece of conduct puzzles me, to attack it in the presence of Jack with such grossness, such partiality and such wearing iteration, as at length shall spur him up in its defence. In a moment he transmigrates, dons the required character, and with moonstruck philosophy justifies the act in question.'

'Laughter was at that time our principal affair,' says Stevenson, and in addition to lively debates they indulged in extravagant practical jokes, which they called 'jinks'. Chief of their jinks was their invention of a mythical Mr. Libbel; they called at houses to inquire for Mr. Libbel, left his card, and wrote letters over his signature to prominent citizens. Here probably they were consciously playing 'the sedulous ape' to Theodore Hook, having read of Hook's famous Berners Street hoax, by which four thousand letters were dispatched to tradesmen, bidding them to deliver goods or attend for service at a particular house in Berners Street on a certain day, when the whole street was a scene of uproar from morning till night.

Though he failed to become a painter, Bob Stevenson seems to have achieved all the Bohemian habits associated with the artist's life. In the staid and formal environment of Edinburgh he indulged his first Bohemian eccentricities, with all the extravagance of enthusiastic youth, and his cousin was his eager henchman. Soon Louis Stevenson took the lead, and Bob became the henchman, for Louis had a restless nervous energy of which Bob's lazy good-nature was incapable. Moreover, Bob was generously content to resign the lead to his younger cousin; Sidney Colvin relates that Bob 'used to vow that the chief interest of anything which happened was to hear what Louis would say about it'. This appreciation of his gifts was perhaps Bob's chief contribution to the moulding of Louis's character. To Thomas Stevenson and other sedate elders Bob must have seemed an undesirable influence; possibly Stevenson first affected untidy dress, his velvet coat, and long hair, because they suited his conception of the Bohemian artist approved by Bob. But Bob buttressed his self-confidence and showed him how to play a leading part in the society of his choice.

Formerly his eccentric posing and sneering attitude had repelled approach. But everybody liked Bob, and through Bob they came to like Louis. Charles Baxter was another member of the L.J.R. He was secretary of the Speculative Society, the son of a noted Edinburgh citizen, and himself to become a successful lawyer and Writer to the Signet. In 'Talk and Talkers' he is the 'person who attains, in his moments, to the insolence of a Restoration comedy, speaking, I declare, as Congreve wrote'. Like Congreve, too, he was a 'friendly, unreproachful man', whose shrewdness and sincerity enabled him to remain the friend of both Stevenson and Henley after their quarrel. As he survived both Henley and the two Stevensons, references to him by the official biographers were guarded, but a letter[1] from Sidney Colvin to Graham Balfour, written when Baxter presented to the Savile Club in 1907 his correspondence with Stevenson, refers to 'poor Baxter' in terms of little cordiality and much condescension. Though he was Stevenson's man of business, acted faithfully as his literary agent from the time of the Henley quarrel till Stevenson's death, and promoted that extremely opportune and valuable asset to Stevenson's literary reputation, the Edinburgh Edition of his works, he was excluded from the select circle of self-appointed custodians of the Stevenson myth. He had known Stevenson too long and intimately to subscribe to the myth, and if he was too discreet openly to endorse Henley's outburst against the 'seraph in chocolate', he was judged by the custodians to belong rather to the Henley camp than to theirs.

Though their acquaintance must have dated at least from

[1] In possession of Stevenson Memorial House, Howard Place, Edinburgh.

Stevenson's election to the Speculative Society in 1869 and his earliest published letters reveal that they were on terms of intimate friendship, the letters are addressed to 'My dear Baxter'. Apparently they were friends for some years before Baxter became 'My dear Charles'. Use of first names never came easily to Stevenson. He could not rid himself of the guarded habit acquired in years of loneliness as an only son. There remained always a core of reserve to which his friends failed to penetrate; they knew Stevenson, but not Louis.

It was the same with another member of the L.J.R., James Walter Ferrier. He became Stevenson's friend about the same time as Baxter, but he figures as 'Ferrier' in their correspondence of 1872. The grandson of Christopher North and son of that Professor Ferrier who edited the twelve volumes of Christopher North's works, he inherited much of his grandfather's brilliance, along with his good looks and love of conviviality—he seems to have been endowed with all the engaging qualities in De Quincey's picturesque portrait of his grandfather as Wilson of Elleray. But Christopher North was a magnificent vessel lacking the ballast to ride rough seas without rolling dangerously, and according to Stevenson's account in 'Old Mortality', young Ferrier lacked the sincerity of outlook, the earnestness of belief and endeavour, to establish a sense of values capable of safely sustaining him across the shoals of youth.

'He was most beautiful in person, most serene and genial by disposition; full of racy words and quaint thoughts. Laughter attended on his coming. He had the air of a great gentleman, jovial and royal with his equals, and to the poorest student gentle and attentive. Power seemed to reside in him exhaustless; we saw him stoop to play with us, but held him marked for higher destinies; we loved his notice; and I have rarely had my pride more gratified than when he sat at my father's table, my acknowledged friend. So he walked among us, both hands full of gifts, carrying with nonchalance the seeds of a most influential life.

'The powers and the ground of friendship is a mystery; but, looking back, I can discern that, in part, we loved the thing he was, for some shadow of what he was to be. For with all his beauty, power, breeding, urbanity and mirth, there was in those days something soulless in our friend. He would astonish us by sallies, witty, innocent and inhumane; and by a misapplied Johnsonian pleasantry, demolish honest sentiment. I can still see and hear him, as he went his way along the lamplit streets, *Là ci darem la mano* on his lips, a noble figure of a youth, but following vanity and incredulous of good; and sure enough, somewhere on the high seas of life, with his health, his hopes, his patrimony and his self-respect, miserably went down.'

Stevenson proceeds to tell the brief story of his broken career —how he lost health and fortune in defiant pursuit of excesses, yet bravely and uncomplainingly faced the fate of his folly, fortified by philosophy dearly purchased from bitter experience. But Ferrier's latter fortunes lay outside Stevenson's own story. On hearing of his death in September 1883, Stevenson confessed that he had neglected him in his days of adversity; he wrote to Henley in emotional self-reproach for his neglect of 'the first friend I have ever lost', and conscience dictated the moving epitaph in 'Old Mortality'.

From these three friendships, providing the pleasures of good-fellowship, the free interchange of ideas, and the common ground of eagerly anticipating the future, Stevenson derived self-confidence sufficiently to defy his father and to demand the right to choose his own career. In April 1871, just as his father had cause to congratulate himself that his boy was showing promise of success in his prospective profession by winning a silver medal for a paper on 'A New Form of Intermittent Light for Lighthouses', Stevenson informed him that he could not enter the engineering profession, as he wished to become a writer. To the father, never doubting that his son would succeed him, as he himself had succeeded his father and his father had succeeded his grandfather, the intimation came as an unbelievable blow. Though she had learned to realise something of her adored son's gifts during holidays spent at Swanston Cottage—a summer residence outside Edinburgh taken when Stevenson was seventeen, which figures in *St. Ives* as the home of Flora Gilchrist's aunt—his fond mother was horrified at his temerity in opposing the wish of his father, and vainly implored him to bow to a will which she had never dreamed of questioning. But Stevenson was firm, and his mother recorded with relief in her diary that his father seemed 'wonderfully resigned'. Thomas Stevenson agreed to his son's abandoning engineering, but stipulated that he should read law with a view to being called to the Scottish bar, so that, in the event of his failing as a writer, he would be qualified to follow an alternative profession. Accordingly, while reading law at the university, Stevenson entered the office of Skene and Peacock, Writers to the Signet, for practical coaching in conveyancing.

Inevitably the parental concession was reluctant; inevitably, preserving a dignified demeanour of disappointment and disapproval, his father wore an air of resigning his own hopes to gratify his son's freedom of choice. More than ever Stevenson avoided his father; feeling the chill draught of disapproval, like Archie Weir, 'he turned his back upon it' and 'stayed as little as was possible in his father's presence'. His father's aloof attitude of sorrowful disapproval intensified his sense of his eccentricity and proportionately his defiance. He saw himself as an affronting eyesore to the conventional and respectable, and exaggerated his deformity in their eyes. Disdaining evening dress as a uniform of respectability, he attended dinner parties in his old velvet coat and tweed trousers; the casual passer-by in the street stared with raised eyebrows, while friends of the family avoided acknowledging him, pitying his parents for being shamed by such a son. He began to haunt the slum districts of Edinburgh, becoming 'the companion of seamen, chimney-sweeps, and thieves'; he professed that he was driven to consort with low company by the poverty of his allowance, but the prime motive lay in the attraction of courting the censure of respectability and cultivating his character as a Bohemian. There were streets in Edinburgh down which none respectable ever walked—down which none respectable could walk with safety after dark; there were districts in Edinburgh—like those in London described in Michael Sadleir's *Forlorn Sunset*—of which the respectable ignored the existence, mention of which was a breach of good form, since the fact of their existence implied a libel on enlightened democracy and a reproach to respectability and Mr. Gladstone.

Thither went Stevenson, 'seeing life' and thinking himself a devil of a fellow, getting drunk on cheap whisky in low taverns with sailors and prostitutes. Down among the dregs he must have occasionally encountered a member of the top-hatted class, furtively seeking relaxation from the bonds of respectability with a painted tart; sometimes accompanied by Baxter or Ferrier, he compared their present demeanour with their deportment in their fathers' dining-rooms. The recollection of these excursions into Edinburgh slums, with their exciting antithesis to the respectability of the society to which he belonged and his knowledge of the impulse in a member of that society to escape occasionally from the atmosphere of respectability for a brief taste of its utmost contrast, recurred years later as a medium for illustrating the theme of dual personality in *Dr. Jekyll and Mr. Hyde*.

Humbug dictated a habit of conscious dishonesty in Victorian biography, and the legend draped like a surplice about Stevenson's memory by his widow and his official biographer, Sir Graham Balfour, conformed with contemporary fashion. Mrs. Stevenson and Graham Balfour were less blameworthy than many others—than, for instance, the guardians of such reputations as Thackeray's or Dickens's. Mrs. Stevenson was a restricting influence on Stevenson in life, and after his death she jealously cherished the reputation she had helped to build. She had a sound practical reason, for Stevenson's sales depended mainly upon his juvenile public, and respectability would have revolted from presenting its schoolboy sons with the works of an author tainted with scandal. By encouraging the inference that she was the only woman in Stevenson's life, she was guilty of no greater humbug than many a wife in respectable society, to whom a husband's life before marriage was a discreetly sealed book, and any subsequent infidelities were accepted as incidents of her wifely fate, to be silently suffered 'for the sake of the children' or for the continuity of her social and domestic amenities. Everybody who knew Stevenson well recognised the necessity for discretion in his biographers; writing to Colvin on the publication of *Letters to His Family and Friends*, Henry James felt 'the vague sense of omissions and truncations—one *smells* the things unprinted', but added resignedly: 'However, that doubtless had to be.' When, therefore, on the publication of the Balfour biography in 1901, Henley protested against the dehumanising of his old friend as a 'seraph in chocolate', his indiscretion was a *gaffe* as gross as if he had poked bawdy fun at a parson or relieved himself audibly of flatulence in a drawing-room, and Henry James, the recipient of so many letters from Stevenson on truth in literary art, described 'the overflow of Henley's gall' as 'really rather a striking and lurid—and so far interesting case—of long discomfortable jealousy and ranklement turned at last to posthumous (as it were!) malignity, and making the man do, coram publico, his ugly act, risking the dishonour for the assuagement'.

Time smoothes the scars unsightly to humbug's spectacles. If a man claims to be a remote descendant of Byron, Casanova, or Ninon de Lenclos, respectability titters polite interest, but skirts are drawn aside and doors closed in his face if he proclaims too close connection with a recently convicted bigamist or a contemporary woman of notoriously elastic morals. When Stevenson's widow died in 1914, the myth was still inviolate, and ten years later, when misguided disciples of Lytton Strachey had established the fashion of 'debunking' in biography, Mr. Swinnerton ruefully remembered the 'extraordinary indignation' excited by the first appearance of his critical study. But the war of 1914–18 brought a revolution in values; a generation hardened to casual regard of physical suffering and mutilation no longer marvelled at Stevenson's triumphant defiance of delicate health and demanded a more sombre philosophy of life than his gallant romanticism. He now belonged to a past age, and the truth, so opprobrious when insinuated by Henley in 1901, could be debated—except among a few octogenarians like Edmund Gosse and Colvin—as a subject for academic discussion by Mr. J. A. Steuart and Mr. G. S. Hellman in 1924 and 1925. From that planetary limbo to which the manuscripts of all important English writers inevitably gravitate, a New York saleroom, emerged a mass of Stevenson's unpublished verse and prose, conveying significant evidence of his early life.

In his excursions as a youthful Hyde, Stevenson must have fallen in with many women of the unclassed, but the researches of Mr. Steuart and Mr. Hellman disclosed a much more important affair than casual mercenary commerce leaving a distasteful memory of a week or a month. He developed an attachment for a young prostitute named Kate Drummond, a Highland girl probably driven to her trade by the treachery of a seducer or some similar indiscretion, which banished her to exile from a respectable home. She was described to Mr. Steuart as 'slim and dark, very trim and neat, with jet-black hair and a complexion that needed no cosmetics to make it rosy and alluring'. With his expressive eyes, his fragility, vivacity, and charm of manner, Stevenson was a type attractive and frequently fascinating to women; in an autobiographical fragment printed in the Balfour biography, he remarks that, among his acquaintance of 'what would be called a very low order', he was 'distinctly petted and respected; the women were most gentle and kind to me'. To this girl, not yet calloused to insensibility by continual degradation and still instinctively shrinking alike from the lusty brutality of rough sailors and the limp caresses of elderly lechers, the velvet-coated youth, with the refined speech and manners of another world, represented the romance that her young heart craved—that she saw forever slipping beyond her reach. In her arms he learned that she had more to give him than other women of her sort; to him she gave freely from desire instead of suffering caresses for money. No doubt he became known as 'her boy'; probably his presence often protected her from insult. The knowledge that he represented love and brightness in her sordid life could not but flatter his vanity, and with that knowledge her situation invoked the sense of chivalry. Besides, love for a prostitute, the most reprehensible of respectability's outcasts, suited his Bohemian character. Had not Hazlitt loved a whore, and Propertius his golden Cynthia? As Tibullus and Propertius eulogised in verse their courtesan mistresses, so Stevenson addressed verses to his Kate as 'Claire'.

Mr. Steuart heard that Kate was 'many times scolded by "the head of her establishment"' for wasting so much time in Stevenson's company, and 'at last actually beaten'. This probably excited Stevenson in anger to the extremity of reckless chivalry. Kate was eager to give up her way of life for his sake, and he proposed to marry her. The sensation of the suggestion in his family circle can be imagined. Thomas Stevenson, devout churchman and austere citizen, must have been more appalled than angry at the madness of the proposal. This was worse than 'nonsense' to be reproved with the conciliatory gesture of a pat on hand or shoulder, but it is doubtful if he went so far as threatening to disown his son if he persisted in his plan; so much was unnecessary, for Stevenson had nothing but his meagre pocket-money of twelve pounds a year, and a threat to throw him upon his own resources was sufficient to quash the project. Stevenson surrendered, and suffered in surrender more than the agony of thwarted desire, for his resignation of Kate condemned her inevitably to a career of shame. Every recollection of her must have been thenceforth torture to his susceptible conscience; for whatever sad fate befell her he felt morally responsible, and in a poem called 'The Vanquished Knight' he wrote:

> ' I have left all upon the shameful field,
> Honour and Hope, My God! and all but life.'

The shame of his surrender afflicted his spirit as no derision or antagonism could have done. Buoyed upon the vanity that he possessed exceptional gifts and was destined to greatness, he could afford to sneer disdainfully at mockers, but this blow humbled his heart, and he could write that, as 'I do now recognise that I shall never be a great man, I may set myself peacefully upon a smaller journey, not without hope of coming to the inn before nightfall'. The 'histrion' in him demanded a pose, and when he fell seriously ill during the winter of 1872–73, he saw himself more than ever as a counterpart of the ill-starred Robert Fergusson. The notion persisted all his life; in 1891 he wrote: 'I believe Fergusson lives in me,' and a few months before his death he told Baxter: 'I had always a great sense of kinship with poor Robert Fergusson—so clever a boy, so wild, of such a mixed strain, so unfortunate, born in the same town with me, and, as I always felt, rather by express intimation than from evidence, so like myself.'

His mood favoured a renunciation of faith. His soul had

sustained its first serious emotional bruise, which he felt with the soreness of sensitive youth. Compelled by considerations of respectablity to cast his love to the certain fate of degradation and disease, he reflected bitterly on the farce of respectability's devout professions of adherence to the doctrines of the Christ who succoured Mary Magdalene, and wrote:

' O fine religious, decent folk,
  In Virtue's flaunting gold and scarlet,
I sneer between two puffs of smoke,—
  Give me the publican and harlot.

Ye dainty-spoken, stiff, severe
  Seed of the migrated Philistian,
One whispered question in your ear—
  Pray, what was Christ, if you be Christian?
If Christ were only here just now,
  Among the city's wynds and gables
Teaching the life he taught us, how
  Would he be welcome to your tables? '

His reading of Spencer and Whitman had led him to a state of thought somewhere along the same lines as that of Henry Sidgwick, a man twelve years his senior, who was writing that same year: 'Is the *permanent* movement of civilised man towards the Socialism of force, or the Socialism of persuasion (Comte), or Individualism (H. Spencer)? I do not know, and yet everything seems to turn on it.' So, in November 1872, the month of his passing the preliminary examination for the Scottish bar, he read an essay to the 'Spec.' on 'Two Questions on the relations between Christ's teaching and modern Christianity', in which he evidently elaborated, as in the first chapter of *Lay Morals*, the disparity between Christ's doctrines and their distorted interpretation by the Churches.

Perhaps because Stevenson was ill, perhaps because their relations were still too tense after the dispute about Kate Drummond for discussion of another topic, his father apparently brooded for nearly three months over what seemed to him an offence as deplorable as Shelley's pamphlet on 'The Necessity of Atheism' had seemed to Oxford's clerical dons—an offence as personal, to one who had accepted unquestioningly his mother's Calvinism, as Archie Weir's tirade against capital punishment to the hanging judge. For it was not till 2nd February 1873 that Stevenson wrote to Baxter of his father's putting to him 'one or two questions as to beliefs, which I candidly answered'.

'I really hate all lying so much now—a new-found honesty that has somehow come out of my late illness—that I could not so much as hesitate at the time; but if I had foreseen the real hell of everything since, I think I should have lied, as I have done so often before. I so far thought of my father, but I had forgotten my mother. And now! they are both ill, both silent, both as down in the mouth as if—I can find no simile. You may fancy how happy it is for me. If it were not too late, I think I could almost find it in my heart to retract, but it is too late; and again, am I to live my whole life as one falsehood? Of course, it is rougher than hell upon my father, but can I help it? They don't see either that my game is not the light-hearted scoffer; that I am not (as they call me) a careless infidel. I believe as much as they do, only generally in the inverse ratio: I am, I think, as honest as they can be in what I hold. I have not come hastily to my views. I reserve (as I told them) many points until I acquire fuller information, and do not think I am thus justly to be called " horrible atheist ". . . . What a curse I am to my parents! O Lord, what a pleasant thing it is to have just *damned* the happiness of (probably) the only two people who care a damn about you in the world.'

Unless acquainted with the novels of Trollope, Mrs. Henry Wood, or Charlotte M. Yonge, the twentieth-century reader may be hard pressed to realise the overwhelming sense of tragedy inflicted upon Thomas Stevenson by his son's religious self-questioning. Since the priests of the Middle Ages terrorised the illiterate with the horrors of eternal damnation, there has been no period when ecclesiasticism has enjoyed such a vogue as during its successful employment of humbug as the creed of the Victorian middle-class. Every Sunday the churches were crowded, the appointment of a layman to some such petty office as sidesman was a credential in citizenship, and the social power of the parsons is illustrated in Wilkie Collins's *Woman in White* where Mrs. Catherick regards herself as acquitted of many years' stigma of scandal when the local cleric acknowledges her existence by lifting his hat in passing.

It was useless for Stevenson to quote in argument from Darwin or Huxley, Spencer or Whitman. Once, after some hours of discussion, his father exclaimed hysterically 'that he is a weak man, and that I am driving him too far, and that I know not what I am doing'. The state of unhappiness in the household was such that 'even the calm of our daily life is all glossing, there is a sort of tremor through it all and a whole world of repressed bitterness'. From such an oppressive atmosphere it was a relief to escape for his summer holiday of 1873 to Cockfield Rectory, near Bury St. Edmunds, the home of a Balfour cousin, Mrs. Churchill Babington—a resort chosen in the hope that he might fall under beneficial influence from the Rev. Mr. Babington. Such an influence he found—not in the rector, but in a fellow-guest, a young married woman with two small sons.

Fanny Sitwell was one of the many children of a fox-hunting Irish squire named Fetherstonhaugh. A mere schoolgirl of sixteen, she married the Rev. Albert Sitwell when her father emigrated to Australia in the hope of repairing his fortunes. Possibly the marriage was undertaken as an alternative to exile with her family; it proved unhappy, and though 'there had been no official separation', at the time when Stevenson met her she was living independently of her husband as secretary of a working men's college in London.

Some time before she had met a young Cambridge don named Sidney Colvin, and between them an attachment developed. Victorian society allowed no solution to their situation. If she gave grounds for divorce, she would lose the custody of her children and suffer social ostracism for the rest of her life. After a few years of hard work in building a reputation as an art critic, Colvin became Slade Professor of Fine Arts at Cambridge in 1873, director of the Fitzwilliam Museum in 1876, and Keeper of Prints and Drawings at the British Museum in 1884. He was dependent upon the emoluments of these offices, all of which he would have been compelled to resign as co-respondent in a divorce case. Like countless contemporaries, they preferred prudence to romance, and

Colvin was sixty, Mrs. Sitwell some six years older, when in 1903, 'all obstacles being cleared away', they were enabled to marry.

It is interesting, though idle, to speculate on how far Colvin's self-denial of a full life affected the character of his work, but his criticism reflects the qualities of his conduct in its rectitude, its prudence, and its absence of imaginative inspiration. He wrote a commendable monograph on Landor, but the more ambitious scheme of his *Life of Keats* resulted in a sprawling, shapeless book—rather a work of reference, painstakingly presenting all the available facts, than a readable account of its subject. After Colvin's death in 1926 his friend Basil Champneys expressed indignation to E.V. Lucas at the 'insinuations that Sidney Colvin's fame rested mainly on his special association with Robert Louis Stevenson', but now he is undoubtedly best remembered as the editor of Stevenson's *Letters*.

It would be impertinent, as well as unfair, to suggest that Mr. Somerset Maugham intended Mr. and Mrs. Barton Trafford in *Cakes and Ale* to be identified as caricatures of Sir Sidney and Lady Colvin. But he must have been thinking of Stevenson when writing of 'the great novelist whose death a few years back had come as such a shock to the English-speaking peoples'. As in the case of Mr. Maugham's 'great novelist' and Mrs. Barton Trafford, Stevenson did leave an extensive correspondence with Mrs. Sitwell, which expressed 'his admiration for her beauty and his respect for her judgment', and 'how much he owed to her encouragement, her ready sympathy, her tact, her taste'. And though Colvin did not—like Mr. Barton Trafford—write the biography of his wife's correspondent, he did edit his letters. Further, her reputation as Stevenson's early Egeria undoubtedly assisted Lady Colvin, after her second marriage, in establishing herself as a fashionable literary hostess, in which capacity she sponsored the pretensions of Stephen Phillips as a poet with much the same vexatious reward as Mrs. Barton Trafford received from her sponsorship of the graceless Jasper Gibbons. But there the parallel ends: there is wide divergence between Barton Trafford's capitalisation of his wife's correspondent and Sidney Colvin's fidelity in friendship and admiration for Stevenson, dating from this meeting at Cockfield Rectory with an unknown young man in disgrace with his family.

A woman of personality and talent, as well as feminine charm and good looks, Mrs. Sitwell at thirty-four was of an age to attract a young man of twenty-two, and she had the additional romantic appeal of being unhappily married, separated from her husband, and obviously the object of attention from the gifted young Cambridge don. Stevenson won a way to her heart by his lively companionship with one of her sons; lacking a more satisfactory vent for sexual emotion, she was well disposed to encourage the admiration of romantic youth and soon listening sympathetically to confidential outpourings about his troubles. Bidden by her to meet 'a real young genius,' Colvin came down from Cambridge to find among the guests

'One, a boy of ten, watching for every moment when he could monopolise the newcomer's attention, either to show off to him the scenes of his toy theatre or to conduct him confidentially by the hand about the garden or beside the moat; while between him and the boy's mother, Mrs. Sitwell, there had sprung up an instantaneous understanding. Not only the lights and brilliancies of his nature, but the strengths and glooms that underlay them, were from the first apparent to her, so that in the trying season of his life which followed he was moved to throw himself upon her sympathies with the unlimited confidence and devotion to which his letters of the time bear witness. He sped those summer nights and days for us all as I have scarce known any sped before or since. He seemed, this youngster, already to have lived and seen and felt and dreamed and laughed and longed more than others do in a lifetime. . . . Pure poetic eloquence (coloured always, be it remembered, by a strong Scottish accent), grave argument and criticism, riotous freaks of fancy, flashes of nonsense more illuminating than wisdom, streamed from him inexhaustibly as he kindled with delight at the delight of his hearers.'

This impression, published in his *Memories and Notes* of 1921, was recorded by Colvin in reminiscence after many years and probably coloured by later enthusiasm. But he was ready to befriend a recommendation of Mrs. Sitwell's, and Stevenson went more than half-way to meet him, for, besides being Mrs. Sitwell's intimate friend, Colvin was the first man he had met who was familiar with famous men of genius. He knew Ruskin and Rossetti, Burne-Jones and Browning, and when Stevenson met him in London the following autumn, he was able to introduce him to important magazine editors.

On his return home the enthusiasm encouraged by Colvin and Mrs. Sitwell was speedily damped, and every few days he wrote to Mrs. Sitwell bulletins about the misery arising from religious differences with his father. He was little disposed to defer to his father's views, for he read Darwin's latest book on the train returning to Edinburgh and began to write the essay on 'John Knox and his Relations to Women' (published two years later in *Macmillan's Magazine* and reprinted in *Familiar Studies of Men and Books*), which exhibits an undergraduate's malicious delight in convicting the Calvinist zealot of lecherous inclinations and indicates his manner of argument against his father's household gods. 'My father and I together can put about a year through in half an hour,' he writes; 'if I had not a very light heart and a great faculty of interest in what is under hand, I really think I should go mad under this wretched state of matters.'

The original letters reveal that, besides suppressing passages indicating Mrs. Sitwell's encouragement of Stevenson to a dangerous degree of intimacy, Colvin omitted much detail illustrative of Stevenson's unhappiness with his parents. On his return from Cockfield, his parents apparently decided to say nothing of Claire so long as Stevenson showed no sign of resuming the affair with her, and to saddle the blame for his unfortunate religious views upon Bob Stevenson's malign influence. 'I have been to-day a very long walk with my father through some of the most beautiful ways hereabouts,' wrote Stevenson on 6th September:

'I think he has made up his mind to say nothing to me about the affair I mentioned. My mother has already informed me officially that Bob and he are not to be allowed to meet. With the strangest readiness they have transferred all blame from me and have no censure for anyone but him; as they have done all through, they are going to do to the end; and, after all, things perhaps lie out most easily on that slope. For me, they are very pleasant. It is a God's mercy I was not at home or things might have really come

to a climax; so you see my six weeks in the sunshine have been a
fortunate season for me in even more ways than I had fancied.'

This state of calm lasted three days before the storm of a
meeting between Bob Stevenson and his uncle, whose mind had
been poisoned against Bob by a pious cousin, recently deceased.

'I was sitting up here working away at John Knox, when the
door opened and Bob came in with his hands over his face and sank
down on a chair and began to sob. He was scarcely able to speak
at first, but he found voice at last, and I then found that he had
come to see me, had met my father in the way and had just brought
to an end an interview with him. There is now, at least, one person
in the world who knows what I have had to face—damn me for
facing it, as I sometimes think, in weak moments—and what a
tempest of emotions my father can raise when he is really excited.
It seems that this poor cousin of mine has hated Bob and me all
through his life, that our words have been a sharp poison to him,
and our opinions horrible, and our presence an intolerable burthen;
he always met us as friends; he was too weak it seemed to show
what he disliked and what shocked him, and he led us on, unconsciously I daresay, to play with him cards-down, and keep
nothing secret. A little before death, he relieved his feelings to my
father; Bob, he said, was a "blight", a "mildew"; it was a matter
of wonder to him "how God should have made such a man";
I was the one depraved and hideous one who could endure Bob's
presence. . . . My father's interview with Bob has been long coming;
and has now come. I am so tired in heart and tired in body that
I cannot tell you the result to-night. . . . To-morrow I shall give
more details.'

Next day he added:

'The war began with my father accusing Bob of having ruined
his house and his son. Bob answered that he didn't know where I
had found out that the Christian religion was not true, but that
he hadn't told me. And, I think from that point, the conversation
went off into emotion and never touched shore again. There was
not much said about me—my views, according to my father, are
rather a childish imitation of Bob, to cease the moment the *mildew*
is removed; all that was said was that I had ceased to care for my
father, and that my father confessed he was ceasing, or had greatly

ceased, to care for me. Indeed, the object of the interview is not very easy to make out; it had no practical issue except the ludicrous one that Bob promised never to talk Religion to me any more. It was awfully rough on him, you know; he had no idea that there was that sort of thing in the world, although I had told him often enough—my father on his knees and that kind of thing. O dear, dear, I just hold on to your hand very tight and shut my eyes. I wonder why God has made *me* to be this curse to my father and mother. If it had not been for the thoughts of you, I should have been twice as cut up . . .'

Later, during the afternoon of the same day:

'No letter. I hope you are well. To continue the story, I have seen Bob again, and he has had a private letter from my father, apologising for anything he may have said, but adhering to the substance of the interview. There was more in this letter (which Bob, perhaps by rather a breach of confidence, allowed me at my earnest desire to see) of his writhings over a ruined life and hopes overthrown which are intolerable to think about. Moreover I learn that my mother had hysterics privately last night over it all.'

Colvin concealed the part played by Stevenson's mother in the disputes between father and son. As an intermediary, she allowed emotion to overwhelm tact and wisdom, so fomenting the distress of both; upbraiding Stevenson in defence of his father, she usually ended in hysteria, and doubtless she adopted the same essentially feminine method of argument with his father. On 12th September Stevenson reported to Mrs. Sitwell:

'To-night my father was talking of how he feared to do what he knew he ought; and I did I think some good to our deplorable condition in this home of ours by what I said. I spoke to my mother afterwards, telling her how I felt with my father and hoped all good from anything he could do; and only hoped in that, that every man should do what he thought best, as best he could. But I had to stop, as she was growing hysterical.'

With such tension between them, a father might have been expected to avoid his son's society, in the hope that troubled waters might be stilled for want of stirring. But Thomas Stevenson's morbid conscience kept him continually brooding over the precarious destiny of his only son, and next day he went 'a very favourite walk' with Stevenson 'along the shore between Granton and Cramond.'

'I am glad to say that the peace of the day and scenery was not marred by any unpleasantness between us two; indeed I do think things are going a little better with us; my father I believe has some of the satisfaction consequent upon a good auto-da-fe now he has finally quarrelled with Bob and banished him. And although it seems mean to profit by what my own heart feels anxious to resent, I am only too glad of any peace between us although every month of it were to cost me a finger. You will understand the wearying, despairing, sick heart that grows up within one, when things go on as sometimes they do; and how the whole of life seems blighted and hopeless and twilight.'

Still his father could not leave well alone, and four days later Stevenson recorded, 'It was really pathetic to hear my father praying pointedly for me to-day at family worship, and to think that the poor man's supplications were addressed to nothing better able to hear and answer than the chandelier.' After about another week, while his mother was away for a few days, he found it 'difficult indeed to steer steady among the breakers . . . for I cannot help getting friendly with my father (whom I *do* like), and so speaking foolishly with my mouth.' Inevitably there was another 'awful scene,' in which 'all that my father had to say has been put forth—not that it was anything new; only it is the devil to hear,' and he could 'scarcely see' in writing to Mrs. Sitwell:

'I say, my dear friend, I am killing my father—he told me to-night (by the way) that I alienated utterly my mother—and this is the result of my attempt to start fair and fresh and to do my best for all of them. I am a beast to bother you, with all your troubles, about this; but to-night has been really very bad—worse than ordinary. If only I could cease to like him, I could pull through with a good heart; but it is really insupportable to see his emotion—an impotent emotion rather, to make things worse—his sort of half thoughts on turning me out and O God bless the whole thing. I have a ringing headache so please excuse this scrawl of nonsense. I should not send it off I know and yet I do wish a little consolation. You don't know what a difference it makes; especially now that Bob is very difficult to get at. I *did* mean to make him very happy all this time my mother was away; and see the result! O dear God, I wish I could think *he* was happy. It has been a terrible blow to him. He said to-night, "He wished he had never married," and I could only echo what he said. "A poor end," he said, "for all my tenderness." And what was there to answer? "I have made all my life to suit you—I have worked for you and gone out of my way for you—and the end of it is that I find you in opposition to the Lord Jesus Christ—I find everything gone—I would ten times sooner have seen you lying in your grave than that you should be shaking the faith of other young men and bringing such ruin on other houses, as you have brought already upon this"— that is a sort of abstract of one speech. There is a jolly scene for you —there is the staff I have been to his declining years. "I thought," he said, "to have had some one to help me, when I was old." Much help he has had.'

On his mother's return, her habit of defending the one to the other, instead of ministering tender consolation to each, dictated an attitude of frigid disapproval towards her son, who, feeling 'seedy and out of heart,' thus recorded his reaction:

'My father said no more than truth about my mother's feelings to me; I see that now very clearly, although it does seem hard to have put it into words. She is quite cold and unresponsive, after all. I try to cheat myself with flimsies, but that's the hard kernel of fact. I tell you this is just a mere trial of nervous strength between us. The weakest will die first, that is all. And I don't know whether to wish for the one alternative or the other. Both seem horrible; but not much more horrible than the unsightly, hopeless present.'

Shrewdly he assessed the state of tension as a 'trial of nervous strength'; himself a masochist, he was the victim of masochists resorting for self-expression to the tortures of sadistic fanaticism. From the rack of his parents' company his only escape lay in the privacy of his own room at the top of the house—a privilege wrung from his mother on his return from Cockfield, on the grounds that he must have a room of his own to secure the seclusion necessary for his writing.

71

The strain upon his nerves was intensified by his yearning for Mrs. Sitwell, to whom he expressed his romantic infatuation in terms of morbid passion. On the matter of her separation from her husband she was receiving advice from the Rev. Mr. Babington; it does not appear whether he was actually advising a return to her husband, but Stevenson was anxiously contemptuous of his 'ministrations'. 'You are the very texture of my thought,' he told her; 'I am never an hour without you slipping in somewhere, dear.' 'Of course, I have not been going on with Claire,' he assures her; 'I have been out of heart for that; and besides it is difficult to act before the reality. Footlights will not do with the sun; the stage morn and the real, lucid morn of one's dark life, look strangely on each other.' To his new love he confided his remorse for renunciation of his old love:

'I have been thinking a little of my wretchedness when your letters did not come; and the whole business knocked most unpleasantly at my conscience. I too left letters unanswered until they ceased to come, from a person to whom the postage even must have been a matter of parsimony; left them unanswered, on purpose that they might cease. O God! a thing comes back to me that hurts the heart very much. For the first letter, she had bought a piece of paper with a sort of flower-arabesque at the top of it. I wish you would write cruelly about this—I wish you would by God. I want something to make me take up arms in my own defence—no, I don't. Only I could not help writing this to you because it is in my mind—on my heart, and I hope you won't hate me for it. Only one thing gives me any little pleasure, and it is a very, very faint one. I never showed the letters to anyone, and some months ago they became insupportable to me and I burnt them. Don't I deserve the gallows?'

Under the stress of nervous strain and morbid emotion his health naturally suffered, and Bob Stevenson recognised that a breakdown could only be averted by escape from his parents. Stevenson wrote to Mrs. Sitwell on 3rd. October:

'Bob got very warm to-day that I should break and leave my parents. My health is certainly not so good as it might be, and he says I have grown a new wrinkle since I came back this summer.

I can only tell you that he was in the humour of even violence, and said that if I were to lose my health here, my father should hear some language from him about his religion that he was not capable of thinking possible, and yet, even in this mood, I convinced him that the thing was impossible. I could not, just after they have given me a room for myself and my mother has taken so much interest in it, go off and leave them that same room empty, as a bitter reproach continually in their side, as a harsh proof that, after they had done all, they had not been able to keep their son.'

A few days later he noted, 'Bob has been, the few times I have been able to see him, a perfect God for me, all through my troubles.'

Apart from occasional meetings with his cousin, his writing afforded the only refuge from morbid preoccupation. Besides drafting his essays on Knox and Whitman, he completed an article on 'Roads', which was sent by Mrs. Sitwell to Colvin, who secured its publication in *The Portfolio*, an art magazine edited by P. G. Hamerton, after its rejection by the *Saturday Review*. As the autumn drew on, he felt a shuddering dread of Edinburgh's bleakness, either blustered with gusty winds or 'drowned in white, wet vapour off the sea', so that 'everything drips and soaks' and 'the very statues seem wet to the skin'. In the hope of gratifying his 'thirst for a little warmth, a little sun, a little corner of blue sky', he seized upon a remark by the Lord Advocate in conversation with his father that there would be advantage in his reading for the English, instead of the Scottish, bar. His parents were persuaded to the plan by alarm for his health; despite his height, he weighed only eight stone six pounds, and in October he fell ill again with 'a bad sore throat, fever, rheumatism and a threatening of pleurisy'. As soon as he was well enough to travel, he was allowed to go up to London, though he had small hopes of passing the bar examination—'indeed after this bodily and spiritual crisis I should not dream of coming up at all; only that I require it as a pretext for a moment's escape'.

Before sitting for the bar examination, his parents required him to undergo a physical examination by a specialist, Sir Andrew Clark. The diagnosis, according to Colvin, was that he was 'suffering from acute nerve exhaustion, with some

threat of danger to the lungs'; Balfour is more particular—
'nervous exhaustion with a threatening of phthisis: the prescription was chiefly mental—a winter in the Riviera by himself, and in complete freedom from anxiety and worry'. The
specialist evidently shrewdly recognised that his patient was
nervously oppressed by a home life which his biographers
conspired to insist on having been generally 'harmonious',
and Stevenson wrote to Mrs. Sitwell:

'Clark is a trump. He said I must go abroad and that I was
better alone. "Mothers," he said, "just put fancies into people's
heads and make them fancy themselves worse than they are." . . . I
was to have been despatched to Torquay with my mother; Clark
disposed of all that at one breath; they think no end of Clark.'

In London, before his departure for France, he was daily with
Mrs. Sitwell; the day of his departure was 'the first day I have
not seen you for ten days'. As he 'burnt all your letters but the
first and the last,' his own letters supply the only evidence of
how far she fanned the flame of his infatuation. As a married
woman separated from her husband, she could afford to risk no
open indiscretion, but Stevenson's romantic ardour tempted
her far beyond the bounds of prudence. When he left for
Mentone, on 5th November, 1873, he carried away the cherished
memory of 'breakfasting in C.P.' (Mrs. Sitwell's home in
Chepstow Place) 'and you were there in the mob cap and the
maroon dressing gown.'

CHAPTER THREE

THE BOHEMIAN

'The true Bohemian . . . lives wholly to himself, does what he wishes, and not what is thought proper, buys what he wants for himself and not what is thought proper, works at what he believes he can do well and not what will bring him in money or favour.'—

Lay Morals.

ON LEAVING England for Mentone, Stevenson felt only exultation at escaping from the repressive atmosphere of home, the gloom of his father and of the Edinburgh winter. 'They are evidently bent on my return in six weeks at longest,' he wrote to Mrs. Sitwell; 'I hope they may find resignation, for methinks I shall manage to disappoint them.' This sentiment contrasts strangely with those attributed to the imaginary 'friend of mine' in *Lay Morals*:

'Falling into ill-health, he was sent at great expense to a more favourable climate; and then I think his perplexities were thickest. When he thought of all the other young men of singular promise, upright, good, the prop of families, who must remain at home to die, and with all their possibilities be lost to life and mankind; and how he, by one more unmerited favour, was chosen out from all these others to survive; he felt as if there were no life, no labour, no devotion of soul and body, that could repay and justify these partialities. A religious lady, to whom he communicated these reflections, could see no force in them whatever. "It was God's will," said she. But he knew . . . that although the possibility of this favour he was now enjoying issued from his circumstances, its acceptance was the act of his own will; and he had accepted it greedily, longing for rest and sunshine. And hence this allegation of God's providence did little to relieve his scruples. I promise you he had a very troubled mind.'

Again, in an autobiographical fragment quoted by Balfour, he remarks: 'I was always kept poor in my youth, to my great indignation at the time, but since then with my complete approval,' adding, 'twelve pounds a year was my allowance up to twenty-three . . . though I amplified it by a very consistent embezzlement from my mother'.

In *Lay Morals* he forestalls comment on the discrepancy between conscience and conduct:

'I would not laugh if I were you, though while he was thus making mountains out of what you think molehills, he were still (as perhaps he was) contentedly practising many other things that to you seem black as hell. Every man is his own judge and mountain-guide through life.'

The Jekyll of conscience asserted that he was a social parasite in subsisting on his father's bounty, and urged him to secure independence by his own efforts as speedily as possible; but the Hyde of self-indulgent impulse resented the parsimony of his father's allowance, supplemented it by persuasively extracting subsidies from his mother, and did not scruple to play upon their concern for his health as a plea for prolongation of holidays. Every offence by Hyde added to the burden of woe upon Jekyll's 'very troubled mind'.

The accounts of his emotions in *Lay Morals* and in the essay, 'Ordered South', are endorsed by his letters to Mrs. Sitwell— the 'religious lady' consulted by the 'friend' of *Lay Morals*. The mood of exultation on his departure from England lasted through the railway journey—'the speed is so easy, and the train disturbs so little the scenes through which it takes us, that our heart becomes full of the placidity and stillness of the country'—till arrival at his destination.

'It is only after he is fairly arrived and settled down in his chosen corner, that the invalid begins to understand the change that has befallen him. Everything about him is as he had remembered, or as he had anticipated. Here, at his feet, under his eyes, are the olive gardens and the blue sea. Nothing can change the eternal magnificence of form of the naked Alps behind Mentone; nothing, not even the crude curves of the railway, can utterly deform the suavity of contour of one bay after another along the whole reach of the Riviera. And of all this, he has only a cold head knowledge that is divorced from enjoyment. He recognises with his intelligence that this thing and that thing is beautiful, while in his heart of hearts he has to confess that it is not beautiful for him. It is in vain that he spurs his discouraged spirit. . . . He is like an enthusiast leading about with him a stolid, indifferent tourist. . . . The world is disenchanted for him. He seems to himself to touch things with muffled hands, and to see them through a veil. His life becomes a palsied fumbling after notes that are silent when he has found and struck them. He cannot recognise that this phlegmatic and unimpressionable body with which he now goes burthened, is the same that he knew heretofore so quick and delicate and alive.'

The account in 'Ordered South' of his emotions and reflections faithfully reproduces those expressed in his letters. At first, blaming the soft climate for his torpor, he felt homesick for the invigorating keenness of Edinburgh's 'hale rough weather' —though this nostalgia seems to have been inspired by a letter from his cousin Bob, lamenting that 'he cannot get on without me at all' and finds that 'he only talked to other people in order that he might tell me afterwards about the conversation'. Thought of Edinburgh reminds him of the miserable condition of tramps and barefoot children in the bleakness of north; he wishes that they could be with him likewise to 'lie down for a little in the sunshine', but realises that 'it is not altogether ill with the invalid after all', and 'if it is only rarely that anything penetrates vividly into his numbed spirit, yet, when anything does, it brings with it a joy that is all the more poignant for its very rarity'.

Reflecting that truly life is better spent in sharpening the perceptions for the appreciation of beauty than in seeking after material success, he yet finds 'something pathetic' in the caprice of mood that governs the pleasures of the senses, so that, in the man of sensibility, 'a degree of nervous prostration, that to other men would be hardly disagreeable, is enough to overthrow for him the whole fabric of his life, to take, except at rare moments, the edge off his pleasures, and to meet him wherever he goes with failure, and the sense of want, and disenchantment of the world and life'. He decided that the invalid's 'numbness of spirit' resembled 'a premature old age', for, like an old man, with senses dulled by infirmity, the invalid can contemplate the possible approach of death as the inevitable ending of a gradual diminution of joy in life.

'It is not so much, indeed, death that approaches as life that withdraws and withers up from round about him. He has outlived his own usefulness, and almost his own enjoyment; and if there is to be no recovery; if never again will he be young and strong and passionate, if the actual present shall be to him always like a thing read in a book or remembered out of the faraway past; if, in fact, this be veritably nightfall, he will not wish greatly for the continuance of a twilight that only strains and disappoints the eyes, but steadfastly await the perfect darkness. He will pray for Medea: when she comes, let her either rejuvenate or slay.'

So he wrote in 'Ordered South', and to Mrs. Sitwell in late November he said simply:

'It is a pitiable blindness, this blindness of the soul; I hope it may not be long with me. . . . To sit by the sea and to be conscious of nothing but the sound of the waves, and the sunshine over all your body, is not unpleasant; but I was an Archangel once. . . . If you knew how old I felt! I am sure this is what age brings with it—this carelessness, this disenchantment, this continual bodily weariness. I am a man of seventy: O Medea, kill me, or make me young again!'

'Ordered South' was the mirrored reflection of an histrionic pose; for the moment it seemed that he was in fact cast for the part of Robert Fergusson, and he felt sorry for himself. Such an essay might have been written by Llewelyn Powys when, nearly forty years later, he too was ordered south in search of health. His diaries show even more sharply than Stevenson's letters a similar trend of emotion, for, unlike Stevenson, he was not posing on paper for a sympathetic feminine audience and he had always a saving sense of humour. Before writing *Skin for Skin* Powys wisely waited till he could survey in retrospect the entire panorama of his experience. Realising its value as the expression of a mood, Stevenson considered 'Ordered South' as worthy of inclusion in his earliest collection of essays, but felt that he 'must in honesty append a word or two of qualification'. Even at this time he wrote to Mrs. Sitwell, 'So remember to keep well; and remember rather anything than not to keep well.' Like Powys, he learned from looking death in the face that life was to be loved for its own sake, though, unlike Powys, he had a Calvinistic conscience requiring a motive for the love of life—'a career which was his only business in this world.'

However consoling and encouraging Mrs. Sitwell's replies to his letters may have been, they were themselves insufficient to rouse Stevenson from the mood of apathy. He stopped work on his Whitman essay, and announcing that 'I have given up all hope, all fancy rather, of making literature my hold: I see that I have not capacity enough', he declared: 'If Colvin does not think that I shall be able to support myself soon by literature, I shall give it up and go (horrible as the thought is to me) into an office of some sort.' Doubtless this was said without sincerity and intended to invoke encouraging protest and tender concern. When he told Baxter, 'I must say straight out that I am not recovering as I could wish', he must have written with a shrewd notion that his friend would report the intimation to his father, so preparing the ground for prolonging his absence abroad. The report to Mrs. Sitwell that 'all yesterday I was under the influence of opium' was palpably histrionic; he assured her that he felt no temptation to repeat the experiment, since 'some verses which I wrote turn out on inspection to be not quite equal to *Kubla Khan*'.

Apathy and the pose of the dying poet were alike dispelled by the advent of Colvin, who came in the third week of December to stay a fortnight. Together they visited Monte Carlo, and correspondence languished in the occupation of conversation. 'Colvin's being with me is a great amusement,' he told his mother, 'I am less tired and dispirited than I was by a good way,' and more expansively he confessed to Mrs. Sitwell: 'I cannot write, in any sense of the word; but I am as happy as can be, and wish to notify the fact, before it passes.'

Before Colvin left, with a promise soon to return from Paris, he helped Stevenson to make some interesting acquaintances, 'a bush-bearded French landscape painter' named Robinet and two 'brilliantly accomplished and cultivated' Russian sisters, the Princess Zassetsky and Madame Garschine. To gain the good graces of the sisters Stevenson was able to follow the same technique as in his approach to Mrs. Sitwell; one of them had a little girl named Nelitchka, who delighted in his playful companionship and called him 'by a word for "rogue" or "naughty man" she had lately picked up in Italy, "Berecchino!"' The elder and 'more dashing' sister had a lover in her own country, but Madame Garschine was 'unattached', and while Stevenson talked much of the child in his letters to Mrs. Sitwell, he confessed to feeling embarrassment at this lady's attentions.

'I don't know what Mme. G.'s little game is with regard to me. Certainly she has either made up her mind to make a fool of me in a somewhat coarse manner, or else she is in train to make a fool of herself.'

Declaring himself 'damnably embarrassed and yet funnily interested', he affected to regard her, with consummate youthful condescension, as 'a very fine organisation whom it gives me pleasure to study, a pleasure which will be neither increased nor diminished by this business, however it turns out'.

Naturally Mrs. Sitwell was eager to know how it turned out; her letters were evidently full of questions and possibly she also hinted a warning to his mother, for Mrs. Stevenson wrote a letter abounding in questions. But, having excited Mrs. Sitwell's curiosity, Stevenson pursued a tantalising strategy, probably well content if it succeeded in provoking indiscreet expressions of jealousy. The sisters were 'people of like views with us' and knew their Mill and Spencer; probably they were disciples of Tolstoy, but Stevenson then knew nothing of Tolstoy. Madame Zassetsky was 'certainly a very clever woman' and had 'a great idea that I am very clever . . . indeed they both have'. After remarking that 'Mme. G. is very nice to me, sweet and serious', a few days later he administered a shock calculated to stimulate awakened jealousy:

'I had a good long talk with Mme. G. I wish I could make up my mind to tell you what she said, for I should like to know if you

" VELVET COAT "

would agree with it: I have been quite confused and upset every time I have thought of it since. If I am like what she says, I must be a very nice person!'

Having, in the course of the next few sentences, dropped the casual information that madame 'never means to go back' to her husband, he proceeds the next day, without revealing more of the 'good long talk':

'All that Mme G. told me the other day (and I believe she meant it)—all that you have told me, *all that you feel for me*—is so much better than I feel myself to be that I begin to loathe myself as an imposture. When you see *Ordered South* you will understand how I prefer "the shadowy life that we have in the hearts of others", because it is so much more beautiful and noble, to the vulgar little market-place of petty passions that I know bitterly to be myself. Is it all a dream, dear? Lift up your eyes, and you will see that I am not worthy, and turn away.'

Having said which, he declares himself 'glad now to be sure' that Madame Garschine had never intended any such 'little game' as he had suspected, either for making a fool of herself or for making a fool of him.

Was Stevenson attempting to make a fool of Mrs. Sitwell while at the same time making a fool of Madame Garschine? Certainly he excited such expressions of jealousy as enabled him to write:

'O my dear, don't misunderstand me; let me hear soon to tell me that you can't doubt me; I wanted to let you know really how the thing stood and perhaps I am wrong, perhaps doing that is impossible in some cases. At least, dear, believe me you have been as much in my heart these last few days as ever you have been, and the thought of you troubles my breathing with the sweetest trouble. I am only happy in the thought of you, my dear; this other woman is interesting to me as a hill might be, or a book, or a picture, but you have all my heart, my darling.'

Already, since coming to Mentone, he had advanced in expression of endearment by habitually addressing her as Consuelo: 'O consuelo de mi alma,' he wrote, 'I have found

the name for you at last—Consuelo. Consolation of my spirit.'
Having excited an expression of jealousy that could be con-
strued as a declaration of her love, he was careful in subsequent
letters to suggest no more than platonic sympathy between
himself and Madame Garschine; 'much that Colvin will tell
you about Mme Garschine,' he warned her, 'is true indeed,
but not quite true.'

Did he also make the most of his situation with Madame
Garschine? The charm that enabled him to be 'petted'
by women of Kate Drummond's class was equally effective
upon women of another order; Fleeming Jenkin must have
been duly astonished when his wife announced her discovery
of 'a young Heine with a Scottish accent' and introduced him
to the truant of his engineering class. Mrs. Sitwell had immediately felt her interest awakened. And now he as strongly
attracted Madame Garschine. Besides a poem in Scots
addressed to both sisters, he addressed to Madame Garschine
four lines of cryptic meaning about the fairness of her face
being rendered grander by love and constancy. The discreet
Colvin described her as 'much of an invalid, consistently
gentle and sympathetic', about fifteen years older than Stevenson, and 'an exquisite musician', but remarking that for
Stevenson she 'conceived a great quasi-maternal tenderness',
he vividly remembered 'the sense of her sharp twitch of pain
as I spoke one day, while she was walking with her arm in
mine, of the fears entertained by his friends for his health and
future'. If she is coarse and he a cad, passion between a woman
of forty and a boy young enough to be her son presents a
degrading spectacle of lust, but Madame Garschine's infatuation for Stevenson may have been like Anna Stormer's for
young Lennan in Galsworthy's novel, *The Dark Flower*, like
Miriam Stern's for Mr. Compton Mackenzie's hero in *The
East Wind of Love*—productive of an experience rich in beauty
for both, providing a cherished memory for the ageing woman
and a lasting debt of gratitude for the young man. In Stevenson's case the memory was spoiled by no bitter recriminations
for the fading of ephemeral passion; he parted from her with
the promise of a visit to Russia in the following summer, but
he neither went to Russia nor ever saw her again.

Her companionship dispelled his mood of apathy. He forgot to despond about his health, began to work again on Whitman, and completed 'Ordered South', which Colvin approved and placed for him with *Macmillan's Magazine*. On his return to Mentone from Paris, Colvin introduced Stevenson to Andrew Lang, who, likewise suffering from lung trouble, had come south in search of health. Colvin felt 'some trepidation' over the introduction, recognising that 'no two young Scots, especially no two sharing so many literary tastes, were ever more unlike by temperament and training'.

'On the one hand the young Oxford don, a successful and typical scholar on the regular academic lines, picturesque by the gift of nature but fastidiously correct and reserved, purely English in speech, with a recurring falsetto note in the voice—that kind of falsetto that bespeaks languor rather than vehemence; full of literature and pleasantry but on his guard, even to affectation, against any show of emotion, and consistently dissembling the *perfervidum ingenium* of his race, if he had it, under a cloak of indifference and light banter. On the other hand the brilliant irregularly educated lad from Edinburgh, to the conventional eye an eccentrically ill-clad and long-haired nondescript, with the rich Lallan accent on his tongue, the obvious innate virility and spirit of adventure in him ever in mutiny against the invalid habits imposed by ill-health, the vivid, demonstrative ways, every impulse of his heart and mind flashing out in the play of eye, feature, and gesture no less than in the humorous riot and poetical abundance of his talk.'

Colvin's fear seemed at first well founded. Stevenson thought Lang 'Oxfordish', and Lang, in his 'Recollections of R. L. Stevenson' published in *Adventures Among Books*, confessed that 'my first impression was not wholly favourable'. With a colour 'a trifle hectic', Stevenson looked 'more like a lass than a lad', his long blue cloak and his Tyrolese hat were 'decidedly dear to him', and Lang summed him up as 'one of your aesthetic young men, though a very clever one'. Sometimes subsequently Stevenson's eccentricities offended his standards of correctness, as when, wearing his shabby cloak and a smoking cap, Stevenson hailed him cheerfully in Bond Street, and Lang refused to stop, saying: 'My character will stand a great deal, but it won't stand being seen talking to a thing like you in Bond Street.'

Fortunately for Stevenson's literary celebrity, while their personal relations continued cordial without ever approaching intimacy, Lang conceived an admiration for his early essays that swelled into extravagant enthusiasm when Stevenson became a writer of romantic fiction. Without the support of Lang's enormous prestige as a critic, the official custodians of Stevenson's reputation could hardly have erected about it the elaborate edifice of legend. For Lang acquired a unique position in the literary world of the eighteen-eighties and 'nineties, wielding an influence beyond that of any critic before or since. Relating how two obscure shilling books were turned into popular successes by notices of Lang's in the *Daily News*, Grant Richards remarked in his *Memories of a Misspent Youth* that since Lang's time—with the single exception of Arnold Bennett's *Evening Standard* articles in the last years of his life— 'no man alive, no newspaper, has all that power'. Just as he started, or stimulated, the sensational success of Anthony Hope's *Prisoner of Zenda*, the sales of Stanley Weyman and S. R. Crockett, and the stupendous popularity of Rider Haggard, Lang contributed immensely to the making of Stevenson's reputation. He did not confine his advertisement of Stevenson to laudatory reviews of his books; he talked continually about him, mentioning his books as standards of comparison when praising another writer's work, recalling remarks by Stevenson as apposite to a subject under discussion, repeatedly referring to characters and incidents in his stories. For instance, reference to a publisher's announcement that Quiller-Couch was to complete *St. Ives* enabled Lang to discuss the impossibility of anybody's completing *Weir of Hermiston*, to suggest mockingly that a national memorial to Stevenson should take the form of a group of statuary representing George Moore in the act of instructing Stevenson in the art of writing, to remark that Stevenson never sought cheap publicity by lending his name to tradesmen's advertisements, and to relate the circumstances of the publication and reception of *Dr. Jekyll and Mr. Hyde*. As Lang lost no opportunity of talking about him, his readers became educated to his estimation of

Stevenson—and Lang's readers comprised the majority of the reading public.

On his way home from Mentone in April 1874, Stevenson stayed two or three weeks in Paris with his cousin Bob, who had effected his escape from Edinburgh to study painting. His mother wired her disapproval of his proposed stay in Paris, but he had been careful to inform her of his intention too late for her communication to reach him before his arrival there. He needed Bob's encouragement to fortify him in a policy of defiance; after enjoying liberty at Mentone to spend anything he required within reason, he intended to demand an allowance sufficient to allow him freedom of movement, and he also anticipated opposition to a plan to pursue his law studies at the university of Gottingen, where Madame Garschine's cousin, Prince Leon Galitzin, was a student. To his surprise he received from his father 'quite a nice note . . . with scarcely a word of anger, or vexation or anything', and no sooner had his parents acquiesced in his going to Gottingen than he decided against going—he had caught a chill in Paris, 'and you know if it is cold here, it must be colder there'.

Reaching home, he was further surprised by his parents' conciliatory demeanour, as he informed Mrs. Sitwell:

'I have made an arrangement with my people: I am to have £84 a year—I only asked for £80 on mature reflection—and as I should soon make a good bit by my pen, I shall be very comfortable. We are all as jolly as can be together, so that is a great thing gained.'

During the month of May at Swanston he finished his essay on 'Victor Hugo's Romances', begun the month before in Paris, and a review of Lord Lytton's *Fables in Song*, which was obtained for him by Colvin from John Morley, the editor of the *Fortnightly Review*.

The essay on Victor Hugo was undertaken in response to Colvin's suggestion that he should write something suitable for the *Cornhill Magazine*. It was immediately accepted by the editor, Leslie Stephen, who wrote him a long letter of criticism because 'I think very highly of the promise shown in your writings and therefore think it worth while to write more fully than I can often to contributors'. When Stevenson reprinted the essay in *Familiar Studies of Men and Books*, he acknowledged that 'the great contemporary master of workmanship, and indeed of all literary arts and technicalities, had not unnaturally dazzled a beginner', but thought it better 'to dwell on merits' than on defects. Most readers of the essay must agree with at least two of Leslie Stephen's objections—that 'you seem to make the distinction between dramatic and novelistic art coincide with the distinction between romantic and 18th century', and that 'you are scarcely just to Scott or Fielding as compared with Hugo'. Stevenson indeed had no very profound understanding or knowledge of his subject; he was sure neither of his opinions nor of his power to express them; so he resorted, like a reviewer out of his depth, to ostentatious literary gesture designed to conceal the obscurity of his reasoning and the deficiency of his knowledge. Probably he was unwise to reprint the essay, for its self-conscious artificiality supplied evidence for those who charged him with being more concerned with manner than with matter; on the other hand, he justly included the essay as illustrating his development as a critical essayist, for its exhibition of self-conscious artificiality in manner serves to emphasise, by force of contrast, the absence of that quality in work of his maturity.

Stephen's letter concluded with an invitation to visit him 'if ever you come to town', and thus provided with an excuse for going to London, he went to stay with Colvin at Hampstead. Again through the agency of Colvin, he had been recently elected a member of the Savile Club, where he and his cousin Bob were to become familiar figures and to engage in many lively conversations, as described in 'Talk and Talkers', with Fleeming Jenkin, Colvin, Lang, and Gosse. He duly called on Leslie Stephen, who tried to secure him an interview with Carlyle, but found the old man in a dark mood and 'sick of visitors'. Colvin introduced him to many literary notabilities, including Thackeray's daughter, Anne Thackeray Ritchie, who, he told his mother, 'has a jolly big mouth and is good humoured looking', and Dr. Appleton, the editor of the *Academy*.

To the *Academy* Stevenson contributed during the next two years several reviews of books, which were signed 'Robert Louis Stevenson'. Perturbed by expressions of opinion too outspoken for his taste, Appleton protested to Colvin; partially reassured, he amused Stevenson by 'the tranquil dishonesty' with which he absolved himself of responsibility by telling him: 'I must put my name to all I write and then all will be well.' The offending review was evidently that of *The Ballads and Songs of Scotland*, by J. Clark Murray, appearing in the *Academy* of 4th August 1874, which, containing as its second sentence, 'Probably there never was published anything with less result, anything that left the reader more entirely where he was', concludes with the query, 'we ask ourselves in wonder, what possible reason could have induced this unsuccessful enquirer to record, at such great length, the story of his failure?'

Stevenson must have been well pleased to have his articles printed above his signature, for the fashion of anonymity established by the *Edinburgh* and the *Quarterly Review* was still generally followed by magazines and periodicals, except in cases of contributors with established reputations. The privately printed history of *The House of Smith, Elder* states that, in the early years of the *Cornhill Magazine*, 'the usual rule was for contributions to be unsigned, save in the case of eminent poets . . . and as time went on, one or two novelists and writers of special authority on their subjects'; 'under Leslie Stephen, who did not sign his own "Hours in a Library" or other essays, signatures became rather more frequent', but it was not until James Payn succeeded Stephen in 1883 'that signature became the rule rather than the exception'. The essay on 'Victor Hugo's Romances' appeared anonymously in the *Cornhill* of August 1874; 'Forest Notes,' in May 1876, was the first of Stevenson's essays for the magazine to be published over the initials 'R.L.S.'.

Of the six essays contributed by Stevenson to the *Edinburgh University Magazine* in 1871, four were unsigned and two signed with the single initial 'L'. When his paper on 'A New Form of Intermittent Light for Lighthouses' was published in the *Transactions of the Royal Scottish Society of Arts*, some offprints were bound into pamphlets, with a title-page bearing the date

1871 and the legend, 'By Robert Louis Stevenson'. It was probably to explain alteration on the proof of this title-page that he wrote in an undated letter to Charles Baxter: 'After several years of feeble & innefectual (*sic*) endeavour with regard to my third initial (a thing I loathe) I have been led to put myself out of the reach of such accidents in the future by taking my first two names in full.' From his full name of Robert Lewis Balfour Stevenson he thus shed the 'Balfour' about 1871, but much earlier he adopted the spelling 'Louis' for 'Lewis'. The story goes that Lewis became Louis because Lewis was the name of a prominent local Liberal politician, duly execrated by Thomas Stevenson in his character of 'a stern and unbending Tory'. His father's nursery nickname for Stevenson was Smout, but entries in his mother's diary between 1854 and 1856 refer as often to 'Lou' as to 'Smout'. Later his mother always called him 'Lou'; whether they spelled the name 'Louis' or 'Lewis', many of his friends sounded the final sibilant *s*, and Henley always called him 'Lewis'.

While he was staying with Colvin at Hampstead, the sight of some 'quite common children' skipping in the lane beneath his window reminded him of Madam Garschine's little girl, and he wrote 'Notes on the Movements of Young Children', which Hamerton accepted for *The Portfolio* of August. Madame Garschine was much in his mind; he intended in the autumn a 'dash to Poland before setting in for the dismal session at Edinburgh', but a letter proposing the meeting proved 'too late to catch her at Franzensbad' and an appeal to Mrs. Sitwell for 'means of finding Madame Garschine's address' was unproductive.

On his return to Edinburgh in June, he suffered intense anxiety for more than a week while Bob Stevenson was critically ill with diphtheria. The strain affected his own health, providing an excuse for a yachting trip through the Inner Hebrides with Charles Baxter and Sir Walter Simpson. Some weeks in August and early September he spent with his parents in Wales, at Barmouth and Llandudno, before escaping alone to visit Andrew Lang at Oxford, whence he started out on the short walking tour through the Chilterns—by High Wycombe, Great Missenden, and Wendover—described in 'An Autumn

Effect', an essay appearing in *The Portfolio* of the following April. Travelling in a dog-cart from Wendover to Tring, he took train to London for a final glimpse of Mrs. Sitwell and society at the Savile Club before facing the gloom of an Edinburgh winter.

He returned reluctantly, as to enforced exile, expecting little congeniality or content, and the event proved worse than expectation. To Mrs. Sitwell he presented a picture of himself working away at his writing with his parents hovering, peering disapproval, against a background of dreary routine.

'I have discovered why I get on always so ill, am always so nasty, so much worse than myself, with my parents; it is because they always take me at my worst, seek out my faults, and never give me any credit. You remember, perhaps, at least I remember, I once wrote to you to tell you how you should do with me; how it was only by getting on my weak side, looking for the best, and always taking it for granted that I should do the best before it is done, that you will ever get the best out of me. This is profoundly true; and I see it on the other side with my parents; I am always bad with them, because they always seem to expect me to be not very good; and I am never good, because they never seem to see when I am good.'

After a few weeks he contrived an excuse to run up to London; he could plead the need for interviewing editors, for his first paper on 'John Knox and His Relations to Women' had been accepted by *Macmillan's Magazine*, and besides being busy on the second paper, he was writing a review of Poe's works for the *Academy*. His main motive was to see Mrs. Sitwell and, in the intervals between their meetings, to make interesting acquaintances and enlivening conversation at the Savile Club.

From Mrs. Sitwell he derived momentary strength to reconcile himself to a distasteful situation: 'I was never more sorry to leave you, but I never left you with a better heart, than last night'; though he 'had a long journey and a cold one', he 'never was sick nor sorry the whole way'. But his serenity was quickly clouded when at Edinburgh he 'found my father waiting for me in the snow, with a very long face'. He was more than ever remote from an understanding of his father's attitude. To him it fairly seemed a matter for congratulation that, assisted by Colvin's introductions and the adaptability of his own talents, he was establishing a footing in literature. He could not appreciate that, to his father's morbid habit of mind, this taste of success presented the promise of a mirage, luring him away from the oasis of a safe profession; his diligent application to his writing was a matter for reproach rather than for praise, since his final examination for the bar was to be faced next summer. Such a subject as Kate Drummond could no more be mentioned between father and son—at twenty-four Stevenson, though an only son, was no longer a boy—but its memory lurked uneasily alert in Thomas Stevenson's mind: his son had convicted himself of moral laxity, he held deplorable views on religion and politics, and he seemed to possess no social sense. It was not surprising that, whenever Stevenson—with a flippancy of manner obviously assumed to mask nervous apprehension—announced an apparently reasonable course of action, his father instinctively fixed him with a searching glance of suspicion, wondering what hidden motive lay behind the plan.

This winter Thomas Stevenson fell ill, and when he was ill— as appears from letters during his last years—his morbid tendency intensified. Contemplating death, he thought of his will, and remarked that, since he regarded his property as held in trust for the views in which he believed, 'did he think he had a son who thought as Tyndall thought, he could not leave his money to him'. Stevenson replied tartly that he would 'reckon any person a thief who would use another's money in such circumstance', and his father was 'quite quiet' as he 'said fervently, "And a damned thief, too"'.

Interpreted by Stevenson to mean that he would not be his father's heir, this scene produced an effect probably least desired by his father, since it stimulated his efforts to earn an independent income by writing. 'My moral disinheritance has quickened me for work again,' he told Mrs. Sitwell. 'I shall not let myself starve, of course; but beyond that must try to be an honest man.' Alone with his conscience, he sincerely believed that he could not in honesty subsist upon his father's money. If he so believed, the stern moralist may ask why he did not self-righteously shake the dust of his father's house from his heels and starve in a Grub Street garret. Suppose he had done so: even if his father had steeled himself to his son's suffering, his mother's anguished appeals would have speedily prevailed upon the son to return and the father, if necessary, to fetch him home. Let it be allowed that Stevenson loved life too well to pursue a principle to lengths of discomfort, but at least he genuinely strove to please his parents so far as his determination to live his own life admitted, and if he compromised with conscience in accepting their bounty, he seems never to have incurred debts of extravagance common among young men of his class. In return for his keep and allowance, he complied with his father's wish that he should read for the bar; the result proved that he amply applied himself to distasteful work, for he passed his final examination the following summer, and was duly called to the Scottish Bar on 16th July 1875.

In view of the time he must have spent in drudgery over law books, the amount of writing accomplished reflects ceaseless assiduity. His method of composition was too careful for fluent facility; when Colvin suggested that *The Portfolio* might take an article from him each month, he wrote:

'Tying myself down to time is an impossibility. You know my own description of myself as a person with a poetic character and no poetic talent; just as my prose muse has all the ways of a poetic one, and I must take my Essays as they come to me. If I got 12 of 'em done in two years, I should be pleased. Never, please, let yourself imagine that I am fertile; I am constipated in the brains.'

All that he had written on Walt Whitman, with 'a lot of notes', was lost when he left his portmanteau in a train, but besides finishing the second paper on John Knox, 'An Autumn Effect', and two or three book reviews, he wrote some *Fables* and about half a dozen short stories under the influence of Poe. Colvin suggested that these *Fables* might be identified among those published posthumously, such as 'The House of Eld' and 'The Yellow Paint', but if Stevenson kept these few fables for so many years, why did he not also preserve the more ambitious short stories, among them *Life and Death*, *The Barrel Organ*,

King Matthias's Hunting Horn, and *The Devil on Cramond Sands?*
In his review of Poe's works he apologises for preoccupation
with Poe's 'method and detail'; he reveals how closely he had
studied the workings of Poe's imagination and the means he
used 'to enhance the significance of any situation, and give
colour and life to seeming irrelevant particulars'. Just as he
learned something from Wilkie Collins in the structure of
longer novels, so from his reading of Poe he learned much about
the art of the short story and its adaptability to the 'crawlers'
of his boyhood.

Under Poe's inspiration he began writing short stories with
fervent enthusiasm. On finishing *King Matthias's Hunting Horn,*
he exclaimed: 'It excites me like wine, or fire, or death, or
love, or something; nothing of my own writing ever excited me
so much; it does seem to me so weird and fantastic.' Again:
'I have been all yesterday evening and this forenoon in Italy,
four hundred years ago . . . what a change this is from
collecting dull notes for *John Knox* . . . the difference between
life and death.' He was soon 'sure I shall stand or fall by the
stories', and proposed to approach a publisher with a collection
of twelve under the uninspired title, *A Book of Stories.* Significantly, in regard to *Dr. Jekyll and Mr. Hyde* and such of his
stories as *Markheim* and *The Merry Men,* he was impressed by
Poe's 'almost incredible insight into the debatable region
between sanity and madness', but the 'loathing and horror'
expressed in his review for the 'infamous' *King Pest* so affected
him at the time of reading the story that 'I did not sleep last
night, and have scarcely been able to eat to-day'. Soon he
found that his own stories 'affect me rather more perhaps than
is wholesome'—'I have only been two hours at work to-day,
and yet I have been crying and am shaking badly, as you can
see in my handwriting, and my back is a bit bad.'

Apart from preoccupation with the morbid in his stories, he
had fallen into a neurotic state of mind, not from the tension of
his home life, but from sexual repression. For some time after
his last sight of Mrs. Sitwell in London, he consoled himself with
dreaming of her face as he had seen it at the Finchley Road
station 'the afternoon before I left', but, starved of sexuality,
he found sentiment a meagre diet.

'O, I do hate this damned life that I lead. Work—work—work; that's all right, it's amusing; but I want women about me and I want pleasure. John Knox had a better time of it than I, with his godly females all leaving their husbands to follow after him; I would I were John Knox; I hate living like a hermit. . . . I wish to God I did not love you so much; but I do, and it's as well for my best interest as I know well enough. And it ought to be nice for you; for you need not fear any bother from this child except petulant moments. I am good now: I am; am I not?'

After visiting the Elgin Marbles with Mrs. Sitwell, he had brought home with him photographs of three female figures, from which he derived pleasure in sensual speculation as a strategic means of wooing Mrs. Sitwell. 'Well, I've got some women now, and they're better than nothing,' he wrote:

'They are wonderfully womanly—they are more womanly than any woman—and those girt draperies are drawn over a wonderful greatness of body instinct with sex. . . . And yet, when all is said, they are not women for us; they are of another race, immortal, separate; one has no wish to look at them with love, only with a sort of lowly adoration, physical, but wanting what is the soul of all love, whether admitted to oneself or not, hope; in a word "the desire of the moth for the star". . . . It is not love that we seek from them, we do not desire to see their great eyes troubled with our passions, or the great impassive members contorted by any hope or pain or pleasure; only now and again, to be conscious that they exist, to have knowledge of them far off in cloudland or feel their steady eyes shining, like quiet watchful stars, above the turmoil of the earth. That is not nonsense, dear, as you will feel to your heart, I know; it is true as truth.'

A few days later his aspirations have become less humble. He thinks 'there is something more substantive about a woman than ever there can be about a man', for while he could 'conceive a great mythical woman, living alone among inaccessible mountain-tops or in some lost island in the pagan seas, and ask no more', he could not think of 'a man without women'. Yet, while he could think of his 'three deep-breasted women, living out all their days on remote hilltops', though they might be 'austere with a holy austerity, rigid with a calm and passionless rigidity', he found them 'none the less women to the end'. 'And think, if one could love a woman like that once, see her once grow pale with passion, and once wring your lips out upon hers, would it not be a small thing to die?'

Mrs. Sitwell was a woman of views much in advance of contemporary convention, but she moved in the social world of Trollope's novels; if she sincerely sought to sympathise with Stevenson's moods and possessed a power of expression commensurate with the qualities of mind attributed to her, her letters must have been masterpieces in the subtlety of feminine evasion. Exploring another avenue of seduction, he quoted Poe's sonnet 'To My Mother' and compared his feeling for Mrs. Sitwell with what he had felt the previous winter for Madame Garschine.

'You do not know, perhaps—I do not think I knew myself, perhaps, until I thought it out to-day—how dear a hope, how sorry a want, this has been for me. For my mother is my father's wife; to have a French mother, there must be a French marriage; the children of lovers are orphans. I am very young at heart—or (God knows) very old—and what I want is a mother, and I have one now, have I not? Someone from whom I shall have no secrets; someone whom I shall love with a love as great as a lover's and yet more; with whom I shall have all a lover's tenderness and more of a lover's timidity; who shall be something fixed and certain and forever true. If I said, I thought myself *de trop* (dear, look back at the place) it was because I am so *exigeant*, because I seek so much and am so wearing and captious, that I thought your dear body and spirit had enough to care for without me, and I think I added that I would continue to love you, did I not? And so I shall, before God. You *have* adopted me, consolation of my soul, I *am* yours and you have a duty to me; you are bound to me, and I am bound to you, by something holier than an oath. And I will be *exigeant*, I will demand from you sympathy and comprehension and forgiveness; I will not give you any truce or quarter, mother. I will make you my mother to the full significance of the name.'

With Poe for excuse, he now began his letters 'Dearest Mother' or 'Madonna', instead of 'My dear friend'. Wanting the 'wholeness' of the man who has experienced the completeness of sexual relationship, Stevenson was—as Mr. Middleton Murry, in *Son of Woman,* described D. H. Lawrence as being in the mood of his poem, 'Wedlock'—'a child full of childish things', who wishes his woman to take him tenderly to her bosom as a mother while submitting to him as 'a wild, untamed, dominant male'.

During this winter of work and emotional disturbance, he was not without recreation in company and amusement. At Christmas there was some days' skating on the loch at Duddingston, and some verses in *New Poems* suggest that he did not skate alone when

'The whole lake rang with rapid skates
In the windless winter air.'

Charles Baxter was his regular companion at concerts—a fact overlooked by his stepson, Lloyd Osbourne, when, remarking that want of any means to satisfy 'a very real love of music' was one of the worst deprivations suffered by Stevenson at Samoa, he declared that all his friends 'except Henley were positively indifferent to music'. 'Baxter and I go together to all the concerts that are going,' Stevenson told Mrs. Sitwell; Beethoven, 'certainly the greatest man the world has yet produced', was their favourite, and Stevenson was 'rapt out of earth' by the *Eroica,* but Wagner ranked next, because he was 'jolly and fresh, like a wind', and Baxter compared him with Walt Whitman.

At the end of January 1875 Stevenson wrote to Mrs. Sitwell:

'Yesterday Leslie Stephen, who was down here to lecture, called on me and took me up to see a poor fellow, a sort of poet who writes for him, and who has been eighteen months in our infirmary. . . . It was very sad to see him there in a little room with two beds, and a couple of sick children in the other bed; a girl came in to visit the children, and played dominoes on the counterpane with them; the gas flared and crackled, the fire burned in a dull economical way; Stephen and I sat in a couple of chairs, and the poor fellow sat up in his bed with his hair and beard all tangled, and talked as cheerfully as if he had been in a King's palace, or the great King's palace of the blue air.'

95

This was William Ernest Henley, who was under treatment for tubercular disease of the foot, and Stevenson's account of their meeting provides an instance of his ability to register a vivid impression in a single sentence. For, in all his photographs and on almost every page of Mr. John Connell's biography, Henley's hair and beard seem to be 'all tangled', his blue eyes twinkling with eager zest in what he is saying or doing. As with many cripples, the energy that he was incapable of exhausting physically expressed itself in extraordinary intellectual force, and though he was little more than a year older than Stevenson, a continuous and courageous endurance of suffering since childhood had already fully developed a vital and vigorous personality. As 'Burly' in 'Talk and Talkers' Stevenson painted his portrait next after his cousin Bob's:

'Burly is a man of a great presence; he commands a larger atmosphere, gives the impression of a grosser mass of character than most men. It has been said of him that his presence could be felt in a room you entered blindfold; and the same, I think, has been said of other powerful constitutions condemned to much physical inaction. There is something boisterous and piratic in Burly's manner of talk which suits well enough with this impression. He will roar you down, he will bury his face in his hands, he will undergo passions of revolt and agony; and meanwhile his attitude of mind is really both conciliatory and receptive; and after Pistol has been out-Pistol'd, and the welkin rung for hours, you begin to perceive a certain subsidence in these spring torrents, points of agreement issue, and you end arm-in-arm, and in a glow of mutual admiration. The outcry only serves to make your final union the more unexpected and precious. Throughout there has been perfect sincerity, perfect intelligence, a desire to hear although not always to listen, and an unaffected eagerness to meet concessions.'

Henley's unquenchable courage inspired affection and enthusiasm in all who knew him. Son of a poor Gloucester bookseller, he had lost one foot in childhood, yet, at an age when boys of better fortune were about to leave school, he went up to London to scrape the barest living from free-lance journalism. Informed by specialists that his other foot must be amputated to save his life, though desperately poor and ill, he journeyed to Edinburgh to ask the advice of Joseph Lister. Like many

EDMUND GOSSE
From the portrait by Sargent in the National Portrait Gallery

medical benefactors who have pursued experiment with contempt for professional convention, Lister was then pronounced a charlatan by the conservative body of medical opinion, though subsequently his services were recognised by a baronetcy and a peerage. When he asked Henley why he had come to him, the reply was characteristic: he came because those who condemned his foot declared Lister to be '(in effect) totally incompetent'. Just as he defied conventional opinion in this matter of life or death, so subsequently he stood by his own independent judgment throughout his literary career. As a result, he reaped none of society's material rewards; each of the journals he edited—boldly stamped with his controlling personality, disdaining affiliation to clique or party, declining to palter to popular taste by degrading the highest standard of quality—were brilliant failures, and the poverty of his last years was alleviated only by a civil list pension.

His independence excited hostility and envy among timid adherents to orthodox opinion, and his offence against propriety in protesting against Graham Balfour's 'barley-sugar effigy' of Stevenson as a 'Seraph in Chocolate', coming two years before his death in 1903, provided excuse for a conspiracy to smother the just survival of his reputation. Henry James recorded significantly that Graham Balfour found Henley's article 'less bad than he expected', and he had 'apparently feared more'. Balfour knew, as James suspected, how much he had suppressed and distorted to show only the Jekyll side of Stevenson; he doubtless feared that Henley might have been stung into disconcerting revelations by animosity against the woman who had severed his friendship with Stevenson.

Research has justified Henley's protest, and criticism based on defective biographical data has vindicated his belief that his friend's reputation would have been better served by biographical honesty. When Mr. Swinnerton was able to argue from the information of the Balfour biography that 'this debonair philosopher, who finds himself never in a quandary', was 'too much petted as a child to permit of . . . wanton and morbid self-distrust', that his 'whole life was deliciously joined together by his naïve and attractive vanity' which enabled

him, 'in deceiving himself', to delight in 'the supreme cleverness of his own self-deception', and that the ease of his environment conspired 'to keep sweet his happy complacency', his
adverse criticism seemed so well founded on fact that almost an
entire generation was converted to the view of Stevenson as
an unduly over-rated writer who owed an ephemeral celebrity
to its cultivation by a clique. The conversion was so complete
that when, in 1927, G. K. Chesterton attempted an essay in re-
habilitation, Edmund Gosse—who had applauded the Balfour
biography, abused Henley's protest, and neglected an opportunity for signal service to Stevenson by his careless and perfunctory editing of his works—wrote to express 'sentiments
. . . of joy, of satisfaction, of relief, of malicious and vindictive
pleasure' excited by 'the book in which you smite the detractors
of R. L. S. hip and thigh'.

Despite vindication of his conduct in the protest, Henley's
reputation has still to recover from the effects of the conspiracy
in disparagement. Perhaps his biography by Mr. John Connell—published at the centenary of his birth—may prove a
decisive step towards a just estimate of his merits, for he is
convincingly revealed as one of the most impressive and influential personalities in late-Victorian letters, a champion of
truth and honesty in an age of pharisaic humbug, an editor
and critic whose independent judgment and generous encouragement fostered the careers of many talented writers. A
representative selection of his work would exhibit a master of
fluent and vigorous prose who was also more than merely a
minor poet. With his contribution to criticism completely
ignored, his name has survived as signatory to the verses, 'Out
of the night that covers me'—a statement of personal attitude
as familiar in anthologies as Landor's 'Dying Speech of an
Old Philosopher'. Even this frequently excites derision;
enlightened by no ulterior knowledge of the writer, the super-
cilious superficiality passing in Bloomsbury for 'critical detach-
ment' fastens upon the phrase 'captain of my soul' as the label
of a truculent jingo, clashing the cymbals in the imperialist
orchestra of which Kipling was leader and Joseph Chamberlain
conductor. Few such critics can have realised that the verses
were written—not by an elderly jingo, intent upon inspiring

enthusiasm for battle from the safety of an invalid's chair—but by a young man of twenty-six on emerging, penniless and unemployed, from a hospital purgatory of two years in danger of losing life or limb.

> ' Beyond this place of wrath and tears
> Looms but the Horror of the shade,
> And yet the menace of the years
> Finds, and shall find, me unafraid.
>
> It matters not how strait the gate,
> How charged with punishments the scroll,
> I am the master of my fate:
> I am the captain of my soul.'

The impact of Henley's individualism determined the course of Stevenson's subsequent conduct. So far he had vacillated between inclination and a sense of duty dictated by conscience, strenuously endeavouring to prove his ability as a writer but conforming with his father's demand that he should qualify to practise as an advocate. Doubtless fearing that modest successes with magazines might be advanced as promise of a reasonable income from writing, his father proposed to give him a thousand pounds when he 'passed Advocate'. Probably Stevenson refused the gift after a scene with his father on announcing that he did not intend to practise at the bar. Colvin states that, though he passed his examination with credit, 'he made no serious attempt to practise', adding significantly, 'by the 25th of the same month [he] had started with Sir Walter Simpson for France'. Balfour attempts to be facetiously specific: Stevenson put up his name on a brass plate at the door of his parents' house; 'he had the fourth or fifth share in the services of a clerk, whom it is alleged that he did not know by sight'; 'he had in all four briefs, and the total of his fees never reached double figures'.

After their profuse documentation of the previous winter, his published *Letters* become singularly sparing of information about this period. Laboriously evasive, Balfour states: 'Money at his command and friends in the South forthwith changed his mode of life . . . henceforth he was never continuously at home for more than three months at a time,' though his 'manner of life, at the times when he was in Edinburgh', did not 'suffer any sudden change'. But a letter to Colvin of the following autumn suggests that only the want of 'money at his command' compelled him to spend any time at Edinburgh; a meeting with Colvin in London was impossible because he was 'worse than a bankrupt', having 'at the present six shillings and a penny' and 'a sounding lot of bills for Christmas'. The more conscientious Colvin, discreetly comments that Stevenson's first visit to Barbizon in the spring of 1875 marked 'the beginning of a great and abiding change in his life and habits'.

But the visit to Barbizon followed two or three months after his meeting with Henley, without which the influence of Bob Stevenson and his artist friends might have been insufficient to confirm his determination to live his own life. Leslie Stephen kindly took Stevenson to meet 'my poor contributor' because 'he will be able to lend him books and perhaps to read his MSS. and be otherwise useful'. Stevenson more than fulfilled Stephen's hopes: daily he went to the hospital, burdened by books, and stayed to talk; he not only read Henley's poems, but sent them to Colvin for his opinion; as soon as clement weather came, he took him for carriage drives into the country and introduced him to his friends, Baxter, Ferrier, Simpson, and Jenkin.

The initial bond of mutual interest lay in their both being tubercular invalids and bent on devoting their lives to letters. Henley was the first man of his own age whom Stevenson had known with similar ambitions to his own: Stevenson was the first friend Henley had made in a class superior to his own lowly beginnings. Stevenson could offer to Henley something of the practical help he had received from Colvin; in return Henley could fortify Stevenson's self-confidence with the advice of tough experience. Deep friendship and affection grew between them; they likened their comradeship to that of Dumas's Musketeers—Stevenson was d'Artagnan, Henley was Porthos, Baxter and Ferrier were Aramis and Athos. As Stevenson drew Henley as Burly, Henley portrayed Stevenson in 'Apparition':

The Bohemian

' Thin-legged, thin-chested, slight unspeakably,
Neat-footed and weak-fingered: in his face—
Lean, large-boned, curved of beak, and touched with race,
Bold-lipped, rich-tinted, mutable as the sea,
The brown eyes radiant with vivacity—
There shines a brilliant and romantic grace,
A spirit intense and rare, with trace on trace
Of passion, impudence, and energy.
Valiant in velvet, light in ragged luck,
Most vain, most generous, sternly critical,
Buffoon and poet, lover and sensualist:
A deal of Ariel, just a streak of Puck,
Much Antony, of Hamlet most of all,
And something of the Shorter-Catechist.'

Shrewdly discerning as well as affectionate, the portrait is quoted by Colvin to support his indignation against descriptions of Stevenson as 'shadowy' or 'thin-blooded' in his leanness: 'the most robust of ordinary men seemed to turn dim and null in presence of the vitality that glowed in the steadfast, penetrating fire of the lean man's eyes, the rich, compelling charm of his smile, the lissom swiftness of his movements and lively expressiveness of his gestures, above all in the irresistible sympathetic play and abundance of his talk'. Colvin objected only that 'Henley has missed what gave its unity to the character and what every other among his nearer friends soon discovered to be the one essential . . . the infinitely kind and tender, devotedly generous, brave and loving heart of the man'. Yet Stevenson revealed himself more intimately to Henley than to Colvin, and perhaps the purity of a loving heart was the quality wanting to weld the conflicting elements into a serenely integrated character.

Within a few weeks of their meeting Stevenson was writing to Mrs. Sitwell that 'Henley has eyes and ears and an immortal soul of his own'. The 'captain of his soul' had already urged Stevenson to assert his right to the life of his choice when, in the spring, he went his first visit to Bob Stevenson at Barbizon. There the seeds of Henley's sowing sprouted.

Of this place he loved so well Stevenson wrote first in 'Forest Notes', an essay published in *Cornhill* just a year later—in May

1876. Some eight years later, for Henley's *Magazine of Art*, he wrote, 'Fontainebleau: Village Communities of Painters', a retrospect of the life he had known there; and lastly, in Samoa, when he knew in his heart that he would never again see Barbizon, he returned to it nostalgically as a setting for scenes in *The Wrecker*. Among the painters' communities, 'Palizzi bore rule at Grez' and Cernay had 'the admirable, placid Pelouse'; only Barbizon, since the recent death of Millet, was 'a headless commonwealth'. Stevenson found that 'any artist is made welcome, through whatever medium he may seek expression; science is respected; even the idler, if he prove, as he so rarely does, a gentleman, will soon begin to find himself at home'.

' This purely artistic society is excellent for the young artist. The lads are mostly fools; they hold the latest orthodoxy in its crudeness; they are at that stage of education, for the most part, when a man is too much occupied with style to be aware of the necessity for any matter; and this, above all for the Englishman, is excellent. To work grossly at the trade, to forget sentiment, to think of his material and nothing else, is, for a while at least, the king's highway of progress. Here, in England, too many painters and writers dwell dispersed, unshielded, among the intelligent bourgeois. These, when they are not merely indifferent, prate to him about the lofty aims and moral influence of art. And this is the lad's ruin. For art is, first of all and last of all, a trade. The love of words and not a desire to publish new discoveries, the love of form and not a novel reading of historical events, mark the vocation of the writer and the painter. The arabesque, properly speaking, and even in literature, is the first fancy of the artist; he first plays with his material as a child plays with a kaleidoscope; and he is already in a second stage when he begins to use his pretty counters for the end of representation. In that, he must pause long and toil faithfully; that is his apprenticeship; and it is only the few who will really grow beyond it, and go forward, fully equipped, to do the real business of art—to give life to abstractions and significance and charm to facts. In the meanwhile, let him dwell much among his fellow-craftsmen. They alone can take a serious interest in the childish tasks and pitiful successes of these years. They alone can behold with equanimity this fingering of the dumb keyboard, this polishing of empty sentences, this dull and literal painting of dull and insignificant subjects.'

Here Stevenson found the same responsiveness, the same understanding of his ambitions and of the enthusiasm with which he had played the sedulous ape in secret, as he had just first encountered in Henley. In Edinburgh he had lived 'among the intelligent bourgeois', who were either indifferent to art as an occupation for eccentrics, or demanded its adaptation to academic or professional advancement, or despised it unless productive of popularity and profit. Colvin had helped him to find a market and counselled him on what editors wanted; Baxter and Mrs. Sitwell had been sympathetic listeners, from admiration and affection, offering consolation and encouragement without comment. But Henley and the Barbizonians spoke his language; they were passing through the pains and pleasures of the same experience.

Barbizon confirmed Henley's counsel. To become an artist, he must devote himself wholly to his art; he could not afford, as his father wished, to court it out of office hours as a tricky mistress, while maintaining at home a safe domestic spouse to supply his creature comforts. Throughout his university years he had led a double life: as Jekyll, he had studied, first engineering, then law, and further deferred to his parents' wishes by sharing their social engagements and allowing them to direct his holidays; as Hyde, he had studied to train himself as a writer, sought romance where he could find it, and resorted for pleasure to tap-room revelry. Agreement to practise law would condemn him forever to such a double life. The decision could not be delayed; he must choose now between a double life and undivided devotion to his art.

Barbizon determined his decision because it showed him the difference between a full and a divided life. Here at leisure, from sunrise to sunset and beyond, he freely enjoyed the fullness of pleasures that formerly he had snatched on occasional excursions with his few friends.

'Our society . . . was full of high spirits, of laughter, and of the initiative of youth. The few elder men who joined us were still young at heart, and took the key from their companions. We returned from long stations in the fortifying air, our blood renewed by the sunshine, our spirits refreshed by the silence of the forest;

the Babel of loud voices sounded good; we fell to eat and play like the natural man; and in the high inn chamber, panelled with indifferent pictures and lit by candles guttering in the night air, the talk and laughter sounded far into the night. It was a good place and a good life for any naturally-minded youth; better yet for the student of painting, and perhaps best of all for the student of letters. He, too, was saturated in this atmosphere of style; he was shut out from the disturbing currents of the world, he might forget that there existed other and more pressing interests than that of art.'

On his return from this first visit to Barbizon, he informed his parents that he would not practise on qualifying as an advocate—virtually that he intended henceforth to be himself and no more attempt to approximate to 'that pale ideal they had preconceived'. The announcement needed courage; he knew so well his father's stricken look, his mother's agony of anxiety as she glanced from one to the other, fearing the effect of emotion on either side. When it was done, and the gloom of reproach and disapproval settled like a pall upon the house, he felt neither triumph nor defiance—only troubled in conscience.

'There has come a real rent in my life . . . I cannot say how glad I am of it, how glad I am to feel my own body again, and recognise my own laugh. And yet I don't quite know how to say it, but I despise myself a little that it should have happened.'

He found difficulty in confiding his feelings to Mrs Sitwell, fearing that she would take part with prudence to condemn his conduct. Meeting her in London on his way back from Barbizon, he was apparently inspired by his new philosophy to advances which she felt compelled to rebuff, and he wrote in apology:

'You need not be afraid, madonna. My dear, I will be as much to you as I can. I do not deny that I am glad of it. There is no longer anything that I am afraid to think of in my mind. But that is all; I will still be your son, dear, if you will still be my mother, or rather whether you will or not; it is very right. I will be as good as I can for your sake; remember that when I was in London I was just in the swing. I have settled down now, and feel very quiet and glad, glad of the past, and quiet and somewhat careless of the future. Only as I say, I do not think I will be bad at all; I do not *feel* bad, not bad at all, dear; and I know I must be good for the love of you, and my oath's sake.'

Puzzled to trace the cause of the change in him, Mrs. Sitwell suspected the influence of another woman, and begging her not to think that 'I am somehow changed towards you', he wrote:

'Only I am changed to myself; all my *sham* goodness, I mean the orderliness, the citizenliness, and sort of respectability, that I had laid on, is going away and away down through wind into everlasting space. I cannot play these games; I am made for the other thing; as I grow well, I fall back into it, day by day. . . . No, dear, I have kept nothing from you. You know all my heart, I am sure. I wonder what could have made you think otherwise. It must have been my depression coming suddenly after so much good spirits. Be brave, my darling mother, or I shall not know what to do. . . . If there is any change, I think I love you better than ever. That is all. It is not at all a disquieting change, is it? You may be glad of it, dear. It is not love that will ever trouble you, for it is so clear: but it will endure all your life; and there will come days when I shall be able to help you better. They must come, darling; where there is so much love, there should be a way to help. O believe me, will you? thoroughly. I am not deceiving you or myself. I am keeping nothing back. You are the living soul of my body, dear mother, and I wish you not to be disquieted for me. I feel as if I was a little incoherent. But it's all right at bottom, right and sound and true.'

He was thus attempting to associate his self-assertion with a coincident improvement in health; probably in fact the feeling of physical well-being did reinforce his courage to face his father and to stake his future on the career of his choice. But, as appears in *Lay Morals*, the conscience of the 'Shorter-Catechist' required a definition of his new character:

'Now the view taught at the present time seems to me to want greatness; and the dialect in which alone it can be intelligibly uttered is not the dialect of my soul. It is a sort of postponement of life; nothing quite is, but something different is to be; we are to keep our eyes upon the indirect from the cradle to the grave, we are to regulate our conduct not by desire, but by a politic eye upon the future; and to value acts as they will bring us money or good opinion; as they will bring us, in one word, *profit*. We must be what is called respectable, and offend no one by our carriage. . . . And we must be what is called prudent and make money; not only because it is pleasant to have money, but because that also is a part of respectability, and we cannot hope to be received in society without decent possessions. . . . If you teach a man to keep his eyes upon what others think of him, unthinkingly to lead the life and hold the principles of the majority of his contemporaries, you must discredit in his eyes the one authoritative voice of his own soul. He may be a docile citizen; he will never be a man. It is ours, on the other hand, to disregard this babble and chattering of other men better and worse than we are, and to walk straight before us by what light we have. . . . The true Bohemian, a creature lost to view under the imaginary Bohemians of literature . . . lives wholly to himself, does what he wishes, and not what is thought proper, buys what he wants for himself and not what is thought proper, works at what he believes he can do well and not what will bring him in money or favour. You may be the most respectable of men, and yet a true Bohemian. . . . I suppose the young man to have chosen his career on honourable principles; he finds his talents and instincts can be best contented in a certain pursuit; in a certain industry, he is sure that he is serving mankind with a healthy and becoming service; and he is not sure that he would be doing so, or doing so equally well, in any other industry within his reach. Then that is his true sphere in life; not the one in which he was born to his father, but the one which is proper to his talents and instincts.'

To the modern young man, increasingly a slave of the state with small thought of duty to parents, this elaborate thesis in self-justification may suggest that Stevenson was simply taking himself much too seriously. But Stevenson lived in an age when the master of the house, 'as a man and a father', reigned in autocratic rule, like Dickens's Mr. Dombey, 'at the head of the home-department'. The relationship between father and son was a favourite theme of fiction; the fashion for fathers to design their sons' destinies, without regard for their individual ties or their inclinations, was exposed by Meredith in *The Ordeal*

of Richard Feverel and *Harry Richmond*: the most hackneyed
device for beginning a contemporary novel shows the hero
disowned by his father—'cut off with a shilling'—for asserting
his right to choose for himself a wife or a career.

It is easy to say, in the light of events, that Stevenson was
justified in asserting his right to choose a career. Courage was
required to reject the counsel of practical reason and the prospect of material advantage. If he had agreed to practise as an
advocate, he was assured of an easy beginning through the
patronage of his father's influential connections; his professional
labours would not be exacting, and he would have ample leisure
for writing. His decision seemed worse than imprudence—it was
an overt gesture of rebellion against the materialist standards
of society. And the manner, as well as the fact, of his rebellion,
was a defiance of materialism. For, apart from Meredith and
the Pre-Raphaelites, few contemporary writers were much
concerned with style—so long as you had something to say,
materialism cared little how it was said. Thackeray was said
to have style, but as a storyteller he was neither so popular nor so
prolific as Dickens; Landor was a stylist and already a classic at
his death, but people preferred to praise rather than to read him.
Since the Industrial Revolution, art and literature, like everything else, had become a business, and style was not a saleable
commodity.

From every aspect Stevenson's conduct was unreasonable and
a cross for any respectable father to bear. He was not 'cut off
with a shilling'; he continued to receive his allowance of eighty-
four pounds a year. But this, supplemented by his earnings and
gifts from his mother, was insufficient to maintain him continuously away from home, and henceforth the oppressive
gloom at home was liable to break into storms of outraged
indignation.

CHAPTER FOUR

THE ILLOGICAL ADVENTURE

'Falling in love is the one illogical adventure, the one thing of which we are tempted to think as supernatural, in our trite and reasonable world. The effect is out of all proportion with the cause.'—*Virginibus Puerisque:* 'On Falling in Love'.

WHEN, immediately after being called to the Scottish bar in July 1875, Stevenson left for France with Sir Walter Simpson, he spent some weeks at Barbizon. Despite his resolution to live his own life, conscience troubled him whenever he thought of his parents, and having revelled as Hyde at Barbizon, he went thence as Jekyll to join his parents on their summer holiday at Wiesbaden and Homburg. There apparently his mother's pleadings on his father's behalf so far prevailed that he was persuaded, returning to Edinburgh, to make for a few months the pretence of practising law described by Balfour. 'Attending trials and spending his mornings in wig and gown at the Parliament House,' he went, as he wrote in a rhymed epistle to Baxter,

> ' To crack o' what he wull but Law
>   The hale forenoon.'

The pretence, says Colvin, 'was before long abandoned as tending to waste time and being incompatible with his real occupation of literature'.

But behind this bare statement hints of the strife between father and son must be sought in his few letters of the period. 'Staying out a whole night making plans in the streets of Edinburgh' with his cousin Bob was not conduct calculated to commend itself to Thomas Stevenson as becoming an advocate; if he could be convinced that the night was thus spent, it must have seemed to him incredibly crazy and irresponsible, but probably he believed that such nights were more discreditably occupied. The gloom of home lowered more than ever oppressive, and Stevenson wrote from Swanston to Mrs. Sitwell: 'I feel I desire to go out of the house, and begin life anew in the cool blue night; never to come back here; never, never.'

Whenever he had money, he escaped from Edinburgh, but it appears that, on at least two occasions, he went out into the night from his father's house and found refuge with Henley in his lodgings. Both of these occasions—one of them lasting so long as three months—must have been during the year 1876, for Henley left Edinburgh for London at the end of that year; one can be more or less located by Henley's reference to 'the Stevenson I nursed in secret, hard by the old Bristo port, till he could make shift to paddle the *Arethusa*'. This must have been in June and July 1876, for he paddled his canoe, the *Arethusa*—with Walter Simpson in the companion canoe, *Cigarette*—down the rivers from Antwerp to Grez on the Loing in September.

The need for secret nursing may be surmised. After a walking tour in January between Ayr and Wigton—calling at Ballantrae—described in 'A Winter's Walk in Carrick and Galloway', he spent a month in London and some weeks at Barbizon. Sometime after his return to Edinburgh in the late spring or summer he wrote to Mrs. Sitwell: 'I don't know where and how I have been living this while back . . . but I have lost my hold of life; and so much the better, perhaps; only as I did live earnestly for a while, the change is not easy.' It seems, as J. A. Steuart says, that he returned to Edinburgh 'to plunge suddenly back into the old life, the old modes of gaiety, which had caused so much distress, censure, and acerbity'; the result was one of those occasions when 'Henry Jekyll stood . . . aghast before the acts of Edward Hyde'.

If the reader has not recently done so, let him now read again the *Strange Case of Dr. Jekyll and Mr. Hyde*; he will be enabled to realise how closely Stevenson drew upon his own conflict of conscience in devising the allegory of the story. In his 'Full Statement of the Case' Henry Jekyll remarks that 'the worst of my faults was a certain impatient gaiety of disposition such has made the happiness of many, but such as I found hard to reconcile with my imperious desire to carry my head high, and wear a more than commonly grave countenance before the public'.

' Hence it came about that I concealed my pleasures; and that when I reached years of reflection, and began to look round me and take stock of my progress and position in the world, I stood already committed to a profound duplicity of life. Many a man would have even blazoned such irregularities as I was guilty of; but from the high views that I had set before me, I regarded and hid them with an almost morbid sense of shame. It was thus rather the exacting nature of my aspirations than any particular degradation in my faults, that made me what I was, and, with even a deeper trench than in the majority of men, severed in me those provinces of good and ill which divide and compound man's dual nature. In this case, I was driven to reflect deeply and inveterately on that hard law of life, which lies at the root of religion and is one of the most plentiful springs of distress. Though so profound a double-dealer, I was in no sense a hypocrite; both sides of me were in dead earnest; I was no more myself when I laid aside restraint and plunged in shame, than when I laboured, in the eye of day, at the furtherance of knowledge.'

However hard he strove to console himself with his moral definition of the character of 'the true Bohemian', Cummy's influence upon his 'covenanting childhood', grafted upon the share of gloomy Calvinism inherited from his father, prevented complete fulfilment of himself in the uncomplicated Bohemianism of Bob Stevenson and Henley.

'With every day, and from both sides of my intelligence, the moral and the intellectual, I thus drew steadily nearer to that truth, by whose partial discovery I have been doomed to such a dreadful shipwreck: that man is not truly one, but truly two. . . . It was on the moral side, and in my own person, that I learned to recognise the thorough and primitive duality of man; I saw that of the two natures that contended in the field of my consciousness, even if I could rightly be said to be either, it was only because I was radically both; and from an early date. . . . I had learned to dwell with pleasure, as a beloved day-dream, on the thought of the separation of these elements. If each, I told myself, could but be housed in separate identities, life would be relieved of all that was unbearable.'

Stevenson must have arrived at this stage of development when, being 'nursed in secret' by Henley, he had reason to realise the depths of degradation into which he might be drawn by a Bohemianism unbridled by conscience. There was no going back; he was committed to Bohemianism, and, as he told Mrs. Sitwell, 'so much the better', for, into whatever agonies of self-recrimination he might lead Jekyll, Hyde was self-fulfilled, whereas Jekyll without Hyde was only a half of himself. To Mrs. Sitwell he obviously could not confide his problem, though—as appears from a letter, written immediately before 30th July, but considered by Colvin to have been written from Swanston in 'July and August 1876'—she earnestly pleaded for continuance of his confidence:

'I'm just in the humour which makes letter writing most impossible; for I just value an experience at the moment. I do not look forward, and as soon as a thing's past, I forget it as much as I can. This is a floating way of life, not very serious, but diverting enough. Morality, virtue, love, and these kind of things are very hard, and very painful even, but they string your life together; now mine's all in rags; and I can't say anything about it. I have the strongest repugnance for writing; indeed, I have nearly got myself persuaded into the notion that letters don't arrive, in order to salve my conscience for never sending them off. . . . This is the first letter I've written for—O I don't know how long. I daresay you may fancy I had a curious time in London last spring . . . I was several times very near Queen's Square, but went away again. I once went down Southampton Row, and felt in a fine flutter in case you should come out of Casino Place. But you didn't. I daresay you know a great deal more about me now, as I know much more of you; and both of us must have learned something of the inscrutable ways of fate. How dark and foolish are the ways in which people once walked, thinking them then lit up with eternal sunlight, and what we now see to be so much gauze and cardboard, imperishable masonry! O for Samson's heave of the shoulder! But at the end, after much wandering, the dawn appeared; or rather two dawns. And one person finds himself alone; possibly, in some cases, two; for a tiff, a twig, a theory—God help us all, amen. For I do cling a little to God, as I have lost all hold on right or wrong. You can't think things both right and wrong you know; the human mind cannot do it, although I daresay it would be devilish clever, if you could; and when you come to a stone wall in morals, you give them up, and be d——d to them. I beg your pardon, but that's the only English idiom which explains my meaning. So I say I cling to God; to a nice immoral old gentleman who knows a bit more about it all than I do, and may, sometime or other, in the course of the ages, explain matters to his creatures over a pipe of tobacco; nay, and he may be something more than this and give one that sense of finish and perfection that can only be had one way in the world. I daresay, it's all a lie, but if it pleases me to imagine it . . .'

To Henley he must have stated his case and inquired a solution: though committed to the course of Hyde, he must retain the ability to reassume the character of Jekyll, for only the curbing conscience of Jekyll could temper the excesses of Hyde. Suggesting the saving grace that he himself proposed to acquire as soon as he could, Henley must have answered in the words of the second essay in *Virginibus Puerisque*: 'You may think you had a conscience and believed in God; but what is conscience to a wife?' It was about this time, and probably while he was living in Henley's lodgings, that he wrote at least the first *Virginibus Puerisque* paper, which appeared in *Cornhill* of August 1876.

During the fifteen months since he wrote 'Forest Notes' immediately after his first visit to Barbizon, Stevenson's small output of writing showed an almost imperceptible, but none the less steady, improvement in quality and poise. Spencer Baynes, a professor at St. Andrews, who was editing the ninth edition of the *Encyclopædia Britannica*, invited him to write the article on Burns. When he reprinted 'Some Aspects of Robert Burns' in *Familiar Studies of Men and Books*, remarking that 'it was with the profoundest pity, but with a growing esteem, that I studied the man's desperate efforts to do right', Stevenson added: 'That I ought to have stated this more noisily I now see.' Evidently he neglected to emphasise his esteem for Burns's conscientious efforts to atone for the consequences of his conduct because, recognising the lineaments of his own Bohemianism in Burns's, he fell into a mood of self-flagellation demanding that he should condemn and decline to condone. 'Some Aspects of Robert Burns' was written in the summer of 1879, when he was well disposed to such a mood, but this essay was probably a revision of the article for the *Encyclopædia*, written at the time when conscience was rebuking his conversion to Bohemianism.

Professor Baynes rejected the article on Burns, because it seemed 'almost like an elaborate attempt to deprecate Burns', but he paid Stevenson five guineas for his trouble and commissioned an article on Béranger, which duly appeared in the *Encyclopædia*. Barbizon inspired an enthusiasm for French history and literature, and the next subject after Béranger was Charles of Orleans. But this essay, finally appearing in the *Cornhill* of December 1876, was on his hands for more than a year. Following the rejection of his 'Burns', he suffered other reverses. Written in the manner of Thackeray's art criticism in his 'Michael Angelo Titmarsh' articles, 'Some Portraits by Raeburn' should have seemed suited to *Cornhill*, but Leslie Stephen rejected it, and the same fate befell with *Blackwood's* and the *Pall Mall*; included in the *Virginibus Puerisque* volume, this Raeburn essay now claims attention for its account of M'Queen of Braxfield, the Lord Justice-Clerk from whose character and history the idea of *Weir of Hermiston* developed.

Not undeservedly described by Colvin as 'one of the most charming of his essays of the Road', 'A Winter's Walk in Carrick and Galloway' has the same vivacity in narrative style as *An Inland Voyage*, but it was left unfinished—perhaps in momentary disgust at the disappointment of the 'Raeburn' rejection, perhaps because Stephen intimated that a general article on 'Walking Tours' would be more acceptable than a particular treatment of a corner of Scotland little frequented by tourists. Written in the spring of 1876, 'Walking Tours' appeared in the June *Cornhill*, the number following that containing 'Forest Notes'. A letter of January 1876 mentions, 'I am trying my hand at a novel just now', but perhaps this was *A Country Dance*, the story 'in six or (perhaps) seven chapters' mentioned along with the shorter stories of the previous winter.

For the *Academy* and *Vanity Fair* he wrote a few reviews, including one of Browning's *Inn Album*, of which he remarked complacently: 'I have slated R. B. pretty handsomely.' Like many young reviewers—and some who have grown older without finding success in another sphere—he too often sought to show off his own cleverness at the expense of the writers under review. As he tells in his *Memoir of Fleeming Jenkin*, he received from Jenkin a salutary reproof when Salvini visited Edinburgh and Stevenson reviewed his *Macbeth* in the *Academy* of 15th April 1876.

'Fleeming opened the paper, read so far, and flung it on the floor. "No," he cried, "that won't do. You were thinking of yourself, not of Salvini!" The criticism was shrewd as usual, but it was unfair through ignorance; it was not of myself that I was thinking, but of the difficulties of my trade, which I had not well mastered.'

The criticism was not unfair: the review contains much conscious fine-writing and undergraduate smartness; the description of Salvini's performance suggests an elaborate imitation of Hazlitt's manner; while the praise of Salvini himself is opulent in enthusiasm, all the other performers, the method of the production, and the stage management, are belittled with contemptuous condescension. However Stevenson excused himself, he took the criticism to heart; his next two reviews for the *Academy*, on 'Jules Verne's Stories' and the *Noctes Ambrosianae*, were admirably terse in expression and just in appreciation—indeed, 'Salvini's *Macbeth*' is the last of his writings to exhibit, not only these faults of self-consciousness, but any of the obvious defects of immaturity.

The first *Virginibus Puerisque* paper—probably written at Henley's lodgings in the early summer of 1876 and published in *Cornhill* of the following August—is the first of those essays from which Stevenson's quality as an essayist must be assessed. Lamenting that Stevenson, as an essayist, was handicapped by his youth, Mr. Swinnerton finds him 'sanguine, gentle, musical', but 'in the deepest sense unoriginal' in delivering the judgments of 'a rather middle-aged inexperience'. If he had lived to be ninety, Stevenson could hardly have hoped to say anything original about a subject perpetually provocative of discussion by poets and moral philosophers since the beginnings of literature, and his inexperience, so far from seeming 'rather middle-aged' or 'decayed', is surely eminently and essentially youthful. He was not presuming to advise the elderly or the middle-aged, who, if they had not already ventured upon the hazards of marriage, might be supposed to have survived the stage of requiring any warning against them; he was writing for those who shared the problems of his own inexperience— for his own generation and its juniors—as his title states, 'virginibus puerisque'. The mature reader who, like Mr. Swinnerton, prefers the advice of an experience stripped of illusion, may consult Hazlitt's 'On the Conduct of Life'; Stevenson's appeal is to palates still preferring the wine of romance to the clear cold water of prudence.

In his twenty-sixth year, he was of an age when most people are closely concerned with the problems of marriage. Among his friends, Simpson had married in 1874; Baxter must have been contemplating the step, since he married in July 1877; Henley was waiting only for a sufficiently assured income to marry an Edinburgh girl, Anna Boyle. With these three friends, as well as with Bob Stevenson and Jenkin, Stevenson must have debated the advantages and disadvantages of the married state, the qualities to be desired in husband and wife, the danger of sexual desire or romantic passion without a safe basis in community of interest, the concessions required on both sides to establish mutual confidence and respect. All these points of argument and inflections of opinion are stated in the essay; so far from striving after an appearance of originality— from seeking to show off in the manner of 'Salvini's *Macbeth*' —Stevenson is content to state the commonplaces of observation and reflection occurring to every succeeding generation of contemplative youth. His distinction resides in the manner of his statement: never before or since have these commonplaces about the problems of marriage been so intelligibly and pleasurably crystallised in lucidity and grace of phrase.

The 'Virginibus Puerisque' essay was in proof when, at Swanston in July 1876, Stevenson finished 'Charles of Orleans' for the *Cornhill* and sent to *Macmillan's Magazine* 'An Apology for Idlers'—a defence, dictated by conscience, of his Bohemian way of life, elaborating the arguments against the bondage of routine afterwards epitomised by W. H. Davies in his lines on 'Leisure':

> ' A poor life this if, full of care,
> We have no time to stand and stare.'

At the end of July he went to the Highlands, joining the Jenkins in their summer holiday near Loch Carron; thence he went to Barbizon before travelling with Sir Walter Simpson to Antwerp to begin their 'inland voyage' in the two canoes, the *Arethusa* and the *Cigarette*.

Son of the obstetrician who popularised the use of chloroform, Simpson inherited his father's fortune and baronetcy in 1870. The most respectable of Stevenson's friends, he had been approved by Stevenson's parents as a suitable companion for a holiday in Germany in the summer of 1872. Having dubiously regarded his parents' choice of a companion, Stevenson was pleasantly surprised in him; writing to Baxter that 'Simpson and I got on very well together, and made a very suitable pair', he remarked: 'I like him much better than I did when I started which was almost more than I hoped for.' Soon Simpson was accepted into the circle of Stevenson's friends, and Baxter was Stevenson's fellow-guest on Simpson's yacht for the trip to the Hebrides in 1874.

In dress and deportment as correct as Andrew Lang, Simpson presented an astonishing contrast with Stevenson as a travelling companion. In the epilogue to *An Inland Voyage* Stevenson thus describes his own curious appearance:

'The *Arethusa* was unwisely dressed. He is no precisian in attire; but by all accounts he was never so ill-inspired as on that tramp; having set forth, indeed, upon a moment's notice, from the most unfashionable spot in Europe, Barbizon. On his head he wore a smoking-cap of Indian work, the gold lace pitifully frayed and tarnished. A flannel shirt of an agreeable dark hue, which the

satirical called black; a light tweed coat made by a good English
tailor; ready-made cheap linen trousers and leathern gaiters completed his array. In person, he is exceptionally lean; and his face
is not, like those of happier mortals, a certificate. For years he
could not pass a frontier, or visit a bank, without suspicion; then
police everywhere, but in his native city, looked askance upon him;
and (although I am sure it will not be credited) he is actually
denied admittance to the casino of Monte Carlo. If you will imagine
him dressed as above, stooping under his knapsack, walking nearly
five miles an hour with the folds of the ready-made trousers flutter-
ing about his spindle shanks, and still looking eagerly round him as
if in terror of pursuit—the figure, when realised, is far from reassur-
ing. When Villon journeyed (perhaps by the same pleasant valley)
to his exile at Roussillon, I wonder if he had not something of the
same appearance.'

Colvin seems to be straining credibility in attempting to excuse
Stevenson of affectation in adopting such studied eccentricity of
attire, but he fairly attributes a partial reason for its adoption
to 'a hankering after social experiment and adventure'. Doubtless he delighted to relate to his friends the adventures recorded
in *An Inland Voyage*—they befitted so appropriately his character
as a Bohemian. The landlady of a village tavern, believing him
to be a beggar, refused to charge him more than a nominal
halfpenny for refreshment; a rural postman in the Loing Valley,
declining to accept his assurance that he was not a purveyor of
pornographic postcards, devised insistent inducements to be
shown the contents of his knapsack. On being arrested as a
suspicious character, he was detained by the police until a
horrified commissary was confronted by Simpson—'a man of
an unquestionable and unassailable manner, in apple-pie order,
dressed not with neatness merely but elegance, ready with his
passport at a word, and well supplied with money: a man the
Commissary would have doffed his hat to on chance upon the
highway; and this *beau cavalier* unblushingly claimed the
Arethusa for his comrade!'

Evidently Simpson had his uses as a travelling companion.
But his respectability did not always succeed in countering the
disreputable impression of his friend. 'Many a bitter bowl had
he partaken of with that disastrous comrade.' To one so

orthodox and fastidious of habit—to 'a man born to float easily through life, his face and manner artfully recommending him to all'—it must have been disconcerting, and doubtless vexatious, to be mistaken for a pedlar and to be refused accommodation, as an undesirable client, at the inn of La Fère. The survival, despite such strains, of their friendship, as well as witnessing the affection and esteem felt by Simpson for Stevenson, implies also a fund of humour and philosophical fortitude. As appears from his character as Athelred in 'Talk and Talkers', Simpson possessed something from which Stevenson, consciously or unconsciously derived reinforcing strength—a core of stability and sincerity which used to be considered characteristic of that unjustly derided and unhappily outmoded product, the typical English gentleman.

'Athelred . . . presents you with the spectacle of a sincere and somewhat slow nature thinking aloud. He is the most unready man I ever knew to shine in conversation. You may see him sometimes wrestle with a refractory jest for a minute or two together, and perhaps fail to throw it in the end. And there is something singularly engaging, often instructive, in the simplicity with which he thus exposes the process as well as the result, the works as well as the dial of the clock. Withal he has his hours of inspiration. Apt words come to him as if by accident, and, coming from deeper down, they smack the more personally, they have the more of fine old crusted humanity, rich in sediment and humour. There are sayings of his in which he has stamped himself into the very grain of the language; you would think he must have worn the words next his skin and slept with them. Yet it is not as a sayer of particular good things that Athelred is most to be regarded, rather as the stalwart woodman of thought. I have pulled on a light cord often enough, while he has been wielding the broad-axe; and between us, on this unequal division, many a specious fallacy has fallen. I have known him to battle the same question night after night for years, keeping it in the reign of talk, constantly applying it and re-applying it to life with humorous or grave intention, and all the while, never hurrying, nor flagging, nor taking an unfair advantage of the facts. Jack [Bob Stevenson] at a given moment, when arising, as it were, from the tripod, can be more radiantly just to those from whom he differs; but then the tenor of his thoughts is even calumnious; while Athelred, slower to forge excuses, is yet slower to condemn, and sits over the welter of the world, vacillating but still judicial, and still faithfully contending with his doubts.'

Simpson's sister—who wrote two tiresomely inadequate books about Stevenson, *The R. L. Stevenson Originals* and *Robert Louis Stevenson's Edinburgh Days*—relates that Simpson and Stevenson 'agreed to differ in pace when they went a walking tour together, the long-legged, restlessly inquisitive Stevenson, hurrying ahead like the hare in the proverb, then pausing in some byway, while Simpson, squarely built, short in his stride, but steady-paced, oftener reached the goal first'. They walked thus separately before Stevenson's arrest while hurrying to Barbizon to recount their adventures of the inland voyage; though he remarks that, 'at noon the next day', they were both telling of their misadventure to the company in Siron's Inn at Barbizon, it seems that they must have walked separately again after their release by the police. The last chapter of *An Inland Voyage* concludes:

'Now we were to return, like the voyager in the play, and see what rearrangements fortune had perfected the while in our surroundings; what surprises stood ready made for us at home; and whither and how far the world had voyaged in our absence. You may paddle all day long; but it is when you come back at nightfall, and look in at the familiar room, that you find Love or Death awaiting you beside the stove; and the most beautiful adventures are not those we go to seek.'

From Will H. Low, the American painter—who told the story in his memoirs, *A Chronicle of Friendships*—he heard that the monastic seclusion of Grez had been invaded by two American women, a Mrs. Osbourne and her daughter, 'a bewitching young girl of seventeen, with eyes so large as to be out of drawing'. Bob Stevenson went over to reconnoitre and report; when he failed to return, Simpson followed; as he likewise stayed, Stevenson went himself and 'met his fate'—as the romantic legend relates, he fell in love 'with his wife at first sight when he saw her in the lamplight through the open window'.

His fate was not the pretty daughter, but her mother. Fanny Osbourne was born Frances Matilda Van de Grift on 10th

March 1840; she was thus nearly eleven years older than Stevenson. Born and brought up at Indianapolis, then a backwoods frontier town, she was the eldest child of Presbyterian parents; her talent for drawing was early evinced when, 'caught in the wave of great temperance revival', she executed two propagandist pictures, 'The Drunkard's Home' and 'The Reformed Drunkard's Home'—on the principle of subsequent advertisements for tooth-pastes and soap-powders, before and after using. At seventeen she married Samuel Osbourne, a Kentuckian of twenty, and her daughter Belle was born the following year.

Samuel Osbourne had 'all the suavity and charm of the Southerner', but neither loyalty nor stability of affection was included among his virtues, and he joined the army of the North in the Civil War. After the war he went to California, and sent for Fanny to join him. Arriving in California, she found that he had departed to seek his fortune in the silver mines of Nevada. Persistently she followed, and lived with him in a cabin of the mining camp till an improvement in his fortunes justified their removal to Virginia City. When, as a result of too ambitious speculation, Osbourne went 'broke', apparently he departed overnight, without awaiting the embarrassment of settling with creditors, and left word for Fanny to join him in San Francisco. Again Fanny and her daughter journeyed to Californa; again they found no husband and father waiting to greet them, but this time Mr. Osbourne was reported to have been 'killed by the Indians'. 'Stranded without means in a strange city', Fanny 'put on widow's weeds' and found herself a job as dressmaker's fitter in San Francisco.

In the same San Francisco boarding-house there happened to be living a young Englishman, John Lloyd, who had known Fanny in Nevada and now charmed her by much the same attentions to her small daughter as Stevenson's to Madame Garschine's little girl. But Mr. Osbourne re-appeared—'a tall, handsome man in high boots and a wide hat'—to bear off Fanny from her boarding-house. When, soon afterwards, Fanny's son was born, he received the baptismal name of Mr. Osbourne and the surname of John Lloyd; the friendship with John Lloyd 'was maintained in later years', wrote Fanny's sister and biographer, Nellie Van de Grift Sanchez, 'and when the once poor clerk became a bank president, Fanny Stevenson put her money in his bank'.

Discreetly silent about Mr. Osbourne's adventures in escaping death at the hands of the Indians, Mrs. Sanchez relates that soon 'Mrs. Osbourne discovered that her husband had again betrayed her, and she returned to her father's house in Indiana'. Whatever Mr. Osbourne's faults, he possessed masculine attraction, for, within a year, his wife 'yielded to entreaties and promises of reform, and again journeyed to California'. While 'making a strong effort to forget past differences', Fanny developed interests apart from her husband: she attended an art school and 'built a studio where she painted'; she became expert in taking and developing photographs at a time when amateur photography was a rare accomplishment; she developed the craft of housewife and hostess, and discovered a passion for gardening. Another son, named Hervey, was born to her, but, when Hervey 'was about four years old, the cloud which had menaced the happiness of the family for so long again descended'. After 'earnest and conscientious efforts to avoid the disruption of her marital ties, plighted with such high hopes in the springtime of her girlhood', she felt 'her husband's infidelities had now became so open and flagrant' that, 'in 1875, partly to remove herself as far as possible from distressing associations, partly to give her daughter the advantage of instruction in foreign schools of art, she took her three children and set out for Europe'.

Settling in Paris, Fanny and Belle attended Jullian's Academy, where George Moore was among their fellow-students. Neither mother nor daughter qualified for inclusion in *Memoirs of My Dead Life*; Moore's American widow came from Baltimore. At five years old her younger son Hervey died, and broken in health and spirits, Fanny was advised, in the summer of 1876, to leave Paris for 'some quiet country place'. So, with her daughter Belle and her son Lloyd, she came to Grez.

While his cousin Bob and their friends paid court to the seventeen-year-old daughter, Stevenson, from the first, devoted his attention to the mother. Now thirty-six, Fanny was only a year younger than Mrs. Sitwell and probably much the same age as Madame Garschine. Colvin described her as 'small, dark-complexioned, eager'.

'In spite of her squarish build she was supple and elastic in all her movements; her hands and feet were small and beautifully modelled, though not meant for, or used to, idleness; the head, under its crop of close-waving thick black hair, was of a build and character that somehow suggested Napoleon, by the firm setting of the jaw and the beautifully precise and delicate modelling of the nose and lips: the eyes were full of sex and mystery as they changed from fire or fun to gloom or tenderness; and it was from between a fine pearly set of small teeth that there came the clear metallic accents of her intensely human and often quaintly individual speech.'

All who met her noticed that 'firm setting of the jaw', which marked her as a woman dangerous to cross: it must be remembered in commenting on Stevenson's subsequent conduct; it looms significant in the eventual breach between Stevenson and Henley; it intimidated men like Colvin into ready acceptance of the belief that she was a providential custodian for Stevenson's unstable character; it inspired Henry James long afterwards to describe her—despite his 'sneaking kindness for her'—as 'poor barbarous and merely *instinctive* lady'. Assertive, possessive, direct in approach to an objective, she was as simple and straightforward of character as Stevenson was complex and involved; to one whose resolution was so habitually shaken by conscience, her personality must have seemed a model of strength and clarity, and Stevenson derived from her the same sense of stabilising reinforcement as from Henley and Simpson.

To engage her deeper interest he was able to employ the same strategy as with Mrs. Sitwell and Madame Garschine. Her small son Lloyd (then called Sam; he became Lloyd after his mother's second marriage) was already excited by Bob Stevenson's stories of 'this wonderful Louis Stevenson, who was so picturesquely gliding towards Grez in a little sailing canoe, and who camped out every night in a tent'; at their first meeting he gazed 'in spell-bound admiration', and admiration became devotion when, instead of finding himself ignored as a tiresome little boy, he was invited to share his boyish interests as with an enlivening and enthusiastic comrade. Stevenson always delighted in children—only the year before he had confided to Mrs. Sitwell 'a longing for children of my own'—and whatever regrets accrued from their romance to Stevenson or Fanny, Lloyd Osbourne had reason to bless his fortune in a stepfather.

Of the time in Paris before they met Stevenson, Lloyd Osbourne wrote, 'We were miserably poor; it seems to me that I was always hungry'. Apparently Stevenson now prevailed upon his father to give him the thousand pounds promised on his call to the bar, for Balfour relates that 'about this time' Thomas Stevenson 'paid to Louis as an instalment of his patrimony a considerable sum, amounting, I believe, to not less than a thousand pounds'. Quoting Colvin's remark that 'the little money he had was always absolutely at the disposal of his friends', Balfour adds, 'In 1877 he had still £800, but, owing to misfortunes befalling his friends, in none of which was he under any obligation to intervene, within less than two years nothing of it remained'. 'A Bohemian,' says *Lay Morals*, 'for as poor as he may be, is always open-handed to his friends'; living up to this axiom where it was accepted among the easy society of artistic Barbizon, Stevenson must have persuaded Fanny to accept his help from time to time.

Another recipient of his largess was Henley, to whom he made gifts or loans throughout their friendship; even after their quarrel, he conveyed gifts to Henley through Charles Baxter. At the end of 1876 Henley removed from Edinburgh to miserable lodgings in Shepherd's Bush, having secured the editorship of a weekly review called *London*—a post he owed to his connection with Stevenson. By his editing of the *Edinburgh University Magazine*—to which Stevenson had contributed in 1871—a college contemporary named Glasgow Brown had won the support of Conservative party potentates to found *London*. On the eve of launching the first number in January 1877, Brown fell ill with tuberculosis, and, like Stevenson three years before, was 'ordered south' to Mentone, where he died little more than a year later. A successor being required at short notice, Henley secured his first chance as an editor.

It appears that Stevenson incurred at least two other

liabilities which may have proved expensive. His published correspondence over this period is too sparse to provide an accurate guide to his movements and occupations. Remarking that 'Mrs. Sitwell remained as closely as ever his trusted friend and helper, and now and again at need an intermediary between himself and his father', Colvin adds lamely, 'their occasions for the interchange of letters became fewer'. In the loose and rambling narrative that he constructed upon the basis of Colvin's papers in *The Colvins and Their Friends*, E. V. Lucas suggests the explanation that 'it would not have been unnatural had Mrs. Osbourne, as she was in 1876, resented Stevenson's dependence upon her predecessor'. At Paris and Grez Stevenson was probably too conscious of Fanny's firm jaw to write so much to Mrs. Sitwell; from Edinburgh he now naturally addressed bulletins of his thoughts and actions to Fanny. Despite the bulk of his published correspondence, he was reputed among his friends to be lax in writing letters, which frequently begin with apologies for delay in replying. But it appears that Stevenson confided to Mrs. Sitwell, not only his affair with Fanny, but also his differences with his parents, and the discreet Colvin suppressed several letters indicating that Fanny's finances were subsidised by Stevenson and that she lived with him as his mistress.

In January 1877 Stevenson wrote to his mother from Paris, 'I dine every day in a Crêmerie with a party of Americans, one Irishman and sometimes an English lady'; describing the English lady as 'elderly' and 'very prim', he says nothing about the Americans. Between February and May he was much at Edinburgh, where, with Henley removed to Shepherd's Bush and Baxter about to be married, he was thrown much upon his own resources. At home the same chilling atmosphere of disapproval prevailed. 'I think I never feel so lonely as when I am too much with my father and mother,' he told Mrs. Sitwell, 'and I am ashamed of the feeling, which makes matters worse.' Separation from Fanny sharpening the urgency for recreative escape, it must have been at this time that he embarked upon two amorous affairs discovered by his later biographers. The more serious was with the dark, slender daughter of an Aberdeen builder and carpenter, who was working in Edinburgh; the heroine of the other was the 'tall, fair, and remarkably well built' daughter of a Midlothian village blacksmith. J. A. Steuart relates that the fair Roxana met the exotic Statira on at least one occasion, when 'a scene of fury resulting in physical violence' occurred between the rival queens near Swanston Cottage, when Stevenson was there with his parents.

This scene must have happened about Christmas of 1877, for no evidence appears that his relations with his parents were more than ordinarily strained during the earlier part of the year. Presumably stimulated by Fanny, he was working hard to compensate for idleness during the first months following their meeting, when he had writen little besides the *Cornhill* essay, 'On Falling in Love'. In May 'An Apology for Idlers', rejected by *Macmillan's Magazine*, was in proof for *Cornhill*, and he had his essay on Villon 'to do for the same magazine', while he had begun a novel called *The Hair Trunk; or, The Ideal Commonwealth*—'a most absurd story of a lot of young Cambridge fellows who are going to found a new society, with no ideas on the subject, and nothing but Bohemian tastes in the place of ideas . . . the trunk is the fun of it—everybody steals it; burglary, marine fight, life on desert island on west coast of Scotland, sloops, etc.' Already he intended to use the islet of Earraid as a setting for fiction, and the idea of the much-stolen trunk seems to have been appropriated by Lloyd Osbourne for *The Wrong Box*, but, though Henley thought its opening scene 'very funny', *The Hair Trunk* was left unfinished. His first story to be accepted for publication was 'my Villon', which appeared in *Temple Bar* of the following October as *A Lodging for the Night*; the same magazine accepted *The Sire de Malétroit's Mousetrap* for publication in January 1878 as *The Sire de Malétroit's Door*. Accompanying his parents on a holiday to Cornwall in August, he sent *Will o' the Mill* 'red hot, to Stephen in a fit of haste'; he was 'quite prepared for a refusal', but Stephen published the story in *Cornhill* of the following January.

From an idea of publishing a volume of his essays at his own expense he was dissuaded by Leslie Stephen, who argued that essays worthy of magazine publication provided a commercial proposition for book publication. Of 'An Apology for Idlers' Stephen remarked that 'something more in that vein would be agreeable to his views', and published 'Crabbed Age and Youth' and 'Aes Triplex' in successive numbers of *Cornhill* for March and April 1878, the first of the two being 'pretty well through' while Stevenson was in Cornwall. Stephen's judgment was vindicated by the approval of his readers, who, remarking in the essays signed 'R. L. S.' a reminiscent savour of the *Roundabout Papers* contributed to the magazine by the editor's predecessor and father-in-law, suspected the initials to signify the 'Real Leslie Stephen'. The 'Virginibus Puerisque' essay brought Stevenson his first 'fan mail', a young man named A. Patchett Martin writing from Australia to express appreciation and enclose a volume of his poems.

In October 1877 he was still on good terms with his parents when he wrote from Paris to acknowledge receipt of his quarter's allowance, now increased to a hundred pounds a year. Writing from Heriot Row on 6th December, he was 'newly returned from France'; on New Year's Day he wrote to Colvin from Dieppe that he was busy with *An Inland Voyage*, that he had only two more sections to write, and that he was anxiously hoping for its acceptance by Kegan Paul, as, besides being 'something put outside of me and off my conscience', 'I want coin so badly'. On 15th February, though he had received the good news of his book's acceptance by Kegan Paul, he wrote from Paris 'a very solemn letter' to his father, beginning with the argument that Christianity is 'not ascetic', but 'a doctrine of life' and 'a wisdom for this world', and proceeding to histrionics calculated to impress with alarm:

'I have had some sharp lessons and some very acute sufferings in these last seven-and-twenty years. . . . I begin to grow an old man; a little sharp, I fear, and a little close and unfriendly; but still I have a good heart, and believe in myself and my fellow-men and the God who made us all. . . . There are not many sadder people in this world, perhaps, than I.'

He refers to Glasgow Brown's dying in the Riviera of the disease afflicting himself, to letters 'it hurt me to write, and I fear it will hurt others to receive'; he is 'lonely and sick and out of heart'; finally he concludes:

'I have taken a step towards more intimate relations with you. But don't expect too much of me. Try to take me as I am. This is a rare moment, and I have profited by it; but take it as a rare moment. Usually I hate to speak of what I really feel, to that extent that when I find myself *cornered*, I have a tendency to say the reverse.'

Printing this letter, apparently with expurgations, Colvin printed another written soon afterwards to Mrs. Sitwell, in which, after saying that he is still in bed after being 'really very seriously ill' for two days, Stevenson speaks of 'the Scotch Presbyterian who has been to Paris under such strange circumstances'. Of this letter Colvin notes, 'Stevenson's father . . . had been taken by Stevenson into confidence about the new complications of his life, and had just been to see his son in Paris,' but he omits another undated letter to Mrs. Sitwell, written from Hotel Canterbury, 44 Boulevard Haussmann:

'I haven't an idea where Colvin is now and I've treated him so mean. But it shouldn't count; I have two invalids instead of one to look after, and I feel so tired, you wouldn't believe. Moreover I have had a deal of writing and telegraphing with my people; they are behaving awfully well; and perhaps that is not the least of my troubles. It takes some of the wind out of my sails; I am ashamed to be stiff, where I find them so full of concessions. The sooner they bring out the gallows I think, and execute us all round, the simpler things would be. . . . Get Colvin to forgive me, and drop me a line. F. really must be excused; I wish I could say she is well; her nerves are quite gone; one day I find her in heaven the next in hell. We have many strong reasons for getting her out of Paris in about a month.'

Colvin intended 'complications' to be understood as referring to Stevenson's love for Fanny. But, knowing that his parents would be appalled by his attachment to a married woman, why should Stevenson have chosen this time—when there was no immediate prospect of his union with Fanny—

to confide in his father? The scene at Swanston between his Scottish mistresses must have precipitated avowal of his love for Fanny. He was no longer the boy who had proposed to marry a prostitute; the builder's daughter belonged to the respectable tradesmen's class, and if Stevenson had seduced her, his father's stern morality would require that he should marry her. His refusal must have roused his father to such indignation against his heartless philandering that Stevenson immediately left home, determined to maintain himself independently: he hurriedly finished *An Inland Voyage* because he wanted 'coin so badly', and he did not draw his allowance for two quarters. Invoked as an 'intermediary', Mrs. Sitwell doubtless counselled him to explain that he could not marry the builder's daughter because his affections were engaged elsewhere, a disclosure so alarming and unexpected that his father travelled to Paris in the hope of averting a worse scandal than gossip about the local girls. Smarting memory of the letters 'that it hurt me to write, and I fear it will hurt others to receive' inspired the comment in 'Some Aspects of Robert Burns': 'It is the punishment of Don Juanism to create continually false positions—relations in life which are wrong in themselves, and which it is equally wrong to break or to perpetuate.' As late as February 1880, he wrote from San Francisco to Henley of receiving 'from an enchanting young lady whom you have seen, or rather from her inspiration, threatening letters, exposure, etc.'

To Burns, also, he attributed the continual conflict between Jekyll and Hyde dividing his own nature. 'If he had been strong enough to refrain or bad enough to persevere in evil; if he had only not been Don Juan at all, or been Don Juan altogether, there had been some possible road for him throughout this troublesome world; but a man, alas! who is equally at the call of his worse and better instincts, stands among changing events without foundation or resource.' The student of biography will find only in Coleridge a comparably shrewd realisation of his own weaknesses while seeking vainly their redress— a fact ignored by many of Stevenson's biographers because they have not troubled to investigate it. Mistaking the business of biography, some have deplored as impertinence any probing into the details of Stevenson's emotional life: 'it seems waste

of time to speculate on the possible details,' writes one otherwise more capable than others, 'nor do any of the particular
incidents seem to have made a lasting impression on his life
or work.' Yet how many of his early essays reflect a present
mood of personal experience—'Virginibus Puerisque' written
when contemplating marriage as a possible refuge from his
temptations; 'An Apology for Idlers' when defending himself
from conscience; 'On Falling in Love' after meeting Fanny;
'Crabbed Age and Youth' as a statement of differences with
his father; 'Aes Triplex' and 'El Dorado' as statements of his
attitude to life and death; even biographical subjects like
Knox, Burns, and Villon were selected as sympathetic with a
present mood! Writers about Stevenson have been too rarely
appreciative readers of his work. If his early biographers had
remembered that remark in 'The Morality of the Profession of
Letters', 'it can never be safe to suppress what is true', they
would have given no grounds for such criticism as Mr.
Swinnerton's—that, as an essayist, Stevenson lacked the
emotional experience required for more than a superficial
treatment of his subjects.

Reciprocating his father's gesture of reconciliation, Stevenson
spent Easter of 1878 with his parents at Gairloch on the Clyde.
Appreciating the pathos of his father's studied gentleness, of
the attitude ascribed to Loudon Dodd's father when saying,
'I am not afraid my boy will ever disgrace me', he felt such
affection that he soon afterwards wrote to assure his father of
'how much and how dearly I think of you'. But, ashamed of
himself as a detected Don Juan, and still more ashamed for
having degraded Fanny in his parents' regard as on the level
of his lighter loves, he felt cautious of finding himself 'cornered',
and so being stung into the aggression of self-defence. Knowing
that they saw his association with a married woman as a
dangerous and lamentable entanglement, he could not feel
easy in their company; he felt 'very angry and bitter', he told
Mrs. Sitwell, 'or rather very bitter and not angry'. Though
'on the mend' after his illness, he felt 'withered', though he
believed 'a little happiness would pick me up at once'.

Before returning to Paris, he stayed with his parents at
Burford Bridge, where, introduced by a mutual friend, he met

George Meredith. Each appears to have been impressed by the other, and Stevenson's admiration for Meredith as an artist mounted during the next decade to such a pitch that Henry James, in a shrewd critical quip, suggested that 'his ideal of the delightful work of fiction would be the adventures of Monte Cristo related by the author of *Richard Feverel*'. Little more than a month after their meeting, Meredith wrote a long and cordial letter of congratulation after reading *An Inland Voyage*. 'The writing is of the rare kind which is naturally simple yet picked and choice,' he said; 'it is literature.' Surprised by the general approval of *An Inland Voyage*, Stevenson felt ashamed that he had not given the reviewers 'something better'; realising as yet little of the average reviewer's value, he was still more surprised when sales so inadequately reflected praise that most of the small edition had to be remaindered.

He received only twenty pounds for the copyright of *An Inland Voyage*, and still 'in a wager with world to carry on my affairs at my own expense, if I can', he served for part of the summer as secretary to Fleeming Jenkin, who was a juror at the Paris Exposition. Realising that she must possess only a part of her lover so long as she could have no share in his home life, Fanny decided to seek a divorce, and in August she returned with her children to California. On the announcement of this decision, Stevenson reported to Mrs. Sitwell that he was 'all squared with my people': his parents were prepared to forget past ructions in present relief from their fears lest Stevenson and Fanny should incur social ostracism by openly living in sin.

After Fanny's departure from Paris, Stevenson went to Monastier in Haute-Loire, where he could live cheaply and benefit from the mountain air. Here he finished *Latter-Day Arabian Nights*, serialised in *London* between 8th June and 26th October, and *Picturesque Notes on Edinburgh*, which, after appearance in *The Portfolio* between June and December, was published in December as an eighteen-shilling volume by Seeley, Jackson, and Halliday. Three essays, 'A Plea for Gas Lamps', 'Pan's Pipes', and 'El Dorado', had appeared in successive numbers of *London*, and Henley welcomed the idea of the *Arabian Nights* because—as Andrew Lang generously admitted—probably he alone then 'foresaw that Mr. Stevenson's *forte* was to be fiction, not essay-writing'.

From Fanny's note on *New Arabian Nights* it seems that the idea of the Suicide Club sprang from a discussion between Louis and Bob Stevenson on the subject of 'Aes Triplex' and 'El Dorado'; if only there was assurance that death was the gate of paradise, how happily a party of friends might together venture upon suicide! Himself the prototype of the Young Man with the Cream Tarts, Bob also supplied something to the plot of 'The Adventure of the Hansom Cabs'; the Prince of Wales was the model for Prince Florizel.   Already an influence on Stevenson as an essayist, Thackeray seems to have dictated the tone of the *Arabian Nights*, which, in flippancy and fancy, with a spice of satire, supply a curious link between the Titmarsh of *The Great Hoggarty Diamond* and the tales of Henry Harland, who was one of Henley's young men before he edited *The Yellow Book*. Unsuited to the staid taste of the 'seventies, if they did not actually expedite the expiry of *London* in the following spring, *Latter-Day Arabian Nights* failed to extend its circulation, and as Kegan Paul thought the tales 'too fantastic, and likely to injure the reputation of their author', they waited four years for book publication by Chatto and Windus as *New Arabian Nights*.

From Monastier, 'hard upon October', Stevenson embarked upon the expedition described in *Travels with a Donkey in the Cevennes*; he left Monastier on Sunday, 21st September, and ended the journey, with the sale of the donkey Modestine, on Friday, 3rd October. After a visit to P. G. Hamerton, editor of *The Portfolio*, at Autun, he crossed to England. 'The world is such a dance,' he told his mother, in excusing his inability to announce ahead any plan of his movements. Without Fanny as an anchorage at Grez or Paris, his existence was nomadic. In London he stayed with Henley at Shepherd's Bush and made frequent use of the Savile Club, where he now formed a friendship with Edmund Gosse. Sometimes Colvin lent him his rooms at Cambridge, where he found life in college surroundings 'romantically pleasurable but hardly credible'; among the dons he made a friend of A. G. Dew-Smith, whose singular character he recalled in devising that of Attwater in *The Ebb-Tide*. At Cambridge he wrote *Providence and the Guitar*, the story of strolling players he had met at Grez, for publication in four numbers of *London* between 2nd and 23rd November as 'Léon Berthelini's Guitar'. In mid-winter Henley stayed with him at Swanston to finish their work in collaboration on the play, *Deacon Brodie*.

All these months he was working hard. After a false start with an account of life at Monastier, printed posthumously as 'A Mountain Town in France', he wrote *Travels with a Donkey* so rapidly that the book was in proof in March and published at the beginning of May. The need for what he and Henley called 'the dibbs' drove him on; to Henley he wrote during the winter: 'I must *save*, save, save, £350 must be made and laid by ere I can breathe freely.' Obviously he needed such a sum of money for Fanny—for a contribution to her divorce expenses, for his own passage across the Atlantic, and for starting their life together. While his parents believed him to be waiting in patience for Fanny's return, he was working hard for the means to rejoin her at the earliest possible moment.

In the preface to *Travels with a Donkey*, addressed to Colvin, describing a book as, 'in an intimate sense, a circular letter to the friends of him who writes it', he wrote, 'they find private messages, assurances of love, and expressions of gratitude, dropped for them in every corner'. The statement was an invitation to Fanny to seek the passages addressed to herself. He hears a woman signing a ballad for her lover, and comments:

'How the world gives and takes away, and brings sweethearts near only to separate them again into distant and strange lands; but to love is the great amulet which makes the world a garden; and "hope, which comes to all", outwears the accidents of life, and reaches with tremulous hand beyond the grave and death.'

He speaks of his feeling of serenity during a solitary night among pine trees;

'And yet even while I was exulting in my solitude I became aware of a strange lack. I wished a companion to lie near me in the starlight, silent and not moving, but ever within touch. For there is a fellowship more quiet even than solitude, and which, rightly understood, is solitude made perfect. And to live out of doors with the woman a man loves is of all lives the most complete and free.'

Perhaps while actually at work on this passage, he was writing in an unpublished letter to Henley:

'I'm not so black at heart as under the circumstances I might be . . . do I not love? and am I not loved? and have I not friends who are the pride of my heart? O no, I'll have none of your blues; I'll be lonely, for I can't help it; and I'll hate to go to bed where there is no dear head upon the pillow, for I can't help that either, God help me; but I'll make no mountain of my little molehill.'

With his mind thus full of Fanny, he also wrote the fourth 'Virginibus Puerisque' essay, 'Truth of Intercourse', where, besides explaining the sympathy and understanding he found with Fanny, he exposed its absence between himself and his parents.

'Truth of intercourse is something more difficult than to refrain from open lies. It is possible to avoid falsehood and yet not tell the truth. . . . To speak truth there must be moral equality or else no respect; and hence between parent and child intercourse is apt to degenerate into a verbal fencing bout, and misapprehensions to become ingrained. And there is another side to this, for the parent begins with an imperfect notion of the child's character, formed in early years or during the equinoctial gales of youth; to this he adheres, noting only the facts which suit with his pre-conception; and wherever a person fancies himself unjustly judged, he at once and finally gives up the effort to speak truth. With our chosen friends, on the other hand, and still more between lovers (for mutual understanding is love's essence), the truth is easily indicated by the one and aptly comprehended by the other. A hint taken, a look understood, conveys the gist of long and delicate explanations; and where the life is known even *yea* and *nay* become luminous. In the closest of all relations—that of a love well founded and equally shared—speech is half discarded, like a roundabout, infantile process or a ceremony of formal etiquette; and the two communicate directly by their presences, and with few looks and fewer words contrive to share their good and evil and uphold each other's hearts in joy.'

The same argument is expounded at greater length in *Lay Morals*, which he was writing at Swanston in March. He had been working hard for 'dibbs' at *Travels with a Donkey* and *Deacon Brodie*, which Henley optimistically believed likely to make both their fortunes; he had a commission from Kegan Paul for another travel book. He knew that such a book as *Lay Morals*, if finished, might be difficult to place with a publisher. Yet he wasted time on it at Swanston, the place where he was most poignantly conscious of his parents' personalities, because his conscience, as usual, demanded self-justification. A few lines in 'Truth of Intercourse' were not enough ; he must justify this most momentous step in his life with a moral autobiography.

The writing of *Lay Morals* was interrupted by a breakdown in health, after which he went again with his parents to Gairloch and thence to stay with Meredith at Box Hill—an invitation which gives the lie to Gosse's tattle that 'Stevenson threw himself with extreme enthusiasm into the acquaintance' and 'I remember hearing at the time that the elder writer was not very responsive at first, that he was a little bewildered at being thus carried by storm'. Meredith was interested in both Stevenson and his work—so interested in his personality that he sketched its outline in the character of Gower Woodseer of *The Amazing Marriage*; he was well pleased to entertain a close friend of Henley, whose praise of his work came at a time when praise of Meredith was so rare that, as he told Stevenson, 'I, who have worked for many years not supposing that any one paid much heed to me, find it extraordinary'. Stevenson remained loyal to his admiration of Meredith; nine years later, in reply to criticism by Henry James of Meredith's affectation in speech and manner, he wrote: 'He is not an easy man to be yourself with—there is so much of him, and the veracity and the high athletic intellectual humbug are so intermixed.'

From Meredith's he crossed to France, dividing his time between Paris and Cernay-la-Ville, where he went 'to get this thing for Paul put out of hand'. If 'this thing' was *Lay Morals*, he made little progress with it. With his mind full of his project to rejoin Fanny, he felt unable to concentrate: 'I sit

and sit, and scribe and scribe, but cannot get my back into it.'
With a struggle he finished 'Some Aspects of Robert Burns'
for *Cornhill* before returning to London at the end of June.

Travels with a Donkey was published in May by Kegan Paul.
Meredith declared that he and John Morley were 'wonderfully
pleased' with it, and Morley intended to ask Stevenson for a
travel article for the *Fortnightly Review*. Reviews were as
favourable, and sales as disappointing, as with *An Inland
Voyage*. After Stevenson's reputation was established, most
critics followed George Saintsbury in finding a 'somewhat
Sternian' flavour in these travel books; some later critics have
pretended that they should be preferred to his fiction as
exercises in artistry. Their fairest appreciation came from
Richard Le Gallienne, when, in May 1892, reviewing *Across
the Plains*, he saw in them the same qualities as in Stevenson's
essays:

'Nothing could be more commonplace than the adventures
which supply the theme, nothing less so than Mr. Stevenson's
account of them. . . . He sees everything as if it had never been
looked on before. Nothing has, so to say, gone cold for him. For
him there is no such thing as merely hard fact. Each fact is a
sensitive centre of infinite interests. And he makes us aware of this
with a simplicity so natural that we are apt to forget that his
record is anything more than a record of actual fact, that it is, as
Mr. Pater would say, " the transcript of the sense of fact rather than
the fact" itself.'

In London he applied for employment to *The Times*; Balfour
says, 'he expressed himself as unwilling to accept "leaders",
but apparently asked for some more general commission'. It
is reasonable to assume that, with the credentials of *An Inland
Voyage* and *Travels with a Donkey*, he hoped for a commission
to write articles on his expedition to California. *The Times*
declined to pay his passage to America for this purpose, but,
though he had earned no more than one-fifth of the £350 he
had thought necessary during the previous winter, he decided
to wait no longer.

In accordance with the way his conscience worked, he spent

the last fortnight of July at Swanston with his parents. Balfour amiably suggests that 'perhaps he hardly realised the distress which he would inevitably cause his parents by leaving them without a word and in almost total ignorance of the hopes and motives which inspired him'. J. A. Steuart considered that his 'callous' conduct towards his parents supplies evidence of 'the flint' in Stevenson's character; Colvin attempted to avert this charge by implying that Stevenson sailed for America on a momentary impulse, without premeditated plan, when he received 'very disquieting news' of Fanny's health. Yet in *Lay Morals* and in 'Truth of Intercourse' he amply explained the reasoning by which he arrived at his course of action. Experience in the previous year had proved that he could expect from his parents no sympathetic understanding of his passion for Fanny; he shrank from exposing himself to the appeals and recriminations that would follow 'a verbal fencing bout' with his father. He knew he must hurt them, but his life was his own—not theirs—to live. His stay at Swanston was a gesture of affection; when he had gone, they could remember that he had chosen to spend with them the last of his time before going. To his close friends he confided his project—to Bob Stevenson and Baxter, Colvin, Gosse, and Henley. Arguing that his health was bad, and he was going 'with every condition to make him worse', Colvin warned him that, if the 'spirit will go playing fast and loose with its body, the body will some day decline the association—and we shall be left without our friend'. More shrewdly Henley appealed neither to sentiment nor to regard for his health, but to practical consideration of his artistic ambition: men like Morley and Stephen would give him work if he was there to woo it from them—surely he could 'see that England and a quiet life are what he wants and must have if he means to make—I won't say reputation—but money by literature'. Gosse relates: 'To the last we were trying to dissuade him from what seemed to us the maddest of enterprises.' He looked thin and ill, as he paced about, 'a cigarette spinning in his wasted fingers'—so exhausted by wearing argument that, as he told Colvin in enclosing to him a letter for his father, he felt incapable of 'a regret, a hope, a fear, or an inclination'. His one clear conviction was expressed in a letter to Colvin written as the boat neared New York:

'At least, if I fail in my great purpose, I shall see some wild life in the West. . . . But I don't yet know if I have the courage to stick to life without it. Man, I was sick, sick, sick of this last year.'

On the steamship *Devonia* he sailed for New York on 7th August 1879.

CHAPTER FIVE

THE AMATEUR EMIGRANT

'There is probably no other act in a man's life so hot-headed and foolhardy as this one of marriage.'—'Virginibus Puerisque,' Second Paper.

ON THE *Devonia* Stevenson travelled 'second cabin', at two guineas more than the steerage fare of six guineas. During the crossing, besides making copious notes of his experiences and fellow-travellers with a view to the travel book called *The Amateur Emigrant*, he wrote *The Story of a Lie*. The weakest and slightest of all his stories, its plot is devised as an allegory on the argument in 'Truth of Intercourse' that 'truth to facts is not always truth to sentiment'; when Dick Naseby tells lies to Esther because he cannot bear to destroy her illusions about her father, and when Dick grieves over his father's anger against him, Stevenson was evidently hoping that his own father would read a message to himself. When Henley condemned the story, Stevenson warmly defended it, protesting that Henley was judging by unfairly high standards of comparison; but, four years later, he declared his intention of re-writing it, 'as it is too weak and ragged'. Meanwhile it was 'this thing for Paul', as, conveyed through Colvin, the story appeared in the October number of the *New Quarterly Magazine*, a struggling periodical owned by Kegan Paul.

The story of his crossing is related in the first part of *The Amateur Emigrant*, 'From the Clyde to Sandy Hook', divided into eight chapters, which he hoped might furnish as many articles for the *Pall Mall Gazette*. When he sent the manuscript to Colvin in the following December, he warned him that 'it is not a monument of eloquence; indeed, I have sought to be prosaic in view of the nature of the subject'. Probably remembering that James Greenwood's articles on his personal experiences in a casual ward had been a sensational success in the

The Amateur Emigrant

Pall Mall Gazette, he was attempting to suit his manner to his market. But neither Henley nor Colvin liked it; in the stark description of squalid subjects there was none of the gay spirit of romantic adventure pervading *An Inland Voyage* and *Travels with a Donkey*; they feared, as Kegan Paul had feared in the case of *New Arabian Nights*, that it would not appeal to admirers of his previous books. Its weakness as a book lies in its lack of interest as a narrative; the studies of the passengers are a series of separate vignettes, and the meticulous objectivity of the author's observations loses the charm Le Gallienne describes in his other books—here a fact is indeed a hard fact, instead of 'a sensitive centre of infinite interests'.

The second part of *The Amateur Emigrant*, 'Across the Plains', describing his journey from New York to San Francisco, was revised and re-written three years later for publication in *Longman's Magazine* of July and August 1883. Americans may dismiss this brief narrative as just another impertinence by a writer from the Old Country following in the disdainful wake of Mrs. Trollope's *Domestic Manners of the Americans* and Dickens's *American Notes* and *Martin Chuzzlewit*; yet it has value as an historical document, written after a century of nationalism, in the miraculous growth of a mushroom civilisation. Reminding the average American that young men of liberal opinions—like Coleridge and Southey eighty years earlier—still regarded the United States as the seat of hope for a new world order, Stevenson asked him to 'imagine a young man, who shall have grown up in an old and rigid circle, following bygone fashions and taught to distrust his own fresh instincts, and who now suddenly hears of a family of cousins, all about his own age, who keep house together by themselves and live far from restraint and tradition; let him imagine this, and he will have some imperfect notion of the sentiment with which spirited English youths turn to the thought of the American Republic'.

'He knows or thinks nothing of the Maine Laws, the Puritan sourness, the fierce, sordid appetite for dollars, or the dreary existence of country towns. A few wild story-books which delighted his childhood form the imaginative basis of his picture of America. In course of time, there is added to this a great crowd of stimulating details—vast cities that grow up as by enchantment; the birds, that have gone south in autumn, returning with the spring to find thousands camped upon their marshes, and the lamps burning far and near along populous streets; forests that disappear like snow; countries larger than Britain that are cleared and settled, one man running forth with his household gods before another, while the bear and the Indian are yet scarce aware of their approach; oil that gushes from the earth; gold that is washed or quarried in the brooks or glens of the Sierras; and all that bustle, courage, action, and constant kaleidoscopic change that Walt Whitman has seized and set forth in his vigorous, cheerful, and loquacious verses.'

Oklahoma was still mapped as 'Indian Territory'; within living memory there had been bloody wars against the Indians, such as the campaign against the Seminoles of the extreme south, described in Robert Wilder's novel, *Bright Feather*. 'All through Ohio, Indiana, Illinois, and Iowa, or for as much as I saw of them from the train and in my waking moments,' the country was 'rich and various . . . a sort of flat paradise'. The plains of Nebraska were so empty that the wayfarer 'may walk five miles and see nothing; ten, and it is as though he had not moved; twenty, and still he is in the midst of the same great level, and has approached no nearer to the one object within view, the flat horizon which keeps pace with his advance'. Through the desert of Wyoming, 'mile upon mile, and not a tree, a bird, or a river', till, coming to Sacramento, 'the city of gardens in a plain of corn', the vision of lovely landscape 'was like meeting one's wife'. Despite mistakes, America was still the hope of humanity; still it might be the promised land of Ross Lockridge's *Raintree County* and Carl Sandburg's *Remembrance Rock*. Yet Stevenson witnessed the sprouting of tares that spread into the twentieth century's harvest of disaster. He waxed indignant against the degradation of freedom by the persecution of the Chinese in San Francisco; when he condemned the outrages against the Indians as 'a chapter of injustice and indignity such as a man must be in some ways base if his heart will suffer him to pardon or forget', he could not foresee the delirium of racial and ideological prejudice into which man could be driven by the fever of fear.

For the sake of economy and material for his book, he crossed

America on an emigrant train, 'sitting on the top of the cars', always writing. In later years he worked best when sitting up in bed, but he always possessed the faculty of writing under any conditions—in train or boat, on a railway platform, or at a roadside inn. He wore 'nothing but a shirt and a pair of trousers', the shirt unbuttoned; he shared 'a tin wash-bowl among four'; he took laudanum to secure sleep. 'What it is to be ill in an emigrant train let those declare who know,' he wrote to Henley; 'my illness is a subject of great mirth to some of my fellow-travellers'.

At San Francisco he found that Fanny, having recovered from 'being much run down in health', had moved to Monterey, a hundred and fifty miles down the coast. Ill and exhausted as he was, he set out on horseback; collapsing in a lonely part of the Coast Line Mountains, he was rescued from death by an old bear-hunter and his partner.

'Two nights I lay out under a tree in a sort of stupor, doing nothing but fetch water for myself and horse, light a fire and make coffee, and all night awake hearing the goat-bells ringing and the tree-frogs singing when each new noise was enough to set me mad. Then the bear-hunter came round, pronounced me "real sick", and ordered me up to the ranche. It was an odd, miserable piece of my life; and according to all rule, it should have been my death.'

The rancheros kept him at their goat-ranch till he was well enough to ride on to Monterey, where he found lodgings with 'a little French doctor'. Each day 'I take one of my meals in a little French restaurant; for the other two, I sponge'. For these two daily meals he 'sponged' on the household where Fanny was staying with her children and her sister; these were the hours of his daily meetings with her, for he was hard at work during the rest of his days. In the following summer he described Monterey in 'The Old Pacific Capital', published in *Fraser's Magazine* of November 1880; its population, 'mostly Mexican and Indian—mixed', was 'about that of a dissenting chapel on a wet Sunday in a strong church neighbourhood'. But already, by the time his article was written, the place had changed in character: 'A huge hotel has sprung up in the desert by the railway . . . and Monterey is advertised in the newspapers, and posted in the waiting-rooms at railway-stations, as a resort for wealth and fashion.'

Despite his weeks of illness, in October he had not only drafted half of *The Amateur Emigrant*, but completed *The Pavilion on the Links*—'carpentry' he called it, 'but not bad at that; and who else can carpenter in England, now that Wilkie Collins is played out?' Much his most successful story to date, *The Pavilion on the Links* afforded to his bibliographer, Colonel W. F. Prideaux, 'the first revelation of Stevenson's gifts as a romanticist', and, after *Strange Case of Dr. Jekyll and Mr. Hyde*, with the possible exception of *The Beach of Falesá*, it is probably the most popular of his shorter stories. As Mr. Compton Mackenzie has written, 'Nothing could be better than Stevenson's handling of the gloomy scene in which his melodrama is played', and few long short stories—'novelettes', as D. H. Lawrence called them—so successfully weather the test of re-reading. Addressing an unromantic generation, Mr. Mackenzie deplores the Victorian sentimentality of this passage:

'To this day I remember the touch of her cheek, which was wet and cold with the rain; and many a time since, when she has been washing her face, I have kissed it again for the sake of that morning on the beach.'

If the sentiment seems strained to-day, it is because two world wars have strangled the romantic gallantry natural to youth; to Stevenson's contemporaries it seemed poetically romantic, and so certainly it must have seemed to the succeeding generations that delighted in Marie Corelli, Elinor Glyn, and Ethel M. Dell. To Stevenson, writing as he lay ill in consequence of travelling half-way round the world for a wife, it must have seemed a true sentiment.

His next effort at fiction, *A Vendetta in the West*, was apparently less successful. He was forcing himself to write: 'Dibbs and speed are my mottoes,' he told Henley; 'God prosper it, poor *Pavilion!* May it bring me money for myself and my sick one, who may need it, I do not know how soon.' To Colvin and Henley, perhaps with the idea of softening their feelings towards her, he intimated that Fanny was as ill as himself; yet, according to her sister's account, Fanny had been restored to health long before Stevenson's arrival in California, being 'sunburned to a fine mahogany' from 'galloping along the country roads on her little mustang'. The business of divorce soon took Fanny away from Monterey; to Gosse on 8th October Stevenson wrote: 'I live here comfortably enough; but I shall soon be left all alone, perhaps till Christmas.' He was to rejoin Fanny in San Francisco, but his departure was delayed by a dangerous attack of pleurisy—'the result, I fear, of overwork, gradual decline of appetite, etc.'

His contradiction of pleurisy in a climate so mild awakened an alarming realisation of the ravages to his constitution in these three months of hardship; the reflection that it was 'six years, all but a few months, since I was obliged to spend twenty-four hours in bed', brought an ominous reminder of the mood described in 'Ordered South'. He began to doubt his ability to survive the ordeal. 'I am going for thirty now,' he wrote to Gosse from his sick-bed, 'and unless I can snatch a little rest before long, I have, I may tell you in confidence, no hope of seeing thirty-one.' While he was sweating out his pleuritic fever with doses of aconite, and staying in bed all day because he 'had no other means of keeping warm for my work', he received the news that Colvin and Henley agreed in regarding the first part of *The Amateur Emigrant* as 'a spiritless record of squalid experiences, little likely to advance his still only half-established reputation'.

Depression deepened when, in mid-December, he left the small, friendly community of Monterey for the loneliness of the city of San Francisco, and he wrote to Gosse:

'Death is no bad friend; a few aches and gasps, and we are done; like the truant child, I am beginning to grow weary and timid in this big jostling city, and could run to my nurse, even although she should have to whip me before putting me to bed.'

In San Francisco he had more than three acquaintances—the painter, Virgil Williams, and his wife, to whom he dedicated *The Silverado Squatters*, and Charles Warren Stoddard, later a university professor of English literature, who figures in the eighth chapter of *The Wrecker*, where his 'strange den upon a

hill' is described and it is recorded that he first introduced
Stevenson to the works of Herman Melville, later described to
Charles Baxter as 'a howling cheese'. Two years later, he wrote
an essay on San Francisco, 'A Modern Cosmopolis', published
in Henley's *Magazine of Art* for May 1883, but his most vivid
personal impressions of the city were recalled in *The Wrecker*.

Besides lacking encouragement, letters from Colvin and
Henley were sparing of sympathy, both inclining to imply that
Stevenson's sorry plight was only what they had warned him to
expect from his reckless venture. When Colvin felt reluctant
to damp his spirits with adverse criticism, Henley advised him,
'Don't defer expostulation because he is ill', arguing that
Stevenson must be forced to realise the urgent need for his
return to England—'Come back he must, and that soon'.
Wounded in his pride, and probably realising that Henley
regarded his pathetic pictures of suffering as products of his
talent as a 'histrion', he wrote a long letter of candid remonstrance to Henley, and then took the line with Colvin that the
pleasure of communication with him enabled him to write
himself 'into a kind of spirits'. Facetiously he described his
daily routine: Breakfast at a coffee-house on coffee and a roll
and butter for fivepence; work all the morning before lunch at
a restaurant, 'where a copious meal, half a bottle of wine,
coffee and brandy may be procured for the sum of four bits,
alias fifty cents, £0 2s. 2d. sterling'; walking and correspondence
in the afternoon; at six the same fivepenny meal as for breakfast
before an evening 'devoted to writing and reading, and by
eleven or half-past darkness closes over this weird and truculent
existence'.

'As for coin, you see I don't spend much, only you and Henley
both seem to think my work rather bosh nowadays, and I do want
to make as much as I was making, that is £200; if I can do that, I
can swim: last year with my ill health I touched only £109; that
would not do, I could not fight through on that; but on £200, as
I say, I am good for the world.'

Despite his friends' disparagement, he intended to finish
The Amateur Emigrant, remarking flippantly that, as 'it bored me
hellishly to write the *Emigrant*', it was only fair that it should

'bore others to read it'. When it was done, 'there shall be no more books of travel for me', he said; 'I'll stick to stories'. Asking, 'do you think it a good plan to be so eminently descriptive, and even eloquent in dispraise', he protested, 'I am not frightened', for 'if the *Emigrant* was a failure, the *Pavilion*, by your leave, was not; it was a story quite adequately and rightly done'. Modestly he esteemed *The Pavilion on the Links* a mere 'blood and thunder story'—'Dibbs is its name'—and he deprecated Henley's offering it to *Cornhill*. He was the more elated, and felt his self-confidence restored, when Leslie Stephen accepted it, and settled to write two essays for *Cornhill*, 'Yoshida Torajiro' and 'Thoreau'.

Towards the end of January, the business of her divorce apparently completed, Fanny and her family came to San Francisco, and Stevenson wrote to Henley:

'Do not damp me about my work; *qu'elle soit bonne ou mauvaise*, it has to be done. You know the wolf is at the door, and I have been seriously ill. I am now at *Thoreau*. I almost blame myself for persevering in anything so difficult under the circumstances: but it may set me up again in style, which is the great point. I have now £80 in the world and two houses to keep up for an indefinite period. It is odd to be on so strict a regimen; it is a week for instance since I have bought myself a drink, and unless times change, I do not suppose I shall every buy myself another. . . . My spirits have risen *contra fortunam*; I will fight this out, and conquer.'

About the same time he informed Baxter: 'I have to drop from a 50 cent to a 25 cent dinner. . . . That brings down my outlay in food and drink to 45 cents or 1s. 10½d. per day.'

In her *Life of Mrs. Robert Louis Stevenson*, Fanny's sister, Nellie Van de Grift Sanchez, preserves a tantalising discretion about the progress of the divorce proceedings. There are grounds for suspicion that Fanny had taken only tentative, if any active, steps before Stevenson arrived in California to force her hand. For the sake of her children, she could not afford to discard their father without something more tangible than the avowals of a romantic young man on the other side of the Atlantic. It seems that Stevenson journeyed to California for no such trivial reason as tender regard for her health, but because he was aware that, without the prompting of personal persuasion, she might continue to hesitate about instituting proceedings. At Monterey in October she left Stevenson for the purpose of prosecuting the divorce, which was facilitated by her compliant husband; now she returned without other means of support than Stevenson could provide. Propriety—perhaps also legal decree—demanded separate residence; while Stevenson continued at his lodgings in Bush Street in the city, Fanny and her family were installed at Oakland, across the bay, in 'an old wooden house embowered in creepers', described in the dedication to *Prince Otto*. At this house, Fanny's sister naively writes, 'we first realised the serious nature of his illness, and yet there was none of the depressing atmosphere of sickness, for he refused to be the regulation sick man'.

In February he was cheered by a 'long and kind letter' from Henley, which must have cost Henley some compromise with impatience to write. Struggling himself to make a living in London, to Henley this self-imposed exile seemed a handicap so hopeless to his chances of success, that previously he had asked Colvin to write on his behalf, 'being too blasphemously given towards California and California things to trust myself'. Active in Stevenson's interests, besides placing *The Pavilion on the Links* with Stephen, he suggested that he might find a publisher for a volume of essays. Replying with a list of plans, Stevenson wrote joyously:

'I am well, cheerful, busy, hopeful; I cannot be knocked down; I do not mind about the *Emigrant* . . . I feel easy now about my year's income, which was my one remaining uneasiness. Fanny is so much better, so almost quite well—in spite of another fit; I count these damned fits like coffin nails—that my heart is very light. As for my work, as I tell you, I am not alarmed for that. It was no great news to me you did not like the *Emigrant*. I never felt more virile, nor had clearer aspirations than at present; the *Emigrant*, from first to last, has been a brick cart stopping the way. As for my poor people, I cannot help that, God knows; and I am glad they mean to disinherit me; you know, Henley, I always had moral doubts about inherited money and this clears me of that forever. I enjoy my economy. Think of 45 cents a day for all food and drink. Less than two shillings, including wine and what not!

. . . Your letter, my dear Henley, was too kindly meant to hurt, far less to offend. I think both you and Colvin are a little too hard on me, in spots, and perhaps make not quite enough allowance for a very dreadful period in my life. I told you I was in trouble; some of it you knew; the rest I could not bear to write about; neither the hopes because I doubted their realisation, nor the fears and indignations, for God knows I dared not think of them to myself. And yet I think you should all be very sure of one thing, that I am a man not liable to take offence nor to change in my affections. I am hard and selfish and forgetful, and too easily filled with my own affairs, but my heart, such as it is, is very faithful to those it loves. It is not a rough letter or two that would change one sentiment in me; and no man could resent an excess of zeal in his friends.'

The essays on Yoshida Torajiro and Thoreau—the former a brilliant study in pure narrative, the latter better than the Burns essay as a more polished and mature example of the biographical approach from a chosen point of view—were sent off to *Cornhill*, where they appeared in March and June respectively; he had high hopes of two stories, *A Vendetta in the West*, over which he had toiled at Monterey, and *The Forest State* or *The Greenwood State*, finished more than four years later as *Prince Otto*.

The phase of buoyancy was brief. In March his landlady's little girl lay dying, and sitting long hours by the child's bedside, Stevenson himself fell dangerously ill. For six weeks 'it was a toss-up for life or death'; he was 'on the verge of a galloping consumption, cold sweats, prostrating attacks of cough, sinking fits in which I lost the power of speech, fever, and all the ugliest circumstances of the disease'. To Gosse he wrote on April 16th: 'I have cause to bless God, my wife that is to be, and one Dr. Bamford (a name the Muse repels), that I have come out of all this . . . with a fair prospect of life and some new desire of living.'

Fanny's sister wrote: 'When I recall the sleepless care with which Mrs. Stevenson watched over him at that critical point in his life, it seems to me that it is not too much to say that the world owes it to her that he lived to produce his best works.' Colvin and Henley might have retorted that Fanny could hardly in decency have done less, since Stevenson was fallen into this predicament as a result of his reckless persistence in pursuit of her. If, only a few months before, she had felt prudent doubts about consigning her fortunes to the precarious care of her romantic young lover, she now found herself committed beyond retreat; comparing Stevenson's devotion to a woman of forty with Mr. Osbourne's demeanour during the flower of her youth, she must have been well satisfied of a change for advantage, and, with all her determination of character, she devoted herself to his welfare as a charge upon her care. Henceforth Stevenson's career was a partnership, of which Fanny was managing director.

As he lay convalescent, his doctor's orders were uncompromising: 'a sea voyage would simply kill him at once', and he must 'go to the mountains'. Colvin reported tersely to Henley, 'that means lungs'. Unable to write, he dictated some of *The Greenwood State* to Fanny's sister, but the doctor warned him against work. As he was thus temporarily incapable of earning, and Fanny had no money of her own, she addressed an appeal to his parents.

In letters to Henley Stevenson relates how he had received at Monterey 'a telegram to come home because my father was ill', followed by other 'telegrams from my people that my father was dying', and how he had written in reply, as 'I could not refuse by telegram; it is so brutal'. Finding his son thus obdurate in his resolution, Thomas Stevenson had spoken 'with anger and dismay' of his 'journey and intentions, his desertion of the old firm, and taking to the devious and barren paths of literature; he 'repulsed all attempts at reconciliation'. But in February, hearing from Baxter and Colvin that Stevenson was living little above starvation level, he 'admitted that the case was not what he supposed', and intimated that, if the marriage was delayed as long as possible, he 'was prepared to do his best'. When no response came to these tentative terms, declaring that 'it was preposterous of Louis to scrimp himself', he offered to telegraph any money required. So, after Fanny's appeal in April, Stevenson was able to write: 'My dear people telegraphed me in these words: "Count on 250 pounds annually".'

On 19th May 1880 Stevenson married Fanny Osbourne in San Francisco at the house of a minister named Scott, with the wives of the minister and Virgil Williams as witnesses. Their honeymoon was his convalescing trip to the mountains north of San Francisco, described in *The Silverado Squatters*. As he remarked, 'it was an odd thing' that, at Calistoga, 'on what we are accustomed to consider the very skirts of civilisation, I should have used the telephone for the first time in my civilised career'. They remained at Silverado longer than they had intended, because both Fanny and her son fell ill with diphtheria. To Henley at this time Colvin quoted from a letter written by Fanny, 'I am trying to take care of my dearest boy.' In fact Stevenson was much occupied in taking care of Fanny, for he wrote to Mrs. Sitwell on 17th June:

'My dear, we have had a miserable time. We were six days in Silverado. The first night I had a cramp and was quite worn out after it; the second day Fanny mashed her thumb while carpentering, and had a nervous chill; the third day, she had another from sleeplessness; the sixth day, she and Sam both began to have diphtheria. I got them down in an open cart; the cases are slight; Sam's especially, but Fanny has been pretty sick and a little light-headed for forty-eight hours. You may fancy if I am tired. I am homesick for Europe; yet it is now a question if I shall be strong enough for the journey home this summer.'

During the ensuing years, while Fanny successfully posed as the devoted nurse of an invalid husband, few of their friends realised that Stevenson's recovery was materially retarded by his concern for an invalid wife.

CHAPTER SIX

FIRST YEARS OF MARRIAGE

'Times are changed with him who marries; there are no more by-path meadows, where you may innocently linger, but the road lies long and straight and dusty to the grave.'—*Virginibus Puerisque.*

O N 7th August 1880, a year to the day after his sailing from Glasgow, Stevenson left New York for Liverpool with his wife and stepson. They were met on landing by his parents and Colvin, who thought 'it made things pleasanter my being there'. Stevenson was 'looking better than I expected, and improved by his new teeth; but weak and easily fluttered ', and so frail that ' you could put your thumb and finger round his thigh '. Colvin's impression of Fanny was unfavourable: he told Henley that Stevenson's mother looked 'the fresher of the two ', and wondered 'whether you and I will ever get reconciled to the little determined brown face and white teeth and grizzling (for that's what it's up to) grizzling hair, which we are to see beside him in future '.

Grizzling indeed and already a grandmother (her daughter Belle had married Joseph D. Strong, a painter, who designed the frontispiece to *The Silverado Squatters*), Fanny must have realised that she was physically ill-fitted for the heroine's part in *All for Love, or, The World Well Lost*. But she had shrewd intelligence, single-minded determination, and the charm that sufficed to captivate the impressionable Stevenson. Colvin felt 'bound to say the old folks put a most brave and most kind face on it indeed '. Fanny knew that so much was bound to be so; they were welcoming a prodigal already forgiven; but she knew also that inwardly they were as curiously critical as Colvin. Colvin could wait; he was staying only for lunch, and she could tackle him later. Stevenson's mother was a conventional Victorian lady, stoically subduing her love for her only son from a sense of duty in submissive devotion to her husband. If Fanny could win the father, the mother would be won, since all she desired was amity between father and son.

Probably she profited from a predisposition in her favour on sight. With memories of poor Kate Drummond, the carpenter's daughter, and the blacksmith's amazon, Thomas Stevenson must have fortified himself to face a flamboyant harpy, with the breezy manners of the backwoods, and felt relief on seeing a demure, solid little matron, replete with respectability. Doubtless she was hardly the daughter-in-law he had hoped for, but Stevenson had disappointed his desires as a son; that she was 'grizzling' and a grandmother seemed no disadvantage, since there would be no 'nonsense' about her, and her mature discretion might balance his son's eccentricity. Fanny's tactful handling of the old gentleman confirmed the favourable impression; her mother-in-law found it 'quite amusing how entirely she agreed with my husband on all subjects'. Colvin was thus enabled to record that 'there sprang up between her and his father the closest possible affection and confidence'.

To his father, at least, Stevenson's marriage afforded satisfaction. With less than seven years to live, the old man had Fanny to thank that they were spent on terms of affectionate intimacy with his son. There were no more scenes of strife, no more disgraceful entanglements, shocking outbursts against religion, or irregular comings and goings. The prodigal had returned—if not in shackles, unmistakably in leading-strings; henceforth he was securely tethered by the apron-strings of respectability.

The rest of the summer was spent with his parents in the Highlands. Convinced by Colvin that its publication might injure Stevenson's reputation, his father insisted on withdrawal of *The Amateur Emigrant*, though it was in proof: 'whatever may be the pecuniary loss', Stevenson wrote to Colvin, 'he is willing to bear it'. Too ill to work, Stevenson wrote little besides a few verses—to Colvin 'a sure sign of ill health'. His doctors warned him against wintering in England and ordered him to Davos, a famous resort for consumptives. On their way he and Fanny paused for several days in London, and his friends flocked to see him, eager to hear the tale of his Californian adventures in such late sessions at the Savile Club as he described in 'Talk and Talkers'—such as Gosse considered to be 'worthy of the finest traditions of eager, cultivated communication'. Fanny asserted her authority; Stevenson's state of health would not permit late nights. Already 'blasphemously given towards California and California things', Henley was not propitiated, and from this time the tale of his friendship with Stevenson reveals a process of undermining by Fanny till its ultimate blasting.

Her first step was to drive a wedge between Henley and Colvin, who had been close correspondents, content to exchange opinions and to share equally the privilege of advising their friend. Within a few weeks, she was writing to Colvin from Davos, confiding details of her husband's condition and plans as to a special friend, flatteringly asking his advice, and cunningly intruding herself as the channel of communication between him and Stevenson. Soon she addressed him fulsomely as 'dear friend' and 'best friend', and sent her love or was his affectionately. Like Thomas Stevenson, Colvin was won: he saw 'in Stevenson's wife a character as strong, interesting and romantic almost as his own; an inseparable sharer of all his thoughts, and staunch companion of all his adventures; the most open-hearted of friends to all who loved him; the most shrewd and stimulating critic of his work; and in sickness, despite her own precarious health, the most devoted and most efficient of nurses'. Complacently he compared her demeanour towards him with that towards Henley and Bob Stevenson: 'Against those of his friends who might forget or ignore the precautions which his health demanded she could be a dragon indeed; but the more considerate among them she made warmly her own and was ever ready to welcome.'[1]

[1] In Stevenson's unpublished letters to Henley—frequently full of schoolboy hilarity, often spiced with bawdy—Colvin appears sometimes as a butt for their fun, and Henley must have withheld many letters when Colvin was preparing the edition of 1899. 'With every word you say of Colvin the dear and good, I eagerly agree,' wrote Stevenson from Zurich in December 1881; 'I said the other day that he " introduced into literary life the chastity of an officer".' With a premonition of the 'seraph in chocolate' controversy, he wrote on the publication of Colvin's *Landor*, 'I am of your way of thinking about Landor. It's a very pleasant work. As you say, his life of R.L.S. will be a joke. "Chapter 2, Youth in Edinburgh" is like to be a masterpiece of the genteel evasion . . . I surely suggest that you should write a blaggard supplement—also a Christian one, for he will be apt to hear that out too—and be morbid from thenceforward in a public insulting controversy with him. The best name for your work and perhaps for me is this Christian blackguard.'

There was no more confidential correspondence directly between Stevenson and Mrs. Sitwell. Mrs. Sitwell wrote, but Fanny answered, in strict accordance with the conventions. Apart from one or two notes, hinting at their old relationship, Stevenson's letters to Mrs. Sitwell were evidently written under Fanny's eye. Shrewdly seizing the opportunities offered by his frequent illness to act as amanuensis, she acquired the freedom of his writing-desk as a casual habit; henceforth he wrote little that escaped her scrutiny.

Stevenson was frequently ill at Davos. 'I go slow and am fit for little,' he told Colvin; his work throughout the winter was limited to the essay on 'The Morality of the Profession of of Letters' for the *Fortnightly Review* of April 1881, the essay on Samuel Pepys appearing in *Cornhill* of the following July, and four articles descriptive of Davos published in the *Pall Mall Gazette* during February and March. Quality notably compensates the deficiency in quantity. Apart from the much longer *Memoir of Fleeming Jenkin*, 'Samuel Pepys' is unluckily the last of his essays in biography; it is more successful than any of his previous biographical essays because, instead of approaching his subject from what he called a particular 'point of view', he surveys Pepys from every angle—as a portrait, the essay shows not merely a profile, but both sides of the face. For students of Pepys there are many observations provocative of argument, such as the improbable but respectable supposition that Pepys's 'period of gallantry' ended with his diary; autobiographically, the section on respectability has important significance.

Here Stevenson expounds the same thesis as in the third chapter of *Lay Morals*:

'When writers inveigh against respectability, in the present degraded meaning of the word, they are usually suspected of a taste for clay pipes and beer cellars; and their performances are thought to hail from the *Owl's Nest* of the comedy. They have something more, however, in their eye than the dullness of a round million dinner parties that sit down yearly in old England. For to do anything because others do it, and not because the thing is good, or kind, or honest in its own right, is to resign all moral control and captaincy upon yourself, and go post-haste to the devil with the greater number. We smile over the ascendancy of priests; but I had rather follow a priest than what they call the leaders of society. . . . The respectable are not led so much by any desire of applause as by a positive need for countenance. The weaker and the tamer the man, the more will he require this support; and any positive quality relieves him, by just so much, of this dependence. In a dozen ways, Pepys was quite strong enough to please himself without regard for others; but his positive qualities were not co-extensive with the field of conduct; and in many parts of life he followed, with gleeful precision, in the footprints of the contemporary Mrs. Grundy.'

A corollary of this theme, as applied to the particular case of the man of letters, appears in 'The Morality of the Profession of Letters':

'There are two duties incumbent upon any man who enters on the business of writing: truth to the fact and a good spirit in the treatment. In every department of literature, though so low as hardly to deserve the name, truth to the fact is of importance to the education and comfort of mankind, and so hard to preserve, that the faithful trying to do so will lend some dignity to the man who tries it. . . . Man is imperfect; yet, in his literature, he must express himself and his own views and preferences; for to do anything else is to do a far more perilous thing than to risk being immoral: it is to be sure of being untrue. To ape a sentiment, even a good one, is to travesty a sentiment; that will not be helpful. To conceal a sentiment, if you are sure you hold it, is to take a liberty with truth. There is probably no point of view possible to a sane man but contains some truth and, in the true connection, might be profitable to the race. I am not afraid of the truth, if any one could tell it me, but I am afraid of parts of it impertinently uttered. There is a time to dance and a time to mourn; to be harsh as well as to be sentimental; to be ascetic as well as to glorify the appetites; and if a man were to combine all these extremes into his work, each in its place and proportion, that work would be the world's masterpiece of morality as well as of art. Partiality is immorality; for any book is wrong that gives a misleading picture of the world and life. The trouble is that the weakling must be partial; the work of one proving dank and depressing; of another, cheap and vulgar; of a third, epileptically sensual; of a fourth, sourly ascetic. In literature as in conduct, you can never hope to do exactly right. All you can do is to make as sure as possible . . .'

Stevenson was still true to his character as 'a Bohemian', asserting his right to live his own life, and to write as he thought and felt, in defiance of respectability's conventions. In the circumstances of his marriage he believed that he had acted in accordance with his Bohemian tenets; his biographers have ignored the importance of a letter written to W. D. Howells, which indicates both the social courage required to venture upon divorce and re-marriage in Victorian times, and Stevenson's sensitive consciousness of his wife's position as a divorcee. With Howells, as editor of the *Atlantic Monthly*, he had been exchanging cordial correspondence, and hearing that Howells was intending a visit to Europe, he invited a visit from him. Then he read Howells's novel, *A Modern Instance*, which he interpreted as a condemnation of divorce, and wrote to Howells on 4th December 1882:

'I find myself under the unpleasant necessity of obtruding on your knowledge a piece of my private life.

'My wife did me the honour to divorce her husband in order to marry me.

'This, neither more nor less, it is at once my duty and my pleasure to communicate. According as your heart is, so will the meaning of this letter be.

'But I will add this much: that after the kindness you showed me in your own country and the sympathy with which many of your books have inspired me, it will be a sincere disappointment to find that you cannot be my guest. I shall bear up however; for I assure you, I desire to know no one who considers himself holier than my wife.'

Howells apparently did not reply; he and Stevenson never met, but, at the request of a mutual friend, Stevenson wrote, in the year before his death, suggesting that they should forget any difference of opinion between them and asking if a character in one of Howells's novels had been drawn from S. S. McClure, the prototype of Pinkerton in *The Wrecker*. Howells replied courteously that he had 'heard McClure's voice in your Pinkerton's words', and that, 'ever since I received your inconceivable letter' nearly eleven years before, he had wished to assure Stevenson of his having no 'grief with me'.

Besides writing only the two essays and four newspaper articles, Stevenson was unusually destitute of literary plans during the winter of 1880–81. He talked of a *History of the Highlands*, but this seems to have been intended to please his father, who industriously occupied himself in research; though he progressed little beyond drafting a synopsis of the book, his notes—especially on the trial of James Stewart for the Appin murder—proved of value when he wrote *Kidnapped* and *Catriona*. Deprived of *The Amateur Emigrant*, Kegan Paul published a collection of Stevenson's essays, dedicated to Henley, under the title, *Virginibus Puerisque*; the sale of the book at six shillings was small, and a remainder, transferred to Chatto and Windus in 1884, was sold out only shortly before the issue of the second edition in 1887.

In January he enjoyed a visit from Colvin, but his chief companion was John Addington Symonds, who had been driven by tubercular affliction to settle permanently at Davos. Symonds died in the year before Stevenson, but he was more than ten years older; two months before his death, he wrote to 'my dear old friend' from 'the same straight valley', reflecting on 'how strangely different our destinies have been!' 'Louis and Mr. Symonds are, so to speak, Siamese twins,' wrote Fanny to Colvin, but her observation was superficial. As Llewelyn Powys wrote in *Swiss Essays*, 'there was something incongruous about the close association between so conspicuous a scholar as was Symonds, and so incorrigible a Bohemian, careless and unpredictable, as was Stevenson'. Their mutual liking was a gradual growth; each at first felt critical of the other. To his friend and biographer, Horatio F. Brown, Symonds announced in November:

'There is a very interesting man come—Louis Stevenson—a friend of Lang and Leslie Stephen—really clever, and curious in matters of style. . . . I find him a great acquisition.'

After more than three months, remarking that Stevenson 'told me the whole history of his wife to-day', Symonds added:

'I have apprehensions about his power of intellectual last. The more I see of him, the less I find of solid mental stuff. He wants years of study in tough subjects. After all a University education has some merits. One feels the want of it in men like him.'

While Symonds found him intellectually lacking in solidity and substance, Stevenson sensed in Symonds a deficiency of vitality and vigour.

'I like Symonds very well, though he is much, I think, of an invalid in mind and character. But his mind is interesting, with many beautiful corners, and his consumptive smile very winning to see. We have had some good talks . . . I, the Bohnist, the un-Grecian, was the means of his conversion in the matter of the Ajax. It is truly not for nothing that I have read my Buckley' [in Bohn's Classics].

As their friendship developed, Stevenson 'converted' Symonds in many trends of thought; though he considered *Virginibus Puerisque* 'a little forced and flashy', Symonds was to write five years later: 'I agree with R. L. Stevenson in holding that the right human life is to take our fill of all the activities and pleasures proper to each age . . . so many of us warped human beings invert the order of life, are never young, and so are never wholesomely middle-aged or old.'

Mrs. Sitwell also came out to Davos, but her visit was fraught with tragedy. One of her sons, a boy of eighteen, was stricken with consumption; the disease was too far advanced for arrest by the mountain air, and he died within a few weeks. Stevenson's poem, 'In Memoriam F.A.S.', was written as a message of condolence to Mrs. Sitwell.

' All that life contains of torture, toil, and treason,
    Shame, dishonour, death, to him were but a name.
Here, a boy, he dwelt through all the singing season,
    And ere the day of sorrow departed as he came.'

Already depressed by continued illness and inability to work, Stevenson fell into a mood of morbid listlessness. Symonds advised him to try reviewing as a refuge from the frustrated urge to work: he and Leslie Stephen feared 'a little some eclipse', and Stevenson was 'not quite without sharing the fear', describing his languor as 'a dead down-draught, a heavy fardel'. His stepson, Lloyd Osbourne, an intimate witness during the years of illness resulting from the Californian expedition, states that Stevenson 'suffered less than is generally believed'.

'The truly dreadful part of his life was the uncertainty of its tenure; the imminence always of a sudden death. He would put a handkerchief to his lips, perceive a crimson stain, and then sooner or later there might be a haemorrhage of the lungs, with all its horror and suspense, and its subsequent and unutterably dejecting aftermath of having to lie immovable for days and nights on end. The mental agony was beyond expression; one wonders how he ever bore up against it; but the actual spells of illness were not extremely painful, nor were they as a rule very long continued.'

It seems that Stevenson was never so dangerously ill as Llewelyn Powys during the last six years of his life—that the disease with him had progressed to the same stage, and produced much the same symptoms, as with Powys before his departure to Africa. His sister-in-law regarded as a virtue his refusal 'to be the regulation sick man', but his temperamental instinct to restless activity rendered him an erratic patient. Lacking Powys's serenity and fortitude under the dread monotony of enduring immobility, he agitated his nerves with fretful worrying. Symonds noted his inability to endure what Powys called 'freezing': 'He does not seem to me to have the sort of toughness or instinctive energy of self-control, the faculty which I possess, of lying still when I feel my centre of vitality attacked.'

In his study of 'Symonds and Stevenson at Davos Platz', Powys too severely condemns Stevenson's conduct as a patient: 'He stayed in bed when he should have been out of doors and when he should have been in bed he played the fool with a toboggan.' On Christmas Day, doubtless to the delight of his stepson, Stevenson 'tobogganed so furiously all morning' that he 'was very tired . . . and could not write'. It was unwise, and he paid the penalty; but he was excited by the same exaltation of spirits, during a temporary spell of well-being, as inspired Powys to the reckless passage of the mountains from Arosa to Davos described in *Skin for Skin*. In one of his newspaper articles, 'The Stimulation of the Alps', he relates the effects of the climate:

'In the rare air, clear, cold, and blinding light of Alpine winters, a man takes a certain troubled delight in his existence, which can nowhere else be paralleled. He is perhaps no happier, but he is stingingly alive. It does not, perhaps, come out of him in work or exercise, yet he feels an enthusiasm of the blood unknown in more temperate climates. It may not be health, but it is fun.

'There is nothing more difficult to communicate on paper than this baseless ardour, this stimulation of the brain, this sterile joyousness of spirits. You wake every morning, see the gold upon the snow-peaks, become filled with courage, and bless God for your prolonged existence. . . . Is it a return of youth, or is it a congestion of the brain? It is a sort of congestion, perhaps, that leads the invalid, when all goes well, to face the new day with such a bubbling cheerfulness. It is certainly congestion that makes night hideous with visions, all the chambers of a many-storied caravanserai, haunted with vociferous nightmares, and many wakeful people come down late for breakfast in the morning. . . . But, on the other hand, the peculiar blessedness of boyhood may itself be but a symptom of the same complaint, for the two effects are strangely similar; and the frame of mind of the invalid upon the Alps is a sort of intermittent youth, with periods of lassitude.'

He felt both the suspicion and the rancour of the invalid impatient with his condition. As he suspected the very air of treachery in stimulating a baseless sense of healthfulness, so he sought no pleasure in his surroundings—unlike Symonds and Powys, he attempted to make no friends among the Swiss peasantry or to appreciate the simple virtues of their manners and customs. For him Davos was a hospital; he had gone for a cure, and felt impatience to escape. In the spring he wrote disconsolately to Colvin of his condition:

'I have been here a little over long. I was reckoning up, and since I have known you, already quite a while, I have not, I believe, remained so long in any one place as here in Davos. That tells on my old gipsy nature; like a violin hung up, I begin to lose what music there was in me. . . .'

In April 1881 Stevenson and Fanny left Davos for France; after a stay at Barbizon, 'a week in Paris reduced me to the limpness and lack of appetite peculiar to a kid glove', and they moved to St. Germain-en-Laye. To his mother he wrote: 'If we are to come to Scotland, I *will* have fir-trees, and I want a burn, the firs for my physical, the water for my moral health'; and arriving in Edinburgh on 30th May, they went three days later to Kinnaird Cottage, Pitlochry. Here he was better in health, and fell to work on a book of short stories, 'all ghastly', such as he had planned in the winter of 1874–75. The first title suggested was *The Black Man and other Tales*; later it became *Tales for Winter Nights*; in the list of contents appeared a survivor from the list of six years before, that alluring title, 'The Devil on Cramond Sands'. *Thrawn Janet* was the first story finished, and sent off to Leslie Stephen: 'as it is all in Scotch he cannot take it, I know', but 'it was *so good*, I could not help sending it'. Stephen promptly accepted the story for *Cornhill* of the following October.

The eerie atmosphere of the weird is so stealthily present in *Thrawn Janet* that Stevenson confessed it 'frightened me to death' in the writing. He maintained his high opinion of the story; twelve years later, describing the story of Tod Lapraik in *Catriona* as 'a piece of living Scots', he asserted, 'if I had never writ anything but that and *Thrawn Janet*, still I'd have been a writer'. His critics have generally endorsed his opinion, and perhaps it is only the Scots dialect—in which the story is told— that damps the enthusiasm of an Anglo-Saxon taste. Yet Henry James allowed that the dialect might be a deterrent, and still pronounced *Thrawn Janet* to be 'a masterpiece' and, among Stevenson's shorter stories, 'the strongest in execution'.

The story written next after *Thrawn Janet*, *The Body-Snatcher*, has undoubtedly suffered unjustly in esteem from its author's modest opinion of it. Within a few weeks of its being finished, Stevenson told Colvin that it was 'laid aside in a justifiable disgust, the tale being horrid'. After more than three years, the story achieved publication in the Christmas number of the *Pall Mall Gazette*, being substituted for one Stevenson had been unable to finish in fulfilment of the commission. Insisting that its quality was much below his best, he declined to accept the full payment agreed upon. Six months before his death, he acknowledged that 'the beastly *Body-Snatcher* has merit', but it

W. E. HENLEY

was omitted from the Edinburgh edition of his works and almost forgotten by Gosse for the Pentland edition, being bundled into incongruous company at the end of the volume containing *Familiar Studies of Men and Books*. Queasy Victorian taste deprecated the subject as too gruesome in its realism, but stronger modern stomachs find no difficulty in digesting a 'crawler' based on the many scandals about procuring bodies for dissection after the conviction of Burke and Hare. Mr. Compton Mackenzie expresses a generally revised judgment in stating that '*The Body-Snatcher* is just as good as *Thrawn Janet*'.

The third story written at Pitlochry, *The Merry Men*, must be rated higher than either of the others. The character of the uncle, driven by avenging conscience to drowning on the scene of his crime, is a massive conception; the atmosphere at the house of Aros is grim with foreboding of impending tragedy; the descriptive and dramatic power of a master depicts the awesome setting of the lonely islet, the uproar of the gale, and desolate splendour of the *dénouement*. 'It is a fantastic sonata about the sea and wrecks,' Stevenson told Colvin, 'and I like it much above all my other attempts at story-telling; I think it is strange; if ever I shall make a hit, I have the line now, as I believe.' In the magazine article on 'My First Book: "Treasure Island"', published in the *Idler* of August 1894, speaking of the 'very easy style' chosen for *Treasure Island*, he wrote: 'Compare it with the almost contemporary "Merry Men"; one reader may prefer the one style, one the other—'tis an affair of character, perhaps of mood; but no expert can fail to see that the one is much more difficult, and the other much easier to maintain.' Published in two numbers of *Cornhill* for June and July 1882, *The Merry Men* gave its title to the volume of six short stories published by Chatto and Windus in 1887.

The prospect of his ever making a living by writing seemed so remote that, in June, hearing of a vacancy in the chair of History and Constitutional Law at Edinburgh University, Stevenson astonishingly offered himself as a candidate. 'The chair is only three months in summer; that is why I try for it,' he explained to Henley; 'if I get it, which I shall not, I should be independent at once.' He thought it 'a mad thing', but was 'advised on all hands to go on': probably Fanny coveted the respectability of a university don's spouse. But universities rarely confer their sinecures upon men of imagination, and imagination was Stevenson's sole apparent recommendation for the post. The educationist Meiklejohn was among his professional sponsors, and testimonials came from all his influential literary friends—Stephen, Symonds, Colvin, Gosse, Andrew Lang, and P. G. Hamerton: apparently Henley was not asked, being of insufficient eminence to impress academic authority. His candidature failed abjectly; he received only three votes.

Throughout June and July at Pitlochry there was 'nothing but cold rains and penetrating winds', and Fanny recorded: 'My husband, who had come to the Highlands solely for the sunshine and bracing air, was condemned to spend the most of his time in our small, stuffy sitting-room, with no amusement or occupation other than that afforded by his writing materials.' She omits to remark that Stevenson felt the want of conversation with his intellectual peers, such as he had enjoyed with Symonds at Davos, but, as soon as it was decided to leave Pitlochry for a cottage with more accommodation at Braemar, he wrote to invite visits from Henley, Gosse, and Colvin. In alarm at these invitations, Fanny wrote to Colvin:

'I don't doubt that it can be so arranged that a bed can be managed for you in the house, I can talk of that when I see you. In the meantime, come on, though I fear it will not be very pleasant for you, though your advice will be very profitable to me in many things. Louis can hardly talk to anyone without being very ill after it, or in fact do anything. I am quite disheartened, and in the lowest possible spirits, so pray excuse this letter if it is not all it should be. At any rate I mean well.'

Colvin and Gosse ventured to trespass upon their hostess's cordiality, each separately visiting Braemar, but Henley did not.

Stevenson did not share Fanny's depression at Pitlochry; on the contrary, 'I never thought I should have been as well again', he informed Mrs. Sitwell; 'I really enjoyed life and work.' He was '*wonderfully* well' before, soon after the move to

Braemar on 2nd August, he caught cold 'in this blighting weather'—'the wind pipes, the rain comes in squalls, great black clouds are continually overhead, and it is as cold as March'. Confined to the house, he resorted for recreation to his stepson's society. 'Stevenson was in the position of a prisoner who makes friends with a mouse,' wrote Lloyd Osbourne, 'and I was the mouse.'

'He shared enthusiastically in all my games—tin soldiers, marbles, chess, drafts, and others even more interesting that he invented for our joint amusement—especially a mimic war-game that required hundreds of tin soldiers, the whole attic floor to play it on, and weeks of time. We were partners in my little printing-press; he wrote verses and engraved blocks for the miniature books I printed and sold; he painted scenery for my toy theatre and we gave performances with my mother as the only audience.'

Of this time at Braemar, Stevenson wrote in 'My First Book: "Treasure Island"':

'It blew a good deal and rained in a proportion; my native air was more unkind than man's ingratitude, and I must consent to pass a good deal of my time between four walls in a house lugubriously known as the late Miss McGregor's Cottage. . . . There was a schoolboy in the Late Miss McGregor's Cottage, home for the holidays, and much in want of "something craggy to break his mind upon". He had no thought of literature; it was the art of Raphael that received his fleeting suffrages; and with the aid of pen and ink and a shilling box of water colours, he had soon turned one of the rooms into a picture gallery. My more immediate duty towards the gallery was to be showman; but I would sometimes unbend a little, join the artist (so to speak) at the easel, and pass the afternoon with him in a generous emulation, making coloured drawings. On one of these occasions, I made the map of an island; it was elaborately and (I thought) beautifully coloured; the shape of it took my fancy beyond expression; it contained harbours that pleased me like sonnets; and with the unconsciousness of the predestined, I ticketed my performance " Treasure Island ". . . . No child but must remember laying his head in the grass, staring into the infinitesimal forest and seeing it grow populous with fairy armies. Somewhat in this way, as I paused upon my map of "Treasure Island", the future characters of the book began to

163

appear there visibly among imaginary woods; and their brown faces and bright weapons peeped out upon me from unexpected quarters, as they passed to and fro, fighting and hunting treasure, on these few square inches of a flat projection. The next thing I knew I had some papers before me and was writing out a list of chapters. How often have I done so, and the thing gone no further! But there seemed elements of success about this enterprise. It was to be a story for boys; no need of psychology or fine writing; and I had a boy at hand to be a touchstone. . . . On a chill September morning, by the cheek of a brisk fire, and the rain drumming on the window, I began *The Sea Cook*, for that was the original title.'

It was not in September, but in late August, that he began to write *The Sea Cook*, for, signing himself 'R. L. S. Author of Boys' Stories', he wrote to Henley on 25th August:

'I am now on another lay for the moment, purely owing to Lloyd, this one; but I believe there's more coin in it than in any amount of crawlers: now, see here, *The Sea Cook, or Treasure Island: A Story for Boys.*

'If this don't fetch the kids, why, they have gone rotten since my day. Will you be surprised to learn that it is about Buccaneers, that it begins in the "Admiral Benbow" public-house on the Devon coast, that it's all about a map, and a treasure, and a mutiny, and a derelict ship, and a current, and a fine old Squire Trelawney (the real Tre, purged of literature and sin, to suit the infant mind), and a doctor, and another doctor, and a sea-cook with one leg, and a sea-song with the chorus "Yo-ho-ho and a bottle of rum" (at the third Ho you heave at the capstan bars), which is a real buccaneer's song, only known to the crew of the late Captain Flint (died of rum at Key West, much regretted, friends will please accept this intimation); and lastly, would you be surprised to hear, in this connection, the name of *Routledge*? That's the kind of man I am, blast your eyes. Two chapters are written, and have been tried on Lloyd with great success; the trouble is to work it off without oaths. Buccaneers without oaths—bricks without straw. But youth and the fond parent have to be consulted.'

Continually urging him to write plays as most likely to produce a profitable return, Henley had lately suggested the subject of *Admiral Guinea*, afterwards the third play they wrote in collaboration, and he expressed exasperation at the new 'lay'.

Stevenson admitted that 'Your Admiral Guinea is curiously near my line, but of course I'm fooling; and your Admiral sounds like a shublime gent'. To a further protest he replied:

'The great desire about *T.I.* is Promptitood. It was the fact of its immediacy that led it, tickled it, cuddled it from my portfolio. If it nets me £50 promptly, I have gained the battle for just now.'

His Squire Trelawney was to have 'a strong dash of Landor', on whom Colvin had recently written a monograph for Macmillan's English Men of Letters series; afterwards he told Henley that 'it was the sight of your maimed strength and masterfulness that begot John Silver . . . the idea of the maimed man, ruling and dreaded by the sound, was entirely taken from you'. In Long John Silver he aimed 'to deprive' Henley 'of all his finer qualities and higher graces of temperament, to leave him with nothing but his strength, his courage, his quickness, and his magnificent geniality, and to try to express these in terms of the culture of a raw tarpaulin'. Publicly he avowed his debt to Washington Irving's *Tales of a Traveller*: 'Billy Bones, his chest, the company in the parlour, the whole inner spirit, and a good deal of the material detail of my first chapters—all were there, all were the property of Washington Irving.' On the other hand, he informed Colvin that it was 'out of Kingsley's *At Last*' that 'I got the Dead Man's Chest—and that was the seed'. For reference he used 'the great Captain Johnson's *History of Notorious Pirates*'; afterwards he wished he had thought to refer to Defoe's *Captain Singleton*.

In a few weeks the story had progressed to the nineteenth chapter—'no writing, just drive along as the words come and the pen will scratch!' 'I love writing boys' books,' he told Henley, and among successors to *The Sea Cook*, he planned to write *Jerry Abershaw: A Tale of Putney Heath*; he thought *The Sea Cook* better than Captain Marryatt; 'I'll be the Harrison Ainsworth of the future'. Every night, after dinner, he read aloud what he had written during the day. During his visit, Gosse was among his listeners, and thus described the daily routine:

'After breakfast I went to Louis's bedroom, where he sat up in bed, with dark, flashing eyes and ruffled hair, and we played chess on the coverlet. Not a word passed, for he was strictly forbidden to speak in the early part of the day. As soon as he felt tired—often in the middle of a game—he would rap with peremptory knuckles on the board as a signal to stop, and then Mrs. Stevenson or I would arrange his writing materials on the bed. Then I would see no more of him till dinner-time, when he would appear, smiling and voluble, the horrid bar of speechlessness having been let down.'

After dinner came the reading, and Gosse reported to his wife on 3rd September: 'Louis has been writing, all the time I have been here, a novel of pirates and hidden treasure, in the highest degree exciting.' Gosse was a cultivated critic: after years of application to reading, he acquired an appreciation of good books and an aptitude for communicating his appreciation in an attractive manner; but he began with no instinctive feeling for literature and so lacked the faculty of critical intuition. To him the writing of *Treasure Island* must have seemed the amiable pastime of an amusing eccentric, and he went away, unaware of the rich vein that Stevenson was working.

A more useful critic was Dr. Alexander Japp, who had written a study of Thoreau and exchanged courteous correspondence with Stevenson on points of difference in his *Cornhill* essay. Both a scholar and a journalist, the biographer of De Quincey and an admiring friend of Mrs. Henry Wood, Japp enjoyed multifarious connections in the publishing world, and he had been lately invited to find new talent for a boys' weekly paper called *Young Folks*, a predecessor of countless 'penny dreadful' periodicals issued in the 'nineties by Alfred Harmsworth, Arthur Pearson, and George Newnes. As Stevenson was unfit to meet him in Edinburgh, Japp came on a visit to Braemar.

'Even the ruthlessness of a united family recoiled before the extreme measure of inflicting on our guest the mutilated members of *The Sea Cook*; at the same time, we would by no means stop our readings; and accordingly the tale was begun again at the beginning, and solemnly re-delivered for the benefit of Dr. Japp. From that moment on, I have thought highly of his critical faculty; for when he left us, he carried away the manuscript in his portmanteau.'

The story was accepted by *Young Folks*, but Stevenson's elation was a little deflated when the hundred pounds for which he had hoped 'dwindled at least into somewhere about £30'. The actual terms were £2. 10s. per page of 450 words. The editor discarded the title of *The Sea Cook* for that of *Treasure Island*. Beginning its serial course on 1st October 1881 and ending on 28th January following, the story was only the secondary attraction of the paper, each instalment being crowded into narrow columns of close type at the end of each number, while in front, luridly illustrated, cantered the adventures of *Don Zalva the Brave*, by Alfred R. Phillips, who was 'the big man for its serials'. The author's name was given as Captain George North. 'The story was not considered important,' wrote the editor, Robert Leighton, 'and it was not announced with any preliminary advertisement.' 'As a serial it was a failure', because 'it had not the serial trick'. 'Boys like a story to plunge at once into the active excitement; but here they were kept dragging on week after week with preliminary matter connected with the inn' before getting to sea for the treasure-hunt. Leighton believed that 'the story was carried on for at least six weeks by its alluring title', and shrewdly judged that '*Treasure Island* is still appreciated less by boys than by grown-up readers'.

In October Stevenson and Fanny left again to winter in Davos. Stevenson was supplied by his uncle and medical adviser, Dr. George Balfour, with 'an ori-nasal respirator for the inhalation of pine-wood oil', on his appearance in which, with 'my pig's snout now upon my face', he wrote an epistle in verse to Henley. In London Henley introduced him to the publishing house of Chatto and Windus, which undertook to publish during the following year his biographical essays as *Familiar Studies of Men and Books* and two volumes of *New Arabian Nights*—the first volume containing the *Latter-Day Arabian Nights* from *London*, while the second included *The Pavilion on the Links*, *A Lodging for the Night*, *The Sire de Malétroit's Door*, and *Providence and the Guitar*. Henley accompanied them to Paris for a few days, and an early letter from Stevenson at Davos thanks him for 'that hundred quid'. It does not appear whether this sum was a loan or a repayment of past loans, but the money came opportunely to Stevenson, whose conscience still recoiled from acceptance of his father's bounty and agitated the desire for independence.

This year at Davos they took a house, the Chalet am Stein, instead of living at the Hotel Belvedere, as in the previous winter. When Symonds visited them on 2nd November, he found Stevenson 'lying, ghastly, in bed—purple cheek-bones, yellow cheeks, bloodless lips—fever all over him—without appetite—and all about him so utterly forlorn', with the black Scotch terrier, Woggs—a present from Walter Simpson— 'squealing', and 'Mrs. Stevenson doing her best to make things comfortable'. The following week Symonds found him 'better' and 'certainly not going to die yet', though he did not like 'his habit as an invalid': 'One thing is in his favour—his serenity of soul about what is called comfort. But the *défaut de cette qualité* is that he is, as a Bohemian, ever restless in mind.' Symonds 'got to like him more', and Stevenson wrote to Japp that Symonds was 'a far better and more interesting thing than any of his books'. After finishing *Treasure Island*, he wrote the first paper on 'Talk and Talkers' for *Cornhill* of the following April, in which Symonds appears as Opalstein—a portrait that impresses, after a reading of Symonds's life and letters, with an exciting sense of its shrewd sympathy and perception, curiously in conflict with Mr. Swinnerton's untenable proposition that 'Stevenson had never a very subtle interest in character'.

'His various and exotic knowledge, complete although unready sympathies, and fine, full, discriminative flow of language, fit him out to be the best of talkers—so perhaps he is with some, not *quite* with me—*proxime accessit*, I should say. He sings the praise of the earth and the arts, flowers and jewels, wine and music, in a moonlight, serenading manner, as to the light guitar; even wisdom comes from his tongue like singing; no one is, indeed, more tuneful in the upper notes. But even while he sings the song of the Sirens, he still hearkens to the barking of the Sphinx. Jarring Byronic notes interrupt the flow of his Horatian humours. His mirth has something of the tragedy of the world for its perpetual background; and he feasts like Don Giovanni to a double orchestra, one lightly sounding for the dance, one pealing Beethoven in the distance. He is not truly reconciled either with life or with himself; and this instant war in his members sometimes divides the man's attention. He does not always, perhaps not often, frankly surrender himself in conversation. He brings into the talk other thoughts than those which he expresses; you are conscious that he keeps an eye on something else, that he does not shake off the world, nor quite forget himself. Hence arise occasional disappointments; even an occasional unfairness for his companions, who find themselves one day giving too much, and the next, when they are wary out of season, giving perhaps too little."

Though Symonds's habit of morbid introspection made him a companion of unpredictable mood, his 'troubled and poetic talk' supplied much solace to Stevenson throughout this lonely winter; both he and Fanny 'learned this his advice is good'.

While she remarks that at Davos 'this time Louis's health seemed to gain greater benefit', Fanny's biographical sister surprisingly omits to mention that Fanny proved the greater invalid during the winter. In the previous year her doctor had told her that she 'should not be so fat, and that it (the fatness) is caused by a disease of the stomach', for which she was 'put upon diet'. Now Stevenson reported to Mrs. Sitwell that 'she has, it is thought, drain-poisoning; she had diarrhoea very bad, pain, great weakness, spotted throat, and I know not all what'. The doctor ordered her to Berne for treatment; Lloyd went with her, and Stevenson was alone for some four weeks. Writing to Charles Baxter on 5th December, he recalled nostalgically the days of his youth in Edinburgh:

'Ah! what would I not give to steal this evening with you through the big, echoing, college archway, and away south under the street lamps, and away to dear Brash's, now defunct! But the old time is dead also, never, never to revive. It was a sad time too, but so gay and so hopeful, and we had such sport with all our low spirits and all our distresses, that it looks like a kind of lamp-lit fairyland behind me. O for ten Edinburgh minutes—sixpence between us, and the ever-glorious Lothian Road, or dear mysterious Leith Walk! But here, a sheer hulk, lies poor Tom Bowling; here in this strange place, whose very strangeness would have been heaven to him then; and aspires, yes, C.B., with tears, after the past. See what comes of being left alone.'

Recalling times when he and Baxter, on clandestine escapades, passed by the names of Johnson and Thomson, he exclaimed:

> 'I swear it by the eternal sky
> Johnson—nor Thomson ne'er shall die!'

But he added: 'Yet I fancy they are dead too; dead like Brash.'

When he fetched Fanny and Lloyd from Berne on Christmas Day, 'the cold was beyond belief' as they drove in an open sleigh 'seven hours on end through whole forests of Christmas trees', and young Lloyd said to Stevenson, 'a blue mouth speaking from a corpse-coloured face, "You seem to be the only one with any courage left!"' Despite the depressing company of a dyspeptic Fanny, he was well enough to work with enthusiasm. 'In treaty with Bentley for a life of Hazlitt', he was 'anxious to write biography', as 'it must be good to live with another man from birth to death', but, occupied with other projects till March, he then decided that 'Hazlitt had better simmer a while' till he was settled for the summer. After the first paper on 'Talk and Talkers', he wrote the 'Preface by way of Criticism' for *Familiar Studies of Men and Books*, and then worked on *The Silverado Squatters* because Chatto and Windus liked the idea of 'a small book about the *Inland Voyage* size'. Written up from notes taken at the time, this book proved frequently distastful—it was 'new wine in old bottles'—and twice he left it to write the *Cornhill* essays, 'A Foreigner at Home' and 'A Gossip on Romance'. 'You have no idea what it costs me to wring out my work now,' he wrote to Henley; 'I have certainly been a fortnight over this *Romance*, sometimes five hours a day.'

'I have tried to do, very popularly, about one-half of the matter you wanted me to try. . . . But the subject was hardly fit for so chatty a paper, and it is all loose dens. If ever I do my book on the Art of Literature, I shall gather them together and be clear.'

This essay has been not unfairly accepted as part of Stevenson's *credo* on the writing of fiction, but too many of his critics have discussed it as if it had been written defensively as an apology for his own novels. In fact, at the time of its writing, none of his novels were yet written, except *Treasure Island*, which was lying, unheeded as 'literature', in the back pages of a juvenile weekly. Apparently Henley, aware of Stevenson's assiduous study of the art of writing, wanted him to write a book on the subject; such a book was never written, and unluckily, while his works remained in copyright, his publishers never collected into one volume the 'loose ends' of his numerous essays on various aspects of the art of letters.[1]

After finishing *Treasure Island*, he wrote no fiction during the winter at Davos, apart from 'my new long story', *The Adventures of John Delafield*, which was 'largely planned' in February, but left unfinished. Always in good spirits when working well, he wrote letters full of fooling to Henley, and delightedly shared in the productions of his stepson's toy printing press. Fanny was his main source of worry: 'Fanny has had a sharp relapse', 'my wife is wretched', Fanny's health 'is still far from good and often alarms me', 'Fanny is still far from well, quite far from well'—such comments appear in different letters of the time. Her sister's omission to mention her state of health at this time gathers significance; hints in the letters build up a picture oddly at variance with the legend of the stoical nurse, devotedly tending the querulous consumptive. Of his visit to Braemar the previous summer, Dr. Japp recalled how, on entering Lloyd's picture gallery, he was still preserving the same decorous demeanour as downstairs, when 'Stevenson said to me with a sly wink and a gentle dig in the ribs, "It's laugh and be thankful here"'.

During the winter his health had so much improved that, after medical examination, his lungs were 'said to be in a splendid state', and his doctor advised that it might be safe for him to settle in the south of France, without returning again to Davos. Crossing to England, before going to Edinburgh, he

---

[1] *Essays in the Art of Writing*, a slim volume, published by Chatto and Windus in 1905, contained only seven essays which Stevenson had omitted from the volumes of essays published during his lifetime. All the essays he wrote on the art and craft of letters are included in the Macdonald Illustrated Classics edition of his *Essays*, 1950.

stayed at Burford Bridge and visited Meredith, who wrote on 23rd May:

'We have had Mr. Louis Stevenson in our valley, staying with his wife and father and mother at the inn. He dined with me several evenings. . . . We speculated on the impression produced by his costume de Bohème, which he seems to have adopted for good—an innocent eccentricity at any rate.'

From Edinburgh in June he went with his parents to Stobo in Peeblesshire. He felt 'very tired and seedy', and wrote nothing except the second paper on 'Talk and Talkers' for the August number of *Cornhill*. This was his last contribution to the *Cornhill Magazine*, as editor of which James Payn succeeded Leslie Stephen about the same time as *Longman's Magazine* was launched in November 1882. 'A Gossip on Romance' appeared in the first number of *Longman's*, which was mainly directed, during the twenty-three years of its life, by Andrew Lang.

The winter's improvement in health was not sustained in Scotland, where blood-spitting returned. In July he went to London for examination by Sir Andrew Clark, by whom he had first been 'ordered south'. Rejoining his wife and parents at Kingussie, he there wrote *The Treasure of Franchard*, which appeared in two numbers of *Longman's* for the following April and May. His inclination to life in France is revealed in his writing in Scotland this story of a French provincial setting. As Fanny was still ailing and disinclined to house-hunting, Stevenson left for Marseilles in September with his cousin Bob.

At Montpellier he had 'some more haemorrhage', but the doctor found 'nothing fresh in the lungs'—only 'some little cold' and catarrh. When Fanny joined him on 11th October, she seemed the greater invalid: Stevenson reported humorously to his mother, 'The wreck was towed into port yesterday evening'. At the end of October they moved into a house called Campagne Defli at St. Marcel, 'five miles out of Marseilles, in a lovely spot, among lovely wooded and cliffy hills', and Fanny wrote to her mother-in-law: 'It is such happiness to be in a place that combines the features of the land where I was born and California, where I have spent the best years of my life.'

The place did not suit Stevenson, who was continually ill and 'unfit to do any work whatever, which always depresses me to the ground'. According to a letter from Fanny to Symonds, 'he had continual hæmorrhages and became so weak that he was twice insensible in one day, and was for a long time like one dead'. At Christmas he went off alone to Nice for a change of air; immediately he began to mend, and occupied himself with writing verses for children, which he sent to Henley (who published some of them in three numbers of his *Magazine of Art* during the year) for an illustrated volume to be called *Penny Whistles*. Ignoring Fanny's wish that he should not venture to Marseilles, where there was an epidemic of fever, he returned to dispose of the lease of Campagne Defli without paying the compensation anticipated by Fanny. To Colvin he wrote from a Marseilles hotel on 15th February:

'The weather is incredible; my heart sings; my health satisfies even my wife. I did jolly well right to come after all and she now admits it. For she broke down as I knew she would, and I from here, without passing a night at the Defli, though with a cruel effusion of coach-hires, took up the wondrous tale and steered the ship through.'

Soon, at Hyères, they found a cottage called the Chalet la Solitude; there were 'two rooms below with a kitchen, and four rooms above, all told'. Stevenson announced himself 'greatly better, have gained flesh, strength, spirits; eat well, walk a good deal, and do some work without fatigue'. When they settled in, towards the end of March, he was able to 'work from four to five hours a day'. Having quickly finished *The Silverado Squatters*, he worked on *Prince Otto*, the story drafted in San Francisco as *The Greenwood State*. Early in May, though Fanny was still 'quite out of sorts', he had 'not the heart to be dispirited by anything', for, while Gosse had obtained forty pounds from the American *Century Magazine* for the serial rights of *The Silverado Squatters*, Henley placed *Treasure Island* with Cassell's for 'a hundred jingling, tingling, golden, minted quid'. He had then 'finished, in draft, the fifteenth chapter' of *Prince Otto*.

But, in the middle of May, came 'a whoreson influenza cold', causing him 'to lie down all day'. This 'busted me a good deal'; having 'no spring' and feeling 'headachy', he was unequal to proceeding with *Prince Otto* and began 'a whole tale of tushery', to be called *The Black Arrow: A Tale of Tunstall Forest*. As Fanny related in a note written for later editions of the book, *The Black Arrow* was written to fulfil a commission from James Henderson, the proprietor of *Young Folks*; she adds: 'No one could accuse my husband of showing a mercenary spirit in the sale of *The Black Arrow*, for which he accepted Mr. Henderson's offer of about three dollars a thousand words, just after receiving two hundred and fifty pounds from Mr. C. J. Longman for the magazine rights of *Prince Otto*.' Fanny's memory was at fault: *The Black Arrow* was written before *Prince Otto* was submitted to *Longman's Magazine*. In fact, Stevenson had been piqued by the failure of *Treasure Island* as a serial; in a letter to Gosse of November 1881, he commented derisively on the adverse criticism by readers of *Young Folks*, and on how the editor had stepped 'chivalrously forth in his defence'. Fanny says fairly: 'My husband was seized by a desire to capture this audience'; he wanted to show that, writing to order, he could please the readers of *Young Folks* as completely as their 'big man' for serials, the author of *Don Zalva the Brave*.

The Black Arrow began its serial course in *Young Folks* on 30th June, continuing till 20th October. Convalescing from his influenza, Stevenson spent July and August with his parents at Royat, in Auvergne, where the writing of *The Black Arrow* 'was continued with almost no effort'; as chapter after chapter went off to the editor, each week brought enthusiastic comments from readers, signing themselves with names of characters in the story, John Amend-All, Dick Shelton, or Joanna Sedley. Sending the story to Henley, Colvin asked him to 'look at it yourself before taking it anywhere', as 'it is rather *less* good than I thought and I'm afraid might do him harm on the whole'. Like *Treasure Island*, *The Black Arrow* appeared in *Young Folks* as the work of Captain George North, and as Henley agreed with Colvin, the story was not published in book form under Stevenson's name till five years later, when

his reputation was too securely established to suffer damage.
Stevenson then wrote a prefatory note of apology, in which he
related the circumstances of its writing:

'The tale was written years ago for a particular audience and
(I may say) in rivalry with a particular author; I think I should do
well to name him—Mr. Alfred R. Phillips. It was not without its
reward at the time. I could not, indeed, displace Mr. Phillips from
his well-won priority; but in the eyes of readers who thought less
than nothing of "Treasure Island", "The Black Arrow" was supposed to mark a clear advance. Those who read volumes and those
who read story papers belong to different worlds. The verdict on
"Treasure Island" was reversed in the other court: I wonder, will
it be the same with its successor?'

The Black Arrow remains a lively and enjoyable book for boys
under fifteen, but it is the only one of Stevenson's works that
defies re-reading.

The publication of *Treasure Island* in November 1883 laid
the foundation of his popular success. It enjoyed no immediately rapid sale like its confessed imitator of two years later,
Rider Haggard's *King Solomon's Mines*. But a second edition
was called for in 1884, the first illustrated edition appeared in
1885, and year by year sales steadily mounted till, by 1897,
seventy-five thousand copies had been sold.

Treasure Island secured for Stevenson the valuable allegiance
of Andrew Lang. As Lang made a habit of destroying letters,
he is sparsely represented in Stevenson's collected correspondence. Since their meeting at Mentone in 1874, their
friendship, confined chiefly to contact at the Savile Club, had
been cordial but never close. Of *Treasure Island* he wrote:
'Except *Tom Sawyer* and the *Odyssey*, I never liked any romance
so much.' Thenceforth a new book of Stevenson's never
passed unnoticed by him, and his immense influence weighted
the balance of popular opinion heavily in Stevenson's favour.

As Lang was chief reader and literary adviser to the firm of
Longmans, his good offices found a new market for Stevenson
when Leslie Stephen left the *Cornhill Magazine* at the end of
1882. Stephen's successor, James Payn, had served for several
years as Stephen's assistant; he knew both Henley and Stevenson

well, frequently joining their circle at the Savile Club, and his influence with Stephen had been invoked in favour of *The Pavilion on the Links*. In the first and second editions of *New Arabian Nights* appeared a note, 'I must prefix a word of thanks to the gentleman who condescended to borrow the gist of one of my stories, and even to honour it with the addition of his signature': when a scavenging journalist identified this borrower with Payn, Stevenson addressed letters in generous exculpation to the *New York Tribune* and the London *Athenaeum*. Stevenson's published letters show that friendly relations with Payn remained unbroken till the end of his life, but a change of policy was dictated by Payn's editorship of *Cornhill*. When the magazine started under Thackeray, the first issue achieved the phenomenal sale of 120,000 copies; under Stephen, the circulation steadily declined, falling as low as twelve thousand. Stephen maintained the style and standards with which the magazine began, but popular taste had changed. The magazine public now demanded the lightest sort of fiction, with articles of gossip about personalities, lacking pretension to literary quality, as in the illustrated 'family' weeklies and monthlies. Payn ascribed the decline of *Cornhill* mainly to 'the failure of the literary, and especially the classical, essay to attract the public', so the author of *Virginibus Puerisque* was among the first contributors to be discarded under his direction.

Longman's Magazine represented a last effort, between 1882 and 1905, to sustain the tradition of the popular literary periodical. To Stevenson it supplied the medium provided by *Cornhill* during the previous eight years. He also derived valuable publicity from Lang's monthly commentary in the magazine, 'At the Sign of the Ship': in his conversational comments on books and authors, Lang regularly referred to Stevenson and his various writings as illustrations of an argument, thereby implying that Stevenson was an established writer, with whose work his readers must of necessity be acquainted. Far more than by favourable reviews, Stevenson's reputation was fostered by this casual persistence in intruding his name upon public notice; as Lang spoke of Stevenson as if everybody must know his work, his readers, in secret shame of their ignorance, hastened to correct the defect in their literary education.

R.L.S. in 1892
From the portrait painted at Vailima by Count Nerli

Treasure Island was approved by Mr. Gladstone, who had a habit of dispatching postcards of congratulation to authors sufficiently respectable, knowing that their publishers would provide him with free advertisement by quoting his opinion. Lord Baldwin, who created a vogue for Mary Webb by talking of her novels at an Academy banquet, followed Gladstone's example in this device for deceiving democracy with the illusion that its leaders were capable of intellectual recreation. When he heard that Gladstone had sat up 'till two in the morning to finish' *Treasure Island*, Stevenson scornfully remarked that 'he would do better to attend to the imperial affairs of England'. He detested Gladstone as a symbol of the bourgeois respectability he despised. Invited by Lang in 1885 to write a study of Wellington for the 'English Worthies' series, he hesitated from distaste to ask Gladstone for his personal reminiscences of Wellington, and decided against doing so on hearing the news of General Gordon's abandonment at Khartoum, as 'I do really not see my way to any form of signature, unless "your fellow criminal in the eyes of God"'. In a letter to Symonds, after execrating Gladstone as a bourgeois, he exclaimed:

'But why should I blame Gladstone, when I too am a Bourgeois? when I have held my peace? Why did I hold my peace? Because I am a sceptic: *i.e.*, a Bourgeois. We believe in nothing, Symonds: you don't, and I don't; and these are two reasons, out of a handful of millions, why England stands before the world dripping with blood and daubed with dishonour.'

When Gladstone resigned after the defeat of the Home Rule Bill in 1886, Stevenson faced the choice of evils inevitably confronting at elections the intelligent thinker of imagination and integrity.

'I am a kind of dam home ruler, worse luck to it. I would support almost anything but that bill. How am I to vote? Great Caesar's Ghost!'

Always on the side of liberal opinion, like Landor he liked the mob only at a distance, and despised its leaders. Conscience continually denied his acquiescence in Coleridge's conviction that the artist can have no place in politics. Hot with indignation at the Majuba disaster of 1881, he wrote a letter to the press, 'Protest on Behalf of Boer Independence'. Now included in his collected works, the letter was suppressed at the time—supposedly by Fanny's influence. At a time when he was canvassing support for a university professorship, such an offence against the orthodox opinions of Respectability would have been suicidal. 'It is strange,' wrote Lloyd Osbourne, 'how many of Stevenson's strongest opinions failed to find any expression in his books.' In England society has always imposed its own censorship; social ostracism and even starvation await the speaker of unpalatable truth. Colvin supported Fanny's prudence; when the *National Review* was founded in 1883 with Alfred Austin as editor, he wrote to Henley: 'I shall be really and seriously hurt if you do anything to make Louis contribute to this foolish Tory magazine.' Fanny was right in counselling Stevenson, as an artist, against useless exhaustion in the limitless labyrinth of politics; she was wrong when she urged the same motives of prudence to curb expression in the legitimate province of his art.

The Black Arrow finished with the summer holiday at Royat; on their return to Hyères in September 1883, 'my husband', wrote Fanny, 'took up other more exciting work'. In fact, he fell deep into a mood of despondency on hearing of the death of his friend, James Walter Ferrier. He was 'the first friend I have ever lost'; reflecting on a wasted life, he wrote to Henley: 'Dear, dear, what a wreck; and yet how pleasant is the retrospect!' Looking back, he thought: 'Ferrier was above me, we were not equals; his true self humoured and smiled paternally upon my failings, even as I humoured and sorrowed over his.' He remembered how, hearing that he was leaving for California, Ferrier was 'terribly upset' as 'we sat late, in Baxter's empty house, where I was sleeping'. Recalling the early days of their friendship, 'I was not certainly the best companion for Walter, but I do believe I was the best he had', he wrote to Ferrier's sister: 'In these early days he was not fortunate in friends—looking back I see most clearly how much we both wanted a man of riper wisdom.'

Brooding upon the past, he was for some time unfit for work: 'I stare upon the paper, not write.' Then he wrote 'Old Mortality', a retrospective review of departed youth, ending with his tribute to Ferrier. On 2nd October he informed his father: 'A feeling of that which lacked with Ferrier and me when we were lads together has put me upon a task which I hope will not be disliked by you: a sketch of some of the more obvious provinces and truths of life for the use of young men.' This was a revision of *Lay Morals*, the moral and spiritual autobiography begun at Swanston in 1879 as an essay in self-justification. Reporting progress to his father ten days later, he wrote: 'I think all the time of Ferrier and myself, these are the pair that I address.' He thought also of his father, who had shown signs at Royat of failing mental faculties; conscience spurred him, before it was too late, to justify his conduct in the eyes of the man he had hurt so much and loved so well. But it was 'a most difficult work; a touch of the parson will drive off those I hope to influence; a touch of overstrained laxity, besides disgusting, like a grimace, may do harm'. The difficulty drove him again to lay the work aside, and this time it was never resumed; having seen both drafts, Balfour declared the earlier to be the more effective.

The mood of retrospection inspired two other essays. In 'Fontainebleau', published in Henley's *Magazine of Art* for the following May and June, he recalled the happy scenes of Barbizon; 'A Penny Plain and Twopence Coloured', preceding 'Fontainebleau' in the *Magazine of Art*, re-created the 'land of Skelt' in which his childish imagination first took flight. To escape the difficulty of *Lay Morals*, while still expounding the lessons of his youth's experience, he started a novel called *The Travelling Companion*. This was the title of one of the 'crawlers' projected at Pitlochry; apparently it progressed far enough to be submitted to a publisher, for Colvin remembered 'that its scene was partly laid in North Italy and that a publisher to whom it was shown declared it a work of genius but indecent'. Two and a half years later, in June 1886, he wrote to Colvin:

'O! the *Travelling Companion* won't do; I am back on it entirely: it is a foul, gross, bitter, ugly daub, with lots of stuff in it, and no urbanity and no glee and no true tragedy—to the crows with it, a carrion tale! I will do no more carrion, I have done too much in this carrion epoch; I will now be clean; and by clean, I don't mean any folly about purity, but such things as a healthy man with his bowels open shall find fit to see and speak about without a pang of nausea.'

Later the manuscript was burned, because 'it was not a work of genius, and *Jekyll* had supplanted it'. The title and the reference to *Strange Case of Dr. Jekyll and Mr. Hyde* suggest that conscience was 'the travelling companion' and the story must have an autobiographical allegory on the conflicting inclinations to good and to evil.

This autumn he wrote yet another essay, which may have preceded 'Old Mortality' in composition, being written immediately after his return from Royat to Hyères and before receiving news of Ferrier's death—'A Note on Realism', for the November *Magazine of Art*. Like 'A Gossip on Romance', this essay has been interpreted as a defence of Stevenson's own manner in fiction, without due consideration for the circumstances and motives of its writing. For a quarter of a century after Dickens's death in 1870, there was an abundance of bad novels, among which anything of lasting worth appeared as rarely as an oasis in a desert. Of the great Victorians immediately junior to Dickens, George Eliot published the last and greatest of her novels, *Middlemarch*, in 1872; Charles Reade, Trollope, and Wilkie Collins had all given their best before 1870. Of the other novelists writing during the 'seventies and 'eighties, only Meredith, Hardy, Henry James, and Stevenson himself have graduated to classic distinction.

Henry James has been lately re-discovered; the other three continue to gather dust upon their shelves because nobody bothers to assess their contribution to the process of artistic development. The modern generation of critics has chosen the example of Gosse rather than that of Saintsbury; before a predominantly ignorant audience, it is more readily rewarding to pretend cleverness than to pursue truth with a critical discernment born of knowledge laboriously acquired. To suit the modern taste for over-simplification, for seeking a storehouse of sustenance in the pill of a broadcast talk, Lord David

Cecil at Oxford asserts that 'George Eliot is the first modern novelist', while Mr. F. R. Leavis at Cambridge categorically affirms that 'the great English novelists are Jane Austen, George Eliot, Henry James and Joseph Conrad'. Mr. Leavis secures convenience by subtle ingenuity, for, having dismissed Fielding as important merely 'because he leads to Jane Austen', he has only to indicate that each novelist handed something to the next, as in a relay race, to convey the impression of having contrived a complete study of the English novel in his notes on four novelists. The supreme virtue in teaching as in literature, simplicity may be overstrained till its misuser topples backwards into the abyss of absurdity.

For the novel, Stevenson's time was an age of transition, with experiment hampered by the prudery of contemporary taste. Mr. Siegfried Sassoon justly claims that Meredith was, 'along with George Eliot and Hardy, one of the makers of the modern novel of psychology, introspection, and ideas', and—perhaps more than any contemporary, since he excelled in studies of feminine character—he suffered from the fashion for prurient secrecy about sex. Unimpeded by prudery, the development of the novel was progressing more rapidly in France, and the influence of Zola, fervently sponsored in England by Charles Reade, induced an insistence on realism as the essence of vitality in fiction.

Stevenson wrote of realism as an experimental fashion—such a fashion as impressionism, cubism, and surrealism at later epochs. When Lytton Strachey revived the art of biography, his too enthusiastic disciples, known as 'debunkers', carried to extremes his selective method of distortion; as Mr. St. John Ervine once remarked, having discovered the wart on Cromwell's nose, they treated Cromwell as if he were nothing but a wart. So the too-enthusiastic disciples of Zola inclined to exaggerate the method of their master, and Stevenson wrote:

'The immediate danger of the realist is to sacrifice the beauty and significance of the whole to local dexterity, or, in the insane pursuit of completion, to immolate his readers under facts; but he comes in the last resort, and as his energy declines, to discard all design, abjure all choice, and, with scientific thoroughness, steadily to communicate matter which is not worth learning.'

The aim of his essay, as he explained in a long letter to Bob Stevenson, was to emphasise that 'this question of realism . . . regards not in the least degree the fundamental truth, but only the technical method, of a work of art.'

'A work of art is first cloudily conceived in the mind; during the period of gestation it stands more clearly forward from these swaddling mists, puts on expressive lineaments, and becomes at length that most faultless, but also, alas! that incommunicable product of the human mind, a perfected design. On the approach to execution all is changed. The artist must now step down, don his working clothes, and become the artisan. He now resolutely commits his airy conception, his delicate Ariel, to the touch of matter; he must decide, almost in a breath, the scale, the style, the spirit, and the particularity of execution of his whole design. . . . It is, then, first of all, at this initial and decisive moment when execution is begun, and thenceforth only in a less degree, that the ideal and the real do indeed, like good and evil angels, contend for the direction of the work.'

The problem of the artistic conscience was the same as that of his personal conscience; the Hyde of realism sought to unseat and overset the Jekyll of idealism. To suppose, like J. A. Steuart, that Stevenson was writing from 'a fundamental misconception of the scope and function of the novel', is to ignore the difference between reality and realism. He was seeking, not to limit the novelist's reality in portraiture, but to warn him against obscuring his effects by superfluity of detail. 'All representative art, which can be said to live, is both realistic and ideal,' he wrote, but 'we of the last quarter of the nineteenth century, breathing as we do the intellectual atmosphere of our age, are more apt to err upon the side of realism than to sin in quest of the ideal'. The artist's danger lay in the 'insubordination' of his 'unruly tools': 'he must omit what is tedious or irrelevant, and suppress what is tedious and necessary.' Chesterton believed that Stevenson, as a novelist, 'simplified so much that he lost some of the comfortable complexity of real life'—that 'he treated everything with an economy of detail and a suppression of irrelevance which had at last something about it stark and unnatural'. But in this insistence on selection of the essential, Stevenson was a revolutionary, violently reacting against the Victorian fashion for loose writing and lavish digression; he was an apostle of economy long before Lawrence and Aldous Huxley, David Garnett and Virginia Woolf. If, as Mr. Swinnerton says, Stevenson 'created a school which has brought romance to be the sweepings of an old costume-chest', he can hardly be blamed for the ineptitude of his imitators.

Evidently realism intruded so far into the representation of *The Travelling Companion* that a publisher found it 'indecent'. The striving for fastidious precision in style and economy of effect still postponed completion of *Prince Otto*; on 13th December 1883 he had 'still one chapter to write' and 'three or four to strengthen or recast'; three months later, on 9th March, 'two chapters of *Otto* do remain: one to rewrite, one to create'. Consciously or unconsciously, this story was written laboriously in imitation of Meredith, whom Stevenson revered as 'the only man of genius of my acquaintance'. To Henley he wrote:

'Otto is, as you say, not a thing to extend my public on. It is queer and a little, little bit free; and some of the parties are immoral; and the whole thing is not a romance, nor yet a comedy; nor yet a romantic comedy; but a kind of preparation of some of the elements of all three in a glass jar. I think it is not without merit, but I am not always on the level of my argument, and some parts are false, and much of the rest is thin; it is more a triumph for myself than anything else; for I see, beyond it, better stuff.'

Begun in California when he had the impression that Henley and Colvin were thinking his work 'rather bosh nowadays', *Prince Otto* was started with the intention of restoring his shaken self-confidence, the idea of the plot deriving from a blank-verse tragedy called *Semiramis*, which he had written in adolescence. The central character was partly himself, but his cousin Bob 'appeared in certain phases': 'whenever my husband wished to depict a romantic, erratic, engaging character,' wrote Fanny, 'he delved into the rich mine of his cousin's personality.' The prototype of the Countess von Rosen was 'my old Russian friend, Madame Zassetsky'; perhaps the manner of the countess's advances to Otto was recalled from the

Princess's attempts at flirtation with himself before she resigned him to Madame Garschine. Stevenson wrote to Henley:

'To be quite frank, there is a risqué character, the Countess von Rosen, a jolly, elderly—how shall I say?—f——stress, whom I try to handle so as to please this rotten public, and damn myself the while for ruining good material. I could, if I dared, make her jump.'

Again, later, to Henley:

'Is Otto fit? . . . As thus, it is very moral. Very, quite in my highest vein; of a nice morality, stap my vitals. But there's a supposed adultery which proves to be an error; and there's a possible, or semi-possible adultery, which doesn't come off. And I fear the word "cuckold" would want to be once employed: yet I might turn that necessity, and I'll try. Otherwise it's as pure as ice. . . . Colvin has heard all the dangerous passages; and they are all to be softened from what he heard.'

'The ladies are beautiful and witty; but they are escaped from a novel of Mr. Meredith's, and have no business here,' wrote Andrew Lang. 'The book is no more Mr. Stevenson's than *A Tale of Two Cities* was Mr. Dickens's.' In a letter of August 1890, Stevenson remarked: 'I have never pleased myself with any women of mine save two character parts, one of only a few lines—the Countess of Rosen—and Madame Desprez in *The Treasure of Franchard*.' In regard to his later work, it is well to remember that these two successes in drawing feminine character—both slight—belong to the period of his beginnings as a novelist. Though he felt the tone to be 'a little, little bit free', the character of the countess would have gained in conviction from greater licence in describing her relations with the prince, a young man suffering from a Freudian inferiority complex, who assumes a pose to screen his want of self-confidence. The story fails in effect because, as Henry Sidgwick said: 'I could not feel sure how much the author intended for amusing extravaganza and how much for serious presentation of human relations and problems.' In imitating Meredith, Stevenson achieved even Meredithian elusiveness, and Henry James delivered a lasting verdict on this book: 'As in his extreme artistic vivacity he seems really disposed to try every thing, he has tried once, by way of a change, to be inhuman, and there is a hard glitter about *Prince Otto* which seems to indicate that in this case, too, he has succeeded, as he has done in most of the feats that he has attempted.'

Despite the depression caused by Ferrier's death, and though Fanny was still 'out of sorts', Stevenson worked steadily and well throughout the autumn of 1883. At Christmas, for the first time, he could look back on a year in which his work had earned some reasonable reward—'a total receipt of £465, 0s. 6d. for the last twelve months!' Further, Lippincott's, the Philadelphia publishers, had been so far impressed by *The Silverado Squatters* that they offered him £450, with a hundred pounds advance, to write a travel book on the islands of the Aegean, a trip that he proposed to undertake in the following autumn. It was a long time since he had seen his friends, and he missed such conversation as he had enjoyed with Symonds at Davos; at the New Year he was delighted at the prospect of a visit from Henley and Baxter.

On the plea that the little cottage provided inadequate accommodation for two guests, Stevenson accompanied his two friends for a few days at Nice, where his health had benefited the year before. He caught cold, and developed congestion of the lungs. When Baxter and Henley brought him back to Hyères, the local doctor informed Fanny that 'there was no hope, and I had better send for some member of the family to be with me at the end'. As there was no time to send for his parents, she called upon Bob Stevenson. A Dr. Drummond was consulted and gave the opinion 'that Louis may well live to be seventy, only he must not travel about'. Bob Stevenson remained till danger was past: 'he helped me to nurse Louis,' wrote Fanny, 'and he kept me from despair as I believe no one else could have done.'

'I am all at a standstill; as idle as a painted ship, but not so pretty,' wrote Stevenson to Gosse in March. 'My romance, which has so nearly butchered me in the writing, not even finished; though so near, thank God, that a few days of tolerable strength will see the roof upon that structure.' But months elapsed before he was again able to work. He suffered from the same weakness of the eyes that afflicted Llewelyn Powys in similar illness; he was harassed by 'extreme nervousness that will not let me lie a moment, and damned sciatica o' nights'. Ferrier's sister 'Coggie' arrived on a prolonged visit, and helped Fanny with the nursing. At the beginning of May he had a dangerous hæmorrhage of the lungs; choking with blood, he made signs to Fanny for pencil and paper, and wrote: 'Don't be frightened; if this is death, it is an easy one.'

As he lay in a darkened room, forbidden to speak and fearful of movements, Fanny amused him by making up stories, two of which, 'The Destroying Angel' and 'The Fair Cuban', he adapted in *The Dynamiter*, so affording an excuse to credit Fanny with 'collaboration'. When he was allowed to use his left hand for writing, he fell to writing verses, his usual occupation when incapacitated by illness for concentrated effort. During the previous autumn, Colvin had arranged at Cambridge for the printing of a few copies of *Penny Whistles*, many of which were distributed among possible illustrators. Stevenson now added to these for the volume published by Longmans, in March 1885, as *A Child's Garden of Verses*, with a dedication to Cummy. He also wrote the final version of 'Requiem'; the concluding lines had been composed during his illness at San Francisco and formed the inscription on his grave:

> 'Under the wide and starry sky,
> Dig the grave and let me lie.
> Glad did I live and gladly die,
> And I laid me down with a will.
>
> This be the verse you grave for me:
> Here he lies where he longed to be;
> *Home is the sailor, home from sea,*
> *And the hunter home from the hill.*'

These lines, endorsing Henley's statement that 'no better histrion ever lived', eminently contributed to the legend of Stevenson's life as an epic of gallantry; they especially appealed to a generation delighting in Rudyard Kipling's truculent heroics.

By early June he was well enough to be moved to Royat, with 'an invalid valet' in attendance; thence he travelled to England, arriving on 1st July—in time for Fanny to attend, the next day, the first night of the London production of *Deacon Brodie*.

In view of Stevenson's refusal to return to England for the previous summer, fearing a repetition of his unlucky summers in 1881 and 1882, there seemed no logical reason for resorting to its unpredictable climate in a condition of precarious convalescence. In Lloyd Osbourne's opinion, 'the reason was absurd'.

'My mother, with a view of keeping up the advance of medicine, and gaining some hints that might help R.L.S., subscribed to the *Lancet*—the well-known medical weekly. It was the worst reading in the world for her. . . . Stevenson, true to himself and wiser, left it severely alone. But my mother glued herself to it, and began to fill her mind with all sorts of bogeys. Vinegar was discovered to be full of perils; salads carried the eggs of tape-worms; salt hardened your arteries and shortened your days; Heaven only knows what she discovered in the way of lurking dangers, previously undreamed of; and when the climax came in an outbreak of cholera in the old part of the town, with a terrible death-roll amongst its poor, dirty, neglected inhabitants, she fell into a panic and began to work on R.L.S. to abandon Hyères as a place too dangerous to live in.'

According to Stevenson's letters, since the time of their marriage more than four years before, Fanny had always been 'quite far from well' or 'out of sorts'. Yet she seems to have suffered no serious illness before her death, at the age of seventy-four, from an apoplectic stroke. She was a hypochondriac, and subject to the hypochondriac's habit of gloom. Before his marriage, so far from belittling his suffering, Stevenson tended to dramatise any ailment; now his flippant gaiety, interpreted by his friends as gallant defiance of disease, was assumed in self-defence. According to Balfour, Fanny herself related how, at Hyères, on hearing the doctor's diagnosis of Stevenson's eye weakness as ophthalmia, she 'sat and gloomed' in another room; then, going to Stevenson, she said bitterly: 'Well, I suppose that this is the very best thing that could have happened!' To which Stevenson wrote the reply: 'Why, how odd! I was just going to say those very words.' Stevenson's father playfully nicknamed Fanny 'Cassandra', and just as he had assumed a pose in self-defence against the criticism of his fellow-undergraduates, Stevenson now lived a perpetual pose to counter the pessimism of his critic on the hearth. His loyalty allowed no criticism of his wife from others; to his mother he wrote repeated reassurances of his perfect happiness, and to Henley, who was least successful in masking his antagonism towards Fanny, he wrote at this time: 'I have the best wife in the world.'

CHAPTER SEVEN

THE HERMIT OF SKERRYVORE

'To forego all the issues of living in a parlour with a regulated
temperature—as if that were not to die a hundred times over, and
for ten years at a stretch! . . . As if it were not to die, and yet be
the patient spectators of our own pitiable change!'—*Aes Triplex*.

T
HE doctor at Hyères had advised Fanny: 'Keep him
alive till he is forty, and then, although a winged bird, he
may live to ninety.' Meanwhile he must live 'as though
he were walking on eggs'. The diagnosis was confirmed by
London doctors: he must 'live the life of a delicate girl' till he
was forty.

After a few days at a Richmond hotel for medical consulta-
tions, Stevenson and Fanny went down to Bournemouth, where
Lloyd Osbourne was then at school. The doctors were divided
in opinion on whether he should live in England or abroad, and
his father's failing heath was the deciding factor. Fanny was
against a return to Hyères, and since he was specifically warned
against the dangers of travel, Stevenson had to remain somewhere near his father. Bournemouth, a resort beneficial to
consumptives, seemed as suitable as anywhere.

In lodgings at Wensleydale, a house on the West Cliff, they
were joined for the month of September by Henley and his wife.
The London production of *Deacon Brodie* seemed to have
justified Henley's faith in the stage as a royal road to 'dibbs'
for Stevenson and himself. Together they worked on *Beau
Austin* and *Admiral Guinea*: the dedication of the former, 'with
admiration and respect to George Meredith', was dated from
Bournemouth, 1st October 1884; *Admiral Guinea* was dedicated
'with affection and esteem to Andrew Lang by the survivors of
the *Walrus*' and dated 'Savannah, this 27th day of September,
1884'. According to Lloyd Osbourne, '*Beau Austin* was written

189

in four days, and I shall never forget Henley reading it aloud—
so movingly, so tenderly, that my eyes were wet with tears'.
As talk and laughter were bad for Stevenson, Fanny felt justifiable fear of the effect produced by Henley. But she was in a
minority, for her son 'idolized' her husband's friend. 'He was
the first man I had ever called by his surname; the first friend
I had ever sought and won,' wrote Lloyd Osbourne:

'a great, glowing, massive-shouldered fellow with a big red beard
and a crutch; jovial, astoundingly clever, and with a laugh that
rolled out like music. Never was there such another as William
Ernest Henley; he had an unimaginable fire and vitality; he swept
one off one's feet. There are no words that can describe the quality
he had of exalting those about him; of communicating his own rousing self-confidence and belief in himself; in the presence of this
demigod, who thrilled you by his appreciation, you became a
demigod yourself, and felt the elation of an Olympian who never
until then had known the tithe of what was in him.'

This was the first time since his marriage that Stevenson had
lived under the same roof with his friend, and Lloyd Osbourne
recalled the gaiety of the visit as marking 'what might be called
the end of an epoch in Stevenson's life'—'he was never afterwards so boyish or so light-hearted; it was the final flare-up of
his departing youth'.

By the time Henley left in early October, Stevenson had finished *Prince Otto*, which appeared serially in *Longman's Magazine*
between April and October, before book publication by Chatto
and Windus in November 1885. In the September number of
Longman's he saw an essay by Henry James on 'The Art of
Fiction', written in protest against remarks by the popular
novelist, Walter Besant, in a lecture on the subject. Deploring
the division of novels into 'the novel and the romance, the novel
of incident and that of character', James insisted that 'a novel
is in its broadest definition a personal impression of life'.
Deriding Besant's assertion that 'a story must, under penalty
of not being a story, consist of "adventure"', he demonstrated
that psychological experience was just as much 'adventure' as
sensational incident: 'it is the special picture that must stand or
fall, according as it seems to possess truth or to lack it.' To

illustrate his point, he cited a good story of incident and an indifferent story of psychological development—'the delightful story' of *Treasure Island* and Edmond de Goncourt's *Chérie*.

'One of these works treats of murders, mysteries, islands of dreadful renown, hairbreadth escapes, miraculous coincidences and buried doubloons. The other treats of a little French girl who lived in a fine house in Paris and died of wounded sensibility because no one would marry her. I call "Treasure Island" delightful, because it appears to me to have succeeded wonderfully in what it attempts; and I venture to bestow no epithet upon "Chérie", which strikes me as having failed in what it attempts—that is, in tracing the development of the moral consciousness of a child. But one of these productions strikes me as exactly as much of a novel as the other, and as having a "story" quite as much.'

He allowed that the artist may choose his own subject or idea; 'our criticism is applied only to what he makes of it'.

Stevenson may have been piqued at being selected as an exponent of the novel of mere incident, ranging him alongside Besant, the commercial craftsman, in opposition to James, the artist. In 'A Humble Remonstrance', published in the December *Longman's*, he began by arguing against an assertion that seemed to advocate the methods deplored in 'A Note on Realism'. 'The air of reality (solidity of specification) seems to me to be the supreme virtue of a novel,' wrote James; 'the only reason for the existence of a novel is that it *does* compete with life.' 'No art—to use the daring phrase of Mr. James—can successfully "compete with life",' wrote Stevenson:

'Man's one method, whether he reasons or creates, is to half-shut his eyes against the dazzle and confusion of reality. . . . Painting, ruefully comparing sunshine and flake-white, gives up truth of colour, as it had already given up relief and movement; and instead of vying with nature, arranges a scheme of harmonious tints. Literature, above all in its most typical mood, the mood of narrative, similarly flees the direct challenge and pursues instead an independent and creative aim. So far as it imitates at all, it imitates not life but speech: not the facts of human destiny, but the emphasis and the suppressions with which the human actor tells of them.

Our art is occupied, and bound to be occupied, not so much in making stories true as in making them typical; not so much in capturing the lineaments of each fact, as in marshalling all of them towards a common end. For the welter of impressions, all forcible but all discrete, which life presents, it substitutes a certain artificial series of impressions, all indeed most feebly represented, but all aiming at the same effect, all eloquent of the same idea, all chiming together like consonant notes in music or like the graduated tints in a good picture. From all its chapters, from all its pages, from all its sentences, the well-written novel echoes and re-echoes its one creative and controlling thought; to this must every incident and character contribute; the style must have been pitched in unison with this; and if there is anywhere a word that looks another way, the book would be stronger, clearer, and (I had almost said) fuller without it. Life is monstrous, infinite, illogical, abrupt, and poignant; a work of art, in comparison, is neat, finite, self-contained, rational, flowing, and emasculate. . . . The life of man is not the subject of novels, but the inexhaustible magazine from which subjects are to be selected; the name of these is legion; and with each new subject—for here again I must differ by the whole width of heaven from Mr. James—the true artist will vary his method and change the point of attack.'

He proceeds to examine the 'three main classes' of novels—the novel of adventure, the novel of character, and the dramatic novel, citing as an example of the second James's *Author of Beltraffio*. In its argument that art is necessarily selective, 'A Humble Remonstrance' is complementary to 'A Note on Realism'. At the time of appearance, these two essays by James and Stevenson were revolutionary in demanding to reform the loose structure of the Victorian novel; they also forecast, with an accuracy reflecting the artistic stature of both writers, the direction of the novel's development in the twentieth century. Neither James nor Stevenson has received due recognition of their contribution to literary criticism, and more than sixty years elapsed before Miss Janet Adam Smith performed a service to letters by bringing these two essays together between the covers of a volume.[1]

---

[1] Besides these two essays, *Henry James and Robert Louis Stevenson: A Record of Friendship and Criticism*, edited with an introduction by Janet Adam Smith (London, 1948) contains the entire correspondence, chronologically arranged, between Stevenson and James, as well as James's two essays on Stevenson—the first from the *Century Magazine* of April 1888, the second, reviewing Colvin's edition of Stevenson's *Letters to His Family and Friends*, from the *North American Review* of January 1900.

VAILIMA

Stevenson, with his Mother, Lloyd Osbourne, Fanny, and servants on the verandah of his house

From a photograph, by courtesy of Picture Post Library

Aside from their value as criticism, the essays represent an exchange of opinion between men of letters exemplary in courtesy—an exchange which might be cynically described as an amiable exhibition of mutual log-rolling. Immediately on reading 'A Humble Remonstrance', James wrote to Stevenson his 'assurance of my enjoyment of everything you write'; of their argument, he described his own essay as 'simply a plea for liberty', while 'no one can assent more than I to your proposition that all art is a simplification'. As cordially Stevenson replied on 8th December; he felt the need for emphasising that effects resulted from the artist's selectiveness as opposed to photographic realism, and gracefully hinted his conception of the weakness in James's novels by suggesting that he might 'pitch the incidents . . . in a slightly more emphatic key'. When James spent several weeks at Bournemouth in the following May and June, a friendship began that never abated in warmth and understanding.

From their lodgings at Wensleydale the Stevensons moved in November 1884 to a furnished house called Bonallie Towers in Branksome Park. Both were 'all to pieces in health'; Stevenson caught a cold which left him with an exhausting cough, and Fanny was 'very very much out of sorts, principally through perpetual misery with me'. When the *Pall Mall Gazette* offered, through Gosse, a commission of forty pounds for a Christmas story, Stevenson was not well enough to write the story he intended; instead, he submitted *Markheim*, and when this was rejected as too short, he substituted *The Body-Snatcher*, which had been laid aside three years before at Pitlochry as too 'horrid'. Though Henley vainly argued that the paper was rich and could well afford to pay for work worthy of acceptance, Stevenson declined to accept the agreed price: 'I took that as a fair price for my best work; I was not able to produce my best; and I will be damned if I steal with my eyes open.' The newspaper seemed well enough pleased with the story, which was advertised by sandwich men carrying posters so lurid that they were suppressed by the police.

In December 'a charming, simple, clever, honest young man', John Singer Sargent, stayed a few days at Bonallie Towers to paint Stevenson's portrait. Of the result Colvin wrote

to Henley: 'It's him to the life in gesture and expression—
living life, with a touch of *charge*: but somehow small and perky
and peaky a little too: as clever as possible, but not satisfying.'
Stevenson himself reported to Henley:

'Sargent has come and gone; I repeat what I said to Bob; he
represents me as a weird, very pretty, large-eyed, chicken-boned,
slightly contorted poet. He is not pleased; wants to do me again
in several postures; walking about and talking is his main notion.
We both lost our hearts to him: a person with a kind of exhibition
manner and English accent, who improves on examination, simple,
bashful, honest, enthusiastic, and rude with a perfect (but quite
inoffensive) English rudeness . . . he gives himself out to be
American.'

Sargent repeated his visit in the following summer, and
this time he attempted to convey character by form and movement instead of by face and mannerism, painting Stevenson
full-length as he paced the dining-room, fingering his moustache, with Fanny, exotically attired in Indian dress, reclining
in a chair at the side of the picture.[1]

During the winter Stevenson wrote the essay 'On Some
Technical Elements of Style in Literature', published in the
Contemporary Review of April, and finished *The Dynamiter*; he
began a romance called *The Great North Road*, and laid it
aside to dally unavailingly with the project of a *Life of
Wellington* for Longman's 'English Worthies' series, edited by
Andrew Lang. In the following June *The Great North Road*,
was 'still unfinished', and only the first eight chapters survive.
Designed to be published by Cassell's as a successor to *Treasure
Island*, the story's surviving chapters show that Stevenson
intended to raise the writing of romance to a more ambitious
level of literary art, introducing into a tale of highway robbery
a study of the complexities of character. A country inn-
keeper's daughter, strong and strapping of physique, staunch
and simple of nature, is shown to be falling in love with a mysterious man socially her superior—'this rather dismal, rather

---

[1] Like the other Sargent portrait, appearing as frontispiece to this book, this
picture is now in America; it is reproduced in Miss Janet Adam Smith's *Henry
James and Robert Louis Stevenson: A Record of Friendship and Criticism*, London, 1948.

effeminate man, who recoiled from a worm, who grew giddy
on the castle wall, who bore so helplessly the weight of his misfortunes', who is yet to be revealed as a highwayman of desperate
effrontery and enterprise. Gosse believed that Stevenson abandoned the story because he 'felt that it was not turning out well',
as the secret of the highwayman's identity was 'rashly and prematurely divulged'. But Stevenson habitually planned his books
in chapters, and the revelation of identity was deliberate, since
the central theme was evidently to turn on the girl's continued
devotion after the initial horror of her discovery that her lover
was a criminal. The writing of the story was delayed by illness,
depriving him of the energy required to cope with a scheme
which, as he told Henley, had developed beyond its original
design:

' *The Great North Road*, which I thought to rattle off like *Treasure
Island* for coins, has turned into my most ambitious design, and will
take piles of writing and thinking. . . . Mr. Archer and Jonathan
Holdaway are both grand premier parts of most unusual difficulty;
and Nance and the Sergeant, the first, very delicate, the second,
demanding great geniality. I quail before the job but, so help me,
it shall be done. It is largely picturesque, most dramatic, and if it
can be made, as human as man.'

Late in January Henley and his wife came again to stay a few
weeks, and Stevenson and Henley collaborated on the last of
their four plays, *Macaire*, a melodrama with a notorious criminal
as hero. They offered the play to Herbert Beerbohm Tree, who
was sufficiently interested to visit Stevenson in the spring, but,
though he subsequently produced two of their plays in London
—*Beau Austin* at the Haymarket in 1890, and *Macaire* at Her
Majesty's Theatre in 1901—Tree made no immediate offer, and
Stevenson lost interest in a form of writing which he had always
regarded rather as an amusement to be shared with Henley
than as a practical means of earning money. 'Do you think you
are right to send *Macaire* and the *Admiral* about?' he asked
Henley in March; he described *Admiral Guinea* as 'a low, black,
dirty, blackguard, ragged piece: vomitable in many parts—
simply vomitable', and *Macaire* as 'a piece of job-work, hurriedly bockled'. 'I come unhesitatingly to the opinion that the

stage is only a lottery, must not be regarded as a trade, and must never be preferred to drudgery,' he wrote in response to Henley's protests. 'If money comes from any play, let us regard it as a legacy, but never count upon it in our income for the year.'

At Easter the Stevensons moved from Bonallie Towers to a house of their own called 'Sea View', purchased by Thomas Stevenson as a present to Fanny, and re-named 'Skerryvore' by Stevenson after the famous lighthouse built by the family firm. Delighted to possess a house of her own, Fanny wrote to her 'dearest friend', Mrs. Sitwell: 'It is very comfortable to know that we have a home really and truly, and will no more be like Noah's dove, flying about with an olive branch, and trying to pretend that we have found a bit of dry ground to perch upon.' The garden was 'delicious', there was 'even a little studio for me to dabble paints in', and 'when we are rich enough (if I am not too fat by that time) there is a stable all ready for my horse'. With the backing of Stevenson's increasing reputation, she found herself received into Bournemouth's most select literary society. She could accept the courtly flattery of the octogenarian Sir Henry Taylor, knighted for nearly half-a-century's service as a clerk in the Colonial Office, but almost a candidate for the Laureateship through having cultivated the friendship of Southey and Wordsworth, and through the authorship of a tragedy in verse produced fifty years before by Macready. Equally respectable were Sir Percy Florence Shelley, the poet's son, and his tiresome wife, who, after affliction 'with the most painful feelings of dismay' at Jefferson Hogg's biography, assumed proprietorship of Shelley's reputation from 'feelings of duty' towards his memory. Detecting in Stevenson an imagined resemblance to her husband's father, Lady Shelley one day made a scene at Skerryvore by upbraiding Stevenson's mother 'for daring to purloin a son who was really *hers*'. But, while admitting that she was 'as mad as some other people you know, and ready to plunge into any wild extravagance at a moment's notice', Fanny found Lady Shelley 'delicious'. She went eagerly to the 'very delightful entertainments' at the Shelleys' 'lovely little theatre at their place here', and delighted in sharing her hypochondria with Lady Taylor—when she had 'not been very well', she 'found the coca wine a blessing and a boon', and 'Lady Taylor feels so well while taking it that she is convinced that it must be a most dangerous remedy'.

In April 1885 Longmans published *The Dynamiter* as *More New Arabian Nights: The Dynamiter*, by Robert Louis Stevenson and Fanny Van de Grift Stevenson, in paper wrappers at a shilling, with a few copies bound in cloth boards at one shilling and sixpence. Reprints were called for in May and July, the book receiving what Fanny called 'great advertisement' from some dynamite outrages by Fenians in London at the time. Though she supplied the ideas of only two of the stories and any part that she wrote was almost certainly re-written entirely by Stevenson, as in his later collaborations with her son, Fanny felt immense pride in authorship and 'some mortification' at receiving scant attention from reviewers. 'I thought in the beginning that I shouldn't mind being Louis's scapegoat,' she wrote to her mother-in-law, 'but it is rather hard to be treated like a comma, and a superfluous one at that.' When she remarked to Sargent, 'I am but a cipher under the shadow', she had the humour to tell Colvin that Sargent 'too eagerly assented', but she expressed dudgeon when correspondents preferred writing to Stevenson rather than to her and when she was expected to sit in silence while Henry James talked with her husband. Her talent as a painter seems to have been entirely forgotten, apart from the 'dabbling' in her studio; she now assumed all the airs of the literary lady, and fortified by her friendship with Lady Shelley and Lady Taylor, she felt herself to be a leading figure in Bournemouth society. She had travelled far from the art-student's poverty in Paris of seven years before —far, too, from such self-consciousness of the possibilities of social ostracism as inspired Stevenson's letter to W. D. Howells less than three years earlier. With her passport in order, she had secured admission to the citadel of respectability.

Invalidism was a condition both interesting and eminently respectable in Victorian society, and Fanny ably abetted Stevenson's literary friends in advertising him as an invalid of genius. During the first four years following their marriage, Stevenson had been fit to travel and to take reasonable exercise, but at Bournemouth he was normally confined within the house and garden. To Gosse he signed himself 'The Hermit of Skerry-vore', and another time he likened his existence to that of 'a pallid weevil in a biscuit'. With his life-long habit of sub-jecting conduct to examination by conscience, he must have reflected upon the contrast between Fanny's social preoccupa-tions and the creed of Bohemianism evolved after his first visit to Barbizon. Sometimes, as appears in passages of his letters suppressed by Colvin, he confided in Henley the stress of domestic conflict. 'I got my little finger into a steam press called the Vandergrifter (patent) and my whole body and soul had to go through after it,' he wrote in the spring or early summer of 1885; 'I came out as limp as a lady's novel, but the Vandergrifter suffered in the process, and is fairly knocked about'. Remarking that 'the Vandergrifter goes (not figuratively, literally) to Bath on Monday next', he ends this letter to Henley: 'I am what she has made me, the embers of the once gay R.L.S.' In another letter to Henley of this time, signed 'The Merely Useless One', he wrote: 'What in the name of fate is to become of an R.L.S. who can no longer (1) spree, (2) walk, (3) cruise, (4) drink, (5) or smoke? Yet that is the state of affairs.'

Lloyd Osbourne observed shrewdly in declaring that, for Stevenson, the gaiety of Henley's visit to Wensleydale was 'the final flare-up of his departing youth'. Sympathy deepened between Stevenson and his stepson; as in the days when he escaped from Fanny's sombre society to laugh in Lloyd's play-room at Braemar, he derived increasing comfort from Lloyd's company as a refuge from Fanny's attempts at domination. To Henley he wrote at this time: 'I am worried first because I don't see my way to have Sam here for his holidays which is about equally painful to Sam and to me; second, because I am doubtful of paying his schooling.' In the spring of 1887 he told Henley:

'I find in the contemplation of the growth of Lloyd much benefit: he is a damn fine youth. Happy am I, to be even thus much of a father! I wonder if that is not your complaint. . . . Perhaps as we approach the foul time of life, young folk become necessary? 'Tis a problem. We know what form this craving wears in certain cases. But perhaps it is a genuine thing in itself: the age of paternity coming,

a demand sets in. Thus perhaps my present (and crescent) infatuation for the youth Lloyd; but no, I think, it is because the youth
himself improves so much, and is such a dam, dam, dam fine youth.'

Circumstances conspired with Fanny's insistence that
Stevenson's health demanded his close incarceration. In
August Stevenson effected his first escape from Skerryvore on
the excuse of an expedition to visit Thomas Hardy, who was
just installed in his new home of Max Gate. From Max Gate
they were to proceed to Dartmoor, where the pure air had
been recommended by Stevenson's medical attendant at
Bournemouth, Dr. Thomas Bodley Scott, to whom *Underwoods*
was dedicated. But at the New London Hotel, Exeter, Stevenson suffered a hæmorrhage, described by Fanny as 'the worst
that he has had except the one at Hyères'. On his return to
Skerryvore, he lay again in 'the land of counterpane', allowed
only the minimum of speech and movement; as late as Boxing
Day of 1885, he described himself as 'a chronic sickist; and my
work cripples along between bed and the parlour, between the
medicine bottle and the cupping glass'.

During the autumn he wrote only two stories, *Olalla* for the
Christmas number of the *Court and Society Review*, and *Strange
Case of Dr. Jekyll and Mr. Hyde*, which was published by Longmans as a 'shilling shocker' early in January 1886. Like the
earlier *Markheim*, both stories are concerned with the conflict
of good and evil in human conduct; both, as related in the
essay, 'A Chapter on Dreams', were in part conceived by 'the
little people who manage man's internal theatre'—the
'Brownies', 'who do one-half my work for me while I am fast
asleep, and in all human likelihood, do the rest for me as well,
when I am wide awake and fondly suppose I do it for myself'.
Of 'the not very defensible story', *Olalla*, he wrote:

'Here the court, the mother, the mother's niche, Olalla, Olalla's
chamber, the meetings on the stair, the broken window, the ugly
scene of the bite, were all given me in bulk and detail as I have tried
to write them; to this I added only the external scenery (for in my
dream I was never beyond the court), the portrait, the characters of
Felipe and the priest, the moral, such as it is, and the last pages,
such as, alas! they are. And I may even say that in this case the

moral itself was given me; for it arose immediately on a comparison of the mother and the daughter, and from the hideous trick of atavism in the first.'

The story of a girl condemned to a life of self-sacrifice to expiate a heritage of evil bequeathed by a long line of ancestors, *Olalla* has a weak ending and an unsatisfactory moral, because there seems no practical reason why a girl who has herself escaped any hereditary taint should assume responsibility for the evils of her family. 'The trouble with *Olalla* is that it somehow sounds false,' wrote Stevenson to Lady Taylor, when dedicating to her the volume of stories in 1887: '*Markheim* is true; *Olalla* false; and I don't know why, nor did I feel it while I worked at them; indeed I had more inspiration with *Olalla*, as the style shows.'

Of *Jekyll and Hyde* he wrote in 'A Chapter on Dreams':

'I had long been trying to write a story on this subject, to find a body, a vehicle, for that strong sense of man's double being which must at times come in upon and overwhelm the mind of every thinking creature. I had even written one, "The Travelling Companion", which was returned by an editor on the plea that it was a work of genius and indecent, and which I burned the other day on the ground that it was not a work of genius, and that "Jekyll" had supplanted it. Then came one of those financial fluctuations to which (with an elegant modesty) I have hitherto referred in the third person. For two days I went about racking my brains for a plot of any sort; and on the second night I dreamed the scene at the window, and a scene afterwards split in two, in which Hyde, pursued for some crime, took the powder and underwent the change in the presence of his pursuers. All the rest was made awake, and consciously, although I think I can trace in much of it the manner of my Brownies. The meaning of the tale is therefore mine, and had long pre-existed in my garden of Adonis, and tried one body after another in vain; indeed, I do most of the morality, worse luck! and my Brownies have not a rudiment of what we call a conscience. Mine, too, is the setting, mine the characters. All that was given me was the matter of three scenes, and the central idea of a voluntary change becoming involuntary. Will it be thought ungenerous, after I have been so liberally ladling out praise to my unseen collaborators, if I here toss them over, bound hand and foot, into the arena of the critics? For the business of the powders, which so many have censured, is, I am relieved to say, not mine at all but the Brownies'.'

Fanny related that Stevenson reproached her rousing him from a troubled sleep, because, he said, 'I was dreaming a fine bogey tale', and he thereupon told her the outline of *Jekyll and Hyde*.

'At daybreak he was working with feverish activity on the new book. In those days the first draft, containing thirty thousand words, was finished, only to be entirely destroyed and immediately re-written from another point of view,—that of the allegory which was palpable, and yet had been missed, probably from haste and the compelling influence of the dream. In another three days the book, except for a few minor corrections, was ready for the press. The amount of work this involved was appalling. That an invalid in my husband's condition of health should have been able to perform the manual labour alone of putting 60,000 words on paper in six days seems incredible. He was suffering from continual hæmorrhages, and was hardly allowed to speak, his conversations being usually carried on by means of a slate and pencil. Two persons were not allowed in his room at the same time, and when one was given that privilege by the doctor, the interview was limited to fifteen minutes' duration. It was my ungracious task to stand guard outside the door, watch in hand, ready to warn the visitor.'

If not 'incredible', Fanny's account was evidently imaginative. Stevenson himself stated that '*Jekyll* was conceived, written, re-written, re-re-written, and printed inside ten weeks'. According to her sister, on receiving the first draft with the assurance that 'it was the best thing he had ever done', Fanny 'read it and thought it the worst', whereupon she 'fell into a state of deep gloom, for she couldn't let it go, and yet it seemed cruel to tell him so'. Pressed for her opinion, she complained that 'he had treated it simply as a story, whereas it was in reality an allegory'. With a recklessness contrary to custom— for, as appears from his posthumous papers, he normally pre-served almost everything he wrote—he threw the manuscript into the fire, and set to work on a second version.

From Stevenson's own account in 'A Chapter of Dreams', it appears unlikely that he 'missed' the point of the allegory in writing the first draft. The allegory was the germ of the story, and he had in fact already attempted the theme in *The Travelling Companion*. Suspicion arises that Fanny's criticism was inspired by reasons which she preferred to conceal. *The Travelling Companion* was rejected by an editor as 'a work of genius and indecent'; was the anonymous editor to be identified with Fanny herself? Remarking that 'their discussions over the work were sometimes hot and protracted', her sister quotes a letter from Fanny to Stevenson's mother:

'If I die before Louis, my last earnest request is that he shall publish nothing without his father's approval. I know that means little short of destruction to both of them, but there will be no one else. The field is always covered with my dead and wounded, and often I am forced to a compromise, but still I make a very good fight.'

Her suggestion of Stevenson's father as a suitable mentor indicates the direction of Fanny's censorship; less than a year before, Thomas Stevenson had protested, 'with his usual vehemence of feeling and expression', against the stage confrontation in *Admiral Guinea* 'of profane blackguardry in the person of Pew with evangelical piety in that of the reformed slaving captain', evoking from Stevenson the rejoinder: 'My dear Father,—Allow me to say, in a strictly Pickwickian sense, that you are a silly fellow.' There seems reason to suspect that, in the first draft of *Jekyll and Hyde*, Stevenson drew upon his own experiences of the double life to describe more realistically the excesses indulged by Jekyll in the character of Hyde. Little more than a year later, George Moore was writing in *Confessions of a Young Man*: 'If any man living in this end of the century needed freedom of expression for the distinct development of his genius, that man is R. L. Stevenson.'

As Stevenson remarked, many critics censured 'the business of the powders'. Henry James mildly expressed the view: 'The powders constitute the machinery of the transformation, and it will probably have struck many readers that this uncanny process would be more conceivable . . . if the author had not made it so definite.' Opinion continues divided concerning this device: in his introduction to the Macdonald

Illustrated Classics edition of the story, Mr. Compton Mackenzie considers that 'to-day that drug handicaps the story
with an old-fashioned artificiality'; Mr. Desmond Mac-
Carthy (in the *Sunday Times*, 13th August 1950) believes that
'the worlds of romance and reality are related, but to mix
them up is fatal', and because 'it would be an artistic blunder
on the part of the author to introduce matter which revolts'
the reader, 'Stevenson's instinct to keep the magic potion . . .
was therefore sound'.

Acceptance of Mr. MacCarthy's distinction between 'the
worlds of romance and reality' requires the reader of *Jekyll
and Hyde* to ignore the allegory in appreciation of the story—to
regard it, like Andrew Lang, as 'a masterpiece of the terrible
and grotesque', with 'an unobtrusive and salutary moral'.
Lang represented only a small minority of his contemporaries
in finding the moral 'unobtrusive'; for most of the thousands
contributing to the book's immediate popular success, the
allegory was the story's chief attraction, being interpreted as
a sensationally daring satire on contemporary morality. The
dignified Jekyll, immaculate of reputation, impeccable in
respectability, seeking relief for his repressed instincts in the
guise of another identity, might be recognised in any reputable
citizen of a correct suburb—as Stevenson wrote to W. H. Low,
he might 'answer to the name of Low or Stevenson'. The
thousands who kept mistresses at Maida Vale or Pimlico
unknown to their families in Kensington or Streatham; the tens
of thousands growing soured by suppression of their natural
selves in conformity with the requirements of social convention;
the masses condemned by industrial civilisation to the drab
monotony of a daily routine terminable only by old age—
all could appreciate the motives for Jekyll's sinister device.
Symonds thought the story 'a dreadful thing', and in reply to
Stevenson's rejoinder that 'the only thing I feel dreadful about
is that damned old business of the war in the members', he
doubted 'whether any one had the right so to scrutinise the
abysmal depths of personality'. A canon of St. Paul's seized
upon the allegory as the text for a sermon, and lesser clergy
followed suit. In Victorian England publicity from the pulpit
was the most influential form of advertisement; in Gosse's

words, *Jekyll and Hyde* 'instantly became the subject of discussion in every class of lettered society, and it is from the moment of its publication that Stevenson, already passionately admired within a comparatively narrow circle, began to take a foremost place in the general world of letters'.

The popular success of *Jekyll and Hyde* provided a timely antidote for an accumulation of depression. Stevenson's recovery from his August attack was hindered by a disastrous visit from his parents in November 1885. Henry James was there during three days of their stay, and wrote to Colvin: 'My visit had the gilt taken off by the somewhat ponderous presence of the parents—who sit on him much too long at once'. As his mental powers declined, Stevenson's father grew increasingly subject to moods of morbid gloom and superstitious foreboding; his mother fluttered helplessly in hysterical agitation, and 'having crushed and exhausted him', she left Stevenson 'the legacy of an influenza cold'. 'After these three weeks of chilling selfishness,' Fanny wrote to Colvin that she would welcome as a relief a visit even from Henley.

In the same month the publication of *Prince Otto* was attended by generally adverse reviews. An article of fervent praise by Henley afforded such striking contrast with other opinions that 'some of it', wrote Stevenson, 'stops my throat'; he wondered 'whether (considering our intimate relations) you would not do better to refrain from reviewing me'. The worst blow came from Edmund Gosse.

'To my constant sorrow,' wrote Gosse in his recollections of Stevenson, 'I was never able to go to Bournemouth during the years he lived there.' As Gosse was normally resident in London and ever busily courting people of increasing reputation, his neglect of Stevenson can only be explained by a feeling of coolness. The seeds of the feeling were sown by Stevenson's shrewd criticism of Gosse's monograph on Gray: 'Your subject peeps every here and there out of the crannies like a shy violet—he could do no more'; later he added, 'your little life is excellent, clean, neat, efficient'. Having an immense conception of his own and his work's importance, Gosse read condescension in Stevenson's opinion, and awaited an opportunity for repayment in the same coin. From America during the winter of 1884–85—where, he informed a friend, he was enjoying 'the greatest social success that any Englishman of letters has enjoyed since Thackeray lectured in Boston'—he wrote a letter to Stevenson in the same key of egregious conceit; Stevenson did not answer it because, as he told Gosse later, 'you were in your high places, sailing with supreme dominion, and seeing life in a particular glory', and he burned it because 'thinks I to myself, if I die one of these fine nights, this is just the letter that Gosse would not wish to go into the hands of third parties'. Feline as one of his own pet cats, Gosse never forgave the mildest affront. Reading an onslaught on *Prince Otto* in the *Saturday Review*, attacking the 'false style' of the story of Seraphina's flight through the forest, Gosse recognised his opportunity. 'Perhaps I should limit down my accusation to the particular passage of the Flight of Seraphina,' he wrote; he did not know 'whether you have already been upbraided for this piece of fine writing', which he described as 'not worthy of you' and 'a wilful and monstrous sacrifice on the altar of George Meredith'.

Stevenson replied cordially, but Gosse's criticism, following his arguments with Fanny over *Jekyll and Hyde*, stung him to bitter comment on what he called 'the hard part of literature':

'You aim high, and you take longer over your work, and it will not be so successful as if you had aimed low and rushed it. What the public likes is work (of any kind) a little loosely executed; so long as it is a little wordy, a little slack, a little dim and knotless, the dear public likes it; it should (if possible) be a little dull into the bargain. I know that good work sometimes hits; but, with my hand on my heart, I think it is by an accident. And I know also that good work must succeed at last; but that is not the doing of the public; they are only shamed into silence or affectation. I do not write for the public; I do write for money, a nobler deity; and most of all for myself. . . . Let us tell each other sad stories of the bestiality of the beast whom we feed. What he likes is the newspaper; and to me the press is the mouth of a sewer, where lying is professed as from an university chair, and everything prurient, and ignoble, and essentially dull, finds its abode and pulpit. I do not like mankind; but men, and not all of these—and fewer women. As for respecting

the race, and, above all, that fatuous rabble of burgesses called
"the public", God save me from such irreligion!—that way lies
disgrace and dishonour. There must be something wrong in me, or
I would not be popular.'

Stevenson had indeed left youth behind, with all its trust in
human nature and all its innocent beliefs that any visible
amelioration may accrue to man in a lifetime's span; he had
reached the season of maturity that realises the isolation of the
artist.

At the New Year of 1886 he was working on the *Memoir of
Fleeming Jenkin*. At Jenkin's death on 12th June 1885, he had
written an obituary notice for the *Academy*, and he undertook
the memoir to be prefixed to a selection of Jenkin's writings.
He found it 'painful, yet very pleasant, to dig into the past of
a dead friend, and find him, at every spadeful, shine brighter'.
With deft precision of detail and discernment in selection of
the essential, the *Memoir* presents a living portrait of Jenkin
against the background of his early life, but the account of his
latter years falters, loses its way in the confusion of digression,
and finally hurries to an abrupt conclusion—perhaps because
Stevenson feared possible offence to the tender susceptibilities
of the widow and relatives, perhaps because he found his
scheme had swelled beyond the space allowed and felt the
need for condensation disproportionate with the scope of the
opening chapters. Further, there was a long interval between
the beginning and the end of the work, which had to be submitted to the widow's censorship; the first chapters were
written in the early months of 1886, but the work was resumed
and completed only after Mrs. Jenkin had visited Bournemouth
in the spring of 1887, leaving with the assurance that 'her
mind was at peace about the *Life*'.

After completing the first chapters of the *Memoir*, Stevenson
started work on *Kidnapped*. As early as March of the previous
year, having received an offer from *Young Folks* for a third
serial, he had written to Henley: 'I must go on and drudge at
Kidnapped, which I hate, and am unfit to do.' The idea of the
story came from his reading the trial of James Stewart for the

Appin murder while projecting his *History of the Highlands* at Davos, but he felt reluctant to write another tale of 'tushery' like *The Black Arrow*. Once the story took shape, his enthusiasm was roused, and he wrote to Henley:

'I have a great story on hand; boy's story; a crackler . . . As at present advised, it would be called somewhat thus: "*Kidnapped*: containing memoirs of the adventures of *David Shaw*; how he was kidnapped and cast away; his sufferings on a barren coast; his journey in the wild *Highlands*; his acquaintance with *Alan Breck Stewart* and the sons of the notorious *Rob Roy*; and all that befell him at the hands of his uncle *Ebenezer Shaw* of *Shaws* wrongly so called: written by himself"—and now I have proposed to Henderson to print from the sheets and to let the book appear when it is about half-way through.'

Thanking Theodore Watts-Dunton for an appreciation of the book in the *Athenaeum*, he related the manner of its writing: 'I began it partly as a lark, partly as a pot-boiler; and suddenly it moved, David and Alan stepped out from the canvas, and I found I was in another world.' Written with the same ease and enjoyment as *Treasure Island*, the story was finished by April, when he wrote to his father: 'I am in great spirits about David, Colvin agreeing with Henley, Fanny, and myself in thinking it far the most human of my labours hitherto.' As Colvin justly considered 'it sin and folly to throw away David and Alan Breck upon so small a field' as a *Young Folks* serial, Stevenson decided 'to leave the door open for a sequel if the public take to it', as 'this will save me from butchering a lot of good material to no purpose'.

Kidnapped appeared serially in *Young Folks* between 1st May and 31st July 1886 before publication in book form by Cassell's. Reviews were enthusiastic, and just as *Jekyll and Hyde* had been compared with Poe and Bulwer, *Kidnapped* was esteemed to be worthy of Defoe and Scott. Henley's appreciation in the August number of *Longman's Magazine* remains the most comprehensive assessment of the story:

'Mr. Stevenson's new book—which these eyes have been privileged to see in proof—is in some ways his best. The material is

inferior to that of "Treasure Island"—is not that common yet
eternal stuff of romance which counts for so much in the interest
and charm of the older story; nor have the adventures of David
Balfour that element of plot which attaches us so closely to the study
of those of Jim Hawkins and Long John. But the whole thing is full
of delightful invention, and is touched, besides, with a humanity
which I do not think that Mr. Stevenson has ever realised before.
The manner of the book is, of course, the manner of Defoe; by
which I mean that there is, as in "Robinson Crusoe", perhaps a
little too much psychology, especially the psychology of suffering.
The two heroes, Alan Breck and David, have a dreadfully hard
time of it, and their aches and pains and tribulations are, it may be,
a trifle too well realised. One thinks with a sigh of the cheerful and
gallant fancy of Dumas; of the smiling indifference to the details of
hunger and fatigue which distinguishes the experiences of Chicot
and D'Artagnan. . . . In two passages at least—the Fight in the
Round House and the Quarrel in the Heather—Mr. Stevenson has
surpassed himself in the matter of brilliant and affecting narrative—
has gone higher, indeed, than is within the flight of any of his contemporaries—and produced a couple of chapters that are *tout
bonnement* a couple of masterpieces. As for the style—a most quaint,
elegant, and delightful compromise between Scotch and English—
it recalls, with certain differences, the manner of Jedediah Cleis-
botham (of Gandercleugh), and is good enough, as it seems to us,
to take high rank and live long as a literary creation.'

In the spring of 1886 Stevenson meditated acceptance of a
commission from the American *Century Magazine* to journey by
boat down the river Rhone for a travel book to be illustrated
by W. H. Low. But Fanny opposed the plan, as 'France is so
hot and unhealthy in the summer'. So, while Fanny went to
London in April to pursue a round of social engagements,
Stevenson accompanied his father to Matlock, where he
patiently endured what he called the old man's Jekyll and
Hyde changes of mood.

With the royalties of two best-sellers, though one was only a
shilling book, he should have been well off. Fifty thousand
copies of *Jekyll and Hyde* were soon sold, and he told Symonds
that, by the end of the midsummer quarter, he had received
£350 from the shilling copies. But cautiously he informed his
father that he seemed to be 'floated financially' and hoped to

'see the year through without help'. He felt no confidence in popular favour, and less in his health; if he suffered a bad winter, he might be able to write nothing to keep his name before the public, and so again endure harassment by the demands of 'Byles the butcher'. Mistrust of his prospects was little less than three years before, when he had written to Henley from Hyères:

'Last year I pocketted £268; but it needn't be so always, and besides—well, it might do for an exceptionally chaste bachelor. But for a married man, who is sick, and has a sick wife, and a boy at school, it is scrimp.'

In June and August he stayed a few days with Colvin in London. On the second occasion he lunched or dined with Burne-Jones, Browning, and James Russell Lowell, before crossing for a short visit to Paris with Henley, who introduced him to the sculptor Rodin. After such modest travels, he returned to Bournemouth in the autumn, eager to resume his attempts to play the piano, a new amusement shared with his stepson. Her sister relates that music was 'as a closed book' to Fanny; 'she could not sing a note nor hardly tell one tune from another'. Soon she recorded her disapproval to Colvin:

'I am afraid the piano is *not* good for him. In the morning he gets up feeling very well indeed, and at about ten sits to the piano where he stays till three or after, drinking his coffee, even, at the instrument. At three or thereabouts he breaks down altogether, gets very white and is extremely wretched with exhaustion until the next morning again."

On another occasion she complained that 'Louis is much too tired through having like an idiot obeyed the doctor's orders to take exercise', and her troubles were increased by her son, who 'takes one cold after another'. Knowing that Colvin was the recipient of his wife's confidences about his health, Stevenson now tended to make light of his ailments in writing to him; in December he reported: 'Fanny is pretty peepy; I am splendid.' Writing at the New Year to Henry James, he allowed James, whom Fanny liked, a glimpse of his marital relations which he would have scrupled to confide to Henley:

'My wife is peepy and dowie. . . . She is a woman (as you know) not without art: the art of extracting the gloom of the eclipse from sunshine; and she has recently laboured in this field not without success or (as we used to say) not without a blessing. It is strange: "we fell out my wife and I" the other night; she tackled me savagely for being a canary-bird; I replied (bleatingly) protesting that there was no use in turning life into King Lear; presently it was discovered that there were two dead combatants upon the field, each slain by the arrow of the truth, and we tenderly carried off each other's corpses. Here is a little comedy for Henry James to write! the beauty was each thought the other quite unscathed at first, but we had dealt shrewd stabs.'

His parents took a furnished house at Bournemouth for the winter, and Stevenson devoted much of his time to his father. The old man was 'very changeable; at times, he seems only a slow quiet edition of himself; again, he will be very heavy and blank; but never so violent as last spring; and therefore, to my mind, better on the whole'. Since finishing *Kidnapped*, Stevenson had written little; probably he felt that, having achieved two such successes as *Jekyll and Hyde* and *Kidnapped* in the space of a few months, he could afford a spell of leisure, and he knew that his father's lease of life was limited. But Fanny disapproved of his idleness. 'Louis fancies that he feels some stirring of the intellect,' she wrote to Colvin during the winter; 'I hope he does, for it was growing alarming. I began to fear he would never work again.'

During these months his only work of fiction was *The Misadventures of John Nicholson*, 'a silly Xmas story (with some larks in it)'. 'I don't love it,' he told Colvin, 'but some of it is passable in its mouldy way.' Failing to finish it for the Christmas of 1886, he allowed it to drift, and the story eventually appeared in *Yule-Tide*, a Christmas annual published by Cassell's in December 1887. Daily association with his father induced thoughts of the past, and he wrote his reminiscences of Colinton in 'The Manse', published in *Scribner's Magazine* of May 1887, and his study of the Swanston shepherd called

'Pastoral' for *Longman's Magazine* of April. Both these essays were included in *Memories and Portraits*, the volume of essays which he now began to prepare for publication by Chatto and Windus in the following autumn. *The Merry Men, and Other Tales and Fables* was published by Chatto and Windus early in the New Year of 1887, and he was also preparing for the press his volume of poems, *Underwoods*.

The principal cause of his distraction from creative work was a concern with politics. Since everything he now wrote commanded the attention of an extensive audience, his ever-wakeful conscience urged employment of his influence in the interests of humanity. For politicians and the press he felt an impatient contempt comparable with Landor's; he was continually excited to furious indignation by the soulless sacrifice of principle to expediency by the one, by the vicious stupidity and vapid sensationalism of the other. After Majuba he had written his 'Protest on Behalf of Boer Independence', suppressed because Fanny feared that expression of unpopular views might impede the growth of his literary reputation. Deeply moved by the betrayal of General Gordon at Khartoum, he wrote: 'When I read at Nice that Graham was recalled from Suakim after all that butchery, I died to politics.' Some months later, he told Henley:

'The men that have killed me are Gladstone and Co. I retire, I repeat, from Public life . . . I wish Oliver Cromwell were alive, or even my wooden-Iron Duke. Is it not sad that we have nobody? . . . Is that little Spitfire, penny-paper pea-shooter Lord Randolph to be the—the hope of the Conservatives? Eh, God. Forster is the only man I take any interest in, in England; and I dimly perceive him to be a man of an intricate, cast-iron conscience, which will negative his good.'

In November 1885 an Irishman named Curtin had been shot by terrorists at his farm in Kerry; because one of the assassins had been killed by the resolute defenders of the house, the terrorists ordered a boycott of the Curtin family, which was cut off from all tradesmen's supplies. Enraged by the government's failure to take action for redress of this victimisation, Stevenson determined to force authority's hand by a quixotic gesture; he proposed to go, with his wife and stepson, and make their home in the Curtins' house. Not unnaturally, Fanny vigorously protested, and invoked the support of all their friends, but Stevenson continued to pursue the project for several months, till his father's death presented other plans.

His only political utterance to elude the vigilance of Fanny was an essay in the *Contemporary Review* of April 1887, 'The Day After To-morrow', in which he forecast the future of socialism in England with an accuracy confounding the critics who deny his claims to profundity of thought. Writing five years before Keir Hardie became the first Labour member of Parliament, he regarded the progress to socialism as so inevitable that, 'if Mr. Hyndman were a man of keen humour, which is far from my conception of his character, he might rest from his troubling and look on: the walls of Jericho begin already to crumble and dissolve'. He showed how, 'piece by piece, each acting against his neighbour, each sawing away the branch on which some other interest is seated, do we apply in detail our Socialistic remedies, and yet not perceive that we are all labouring together to bring in Socialism at large'. He saw democracy as a plant inadequately rooted to withstand the blast of its accumulating responsibilities:

'Decay appears to have seized on the organ of popular government in every land; and this just at the moment when we begin to bring to it, as to an oracle of justice, the whole skein of our private affairs to be unravelled, and ask it, like a new Messiah, to take upon itself our frailties and play for us the part that should be played by our own virtues.'

He saw the golden age of socialism as 'the golden age of officials'— 'in all our concerns it will be their beloved duty to meddle, with what tact, with what obliging words, analogy will aid us to imagine'. Man would not long rest content with the benefits of 'regular meals and weatherproof lodgings'; as soon as bread became amply supplied, 'the cry for circuses will be the louder'. And while 'in the sovereign commune all will be centralised and sensitive', the 'communes will not be all equal in extent, nor in quality of soil, nor in growth of population; nor will the surplus produce of all be equally marketable'. The inevitable consequence seemed to Stevenson 'the New-Old with a vengeance, and irresistibly suggests the growth of military powers and the foundation of new empires'.

If Stevenson had remained resident in England, he might have been tempted to more such expressions of thought as 'The Day After To-morrow'. But, just as he was finishing the *Memoir of Fleeming Jenkin*, came serious news of his father, who had left Bournemouth for Edinburgh a few weeks before. With Fanny he travelled to Edinburgh on 6th May; on the 8th, Thomas Stevenson died. The first shock of grief was followed by a feeling of relief. 'If we could have had my father, that would have been a different thing,' wrote Stevenson to Colvin, 'but to keep that changeling—suffering changeling—any longer, could better none and nothing.'

Fanny was delighted with the advice and consideration of Stevenson's uncle, Dr. Balfour. 'All this old pretending that Louis was only nerves and not ill is at an end,' she informed Colvin; 'though Louis may have ups and downs he can never really be better, and will always have hæmorrhages more or less bad according to the care he takes of himself.' Dr. Balfour was also diplomatic about Fanny's ailments: she 'had had wrong treatment from all the doctors' but one, and if she had followed that one prescription, she 'should now be much better'; 'as it is, he says the thing has not progressed so far but that I may be quite cured in time, though,' she added complacently, 'it may be several years.' One of the doctors had prescribed for her the waters of Aix, but Dr. Balfour assured her that Aix was not 'very important for me', for, while 'it might do some good', 'at the same time it might do harm unless the doctor there understood the case thoroughly'.

As Aix was unnecessary to her health, Fanny's thoughts turned westward; it was now seven years since she had left America. Soon after their return from Edinburgh to Bournemouth in June, she wrote to Colvin: 'Mrs. Stevenson will this year get some money from the business, so she proposes to stand all the expense she can of a winter in Colorado.' When Symonds spent a day with them at Bournemouth in July, he found the Stevensons preparing for departure—Stevenson, his mother, Fanny, Lloyd Osbourne, and two servants. Edmund Gosse saw Stevenson for the last time at a Finsbury Hotel on Sunday 21st August 1887, the day before he sailed from Tilbury. As he watched the tall, thin figure leaning over the boat's rail in waving farewell, the faithful Colvin thought their parting was only for the winter, but it was his last sight of Stevenson, and Stevenson's last of England.

CHAPTER EIGHT

SARANAC AND SAMOA

'I'm a man of the world still, and I made my mission pay. No good ever came of coddling. A man has to stand up in God's sight and work up to his weight avoirdupois'.—Attwater in *The Ebb-Tide*.

As WITH Thackeray, Reade, and other Victorian novelists, Stevenson's work had received more rapid and generous appreciation in America than in England, though the absence of an international copyright agreement, despite Reade's persistent crusade for a quarter of a century, allowed American popularity to present no profit to English writers. *Kidnapped* had just appeared in New York, pirated editions of *Jekyll and Hyde* were selling in thousands, and Stevenson was greeted on landing as a celebrity. He was amused by 'the poor interviewer lads', who were 'no more vulgar in their reports than they could help'; but 'Lord, what a silly thing is popularity'! he exclaimed, regretting 'the cool obscurity of Skerryvore'. His health had benefited from the sea voyage, but, having 'nearly died of interviewers and visitors, during twenty-four hours of New York', he caught a cold, decided 'fog is not for me', and leaving New York to stay at Newport with some admirers, Mr. and Mrs. Charles Fairchild, he spent the whole of his visit in bed.

At Newport he decided that, as the cold of Colorado might prove 'too rigorous', and anyhow he 'could not risk the long railway voyage', the winter should be spent on Saranac Lake, in the Adirondacks. Returning to New York in late September, he sat to the sculptor, Augustus St. Gaudens, for a medallion in bronze, and interviewed editors more generous than their London compeers. From the *New York World* he refused an offer of two thousand pounds a year for a weekly article, as his health was unlikely to permit work of such regularity;

though he accepted an offer of seven hundred pounds from *Scribner's Magazine* for twelve monthly articles, he confided to Henley his fear that 'the slavery may overweigh me'. With S. S. McClure he signed a contract by which he was to receive £1,600 (eight thousand dollars) for the serial rights of his next novel—an agreement he regretted within a fortnight, when he discovered that he had already committed himself to Scribner's. For years he had been accustomed to leave in Henley's hands all transactions with publishers and editors; now he could only plead that 'I have no memory', citing as an example how he had 'omitted to reserve the American rights in *Jekyll*'. As Scribner's held to their bargain, McClure, the prototype of Pinkerton in *The Wrecker*, gracefully waived his claim, profiting thereby in receiving from Stevenson such writings as fell outside the scope of his agreement with Scribner's.

Though he had written little for a year, his name was before the public in England by the appearance of his second volume of verse, *Underwoods*, his *Memories and Portraits*, the book of stories called *The Merry Men*, and a new edition of *Virginibus Puerisque*. Of the stories in *The Merry Men*, Andrew Lang declared *Thrawn Janet* to be 'written in the best Scotch since the pen fell from the hand of the author of *Wandering Willie's Tale*', *Markheim* 'as good as Hawthorne', and *The Merry Men* worthy of Hawthorne 'if he had been a kindly Scot'. *Underwoods* afforded an opportunity for Gosse to write of 'Mr. R. L. Stevenson as a Poet'; since *A Child's Garden of Verses* was followed by such 'an easy book to appreciate and enjoy' as *Underwoods*, Stevenson claimed consideration as a poet and 'a candidate for the bays'. He hesitated 'to decide whether or no Mr. R. L. Stevenson's poems will be read in the future', but he found them 'so full of character, so redolent of his own fascinating temperament, that it is not too wild to suppose that so long as his prose is appreciated those who love that will turn to this'. Though Gosse could not quarrel with a rising reputation, neither could he forget a slight offence; feline irony lurks in almost every paragraph of his article, as Stevenson perceived, for he wrote a letter of banter to Gosse, saying: 'I do not believe you ever wrote anything so funny.'

At Saranac he settled to writing the series of essays for

Scribner's.[1] He felt that some of them bore 'many traces of effort', with 'the ungenuine inspiration of an income at so much per essay, and the honest desire of the incomer to give good measure for his money'. He thought 'The Lantern-Bearers' 'was a good paper, really contained some excellent sense, and was ingeniously put together', and his 'Darwinian sermon', 'Pulvis et Umbra', was 'pulled off after a fashion'.

In health he felt 'decidedly better'. To Symonds he wrote that, as at Davos, 'my wife again suffers in high and cold places; I again profit'—a statement which, supported by the experiences of such sufferers as Symonds and Llewelyn Powys, suggests that he might have been spared his illnesses at Hyères and Bournemouth if he had persevered with winters at Davos. While Fanny departed to New York 'for a change', Stevenson continued his labours, and Lloyd Osbourne 'pattered' on his typewriter the first draft of 'a humorous romance', in the manner of *New Arabian Nights*, called *The Finsbury Tontine*, which Stevenson described to Henley as 'quite incredibly silly'—'the adventures of Charles Baxter and a drawing master, as they dispose of a dead body, are quite killing: Charles really high old fun.'

Writing to Colvin on Christmas Eve, he announced that he had 'fallen head over heels into a new tale, *The Master of Ballantrae*'.

'No thought have I now apart from it, and I have got along up to page ninety-two of the draft with great interest. It is to me a most seizing tale; there are some fantastic elements; the most is a dead genuine human problem—human tragedy, I should say rather. It will be about as long, I imagine, as *Kidnapped*.'

In a note on 'The Genesis of "The Master of Ballantrae"', written three years later at the request of E. L. Burlingame, the editor of *Scribner's*, Stevenson described how he conceived

---

[1] The essays appeared in the following order in twelve successive numbers of *Scribner's Magazine* between January and December 1888; 'A Chapter on Dreams', 'The Lantern-Bearers', 'Beggars', 'Pulvis et Umbra', 'Gentlemen', 'Some Gentlemen in Fiction', 'Popular Authors', 'Epilogue to *An Inland Voyage*', 'Letter to a Young Gentleman who Proposes to Embrace the Career of Art', 'Contributions to the History of Fife: Random Memories', 'The Education of an Engineer: More Random Memories', and 'A Christmas Sermon'.

the idea of the story, with the scene shifting between Scotland, India, and America, as he 'was walking one night in the verandah of a small house in which I lived, outside the hamlet of Saranac . . . a fine frosty night, with no wind and the thermometer below zero'. At first he worked with the same ease and enthusiasm as at *Treasure Island* and *Kidnapped*, but, after finishing the first four serial numbers, he had to lay it aside, 'as I was quite worked out'. He was well in health; Fanny had reported in December that 'Louis has not, since he left England, brought up one drop of blood from his lungs'. Fanny herself caused the pause in his work. From a visit to New York she returned to Saranac in February 'pretty ill'; while she kept her bed, the maid also fell ill, and Stevenson had to share with Lloyd the domestic duties of washing dishes, cleaning the kitchen, and preparing meals. To Colvin he wrote a letter 'interrupted days ago by household labours', relating that, since its beginning, 'I have had and (I tremble to write it, but it does seem as if I had) beaten off an influenza'.

In this mood of exhaustion and discomfort he received a letter from Henley, which caused the final rupture of their friendship. Some years before, Bob Stevenson's sister, Katherine de Mattos (to whom Stevenson dedicated *Jekyll and Hyde*) had written a story, which Henley offered vainly to editors and publishers. Fanny read the story, suggested that it might be improved by making the heroine a 'nixie' or water-sprite, and asked, if Katherine's story failed to achieve publication, to be allowed to try her version. Katherine complied with the request, though so reluctantly that Stevenson asked Fanny 'to go no further'. But Fanny 'had taken a fancy to the idea', and 'nothing would serve her but to act on the unwilling consent'. She wrote her version of the story and, as the joint-author of *The Dynamiter*, succeeded in placing it with a magazine, where it was seen by Henley 'with considerable amazement'.

'It's Katherine's; surely it's Katherine's? The situation, the environment, the principal figure—*voyons*! There are even reminiscences of phrase and imagery, parallel incident—*que sais-je*? It is all better focused, no doubt; but I think it has lost as much (at least) as it has gained; and why there wasn't a double signature is what I've not been able to understand.'

On Fanny, ill in bed and accustomed to making the most of her indispositions, the effect of this letter may be imagined. Ever since her marriage, antagonism between her and Henley had mounted in steadily threatening crescendo. With increasing irritation she resented the continuance of the arrangement between her husband and Henley, by which each drew upon the funds of the other as necessity demanded; such a situation may have seemed to her both picturesque and proper in a Bohemian bachelor, but, with Stevenson driving himself to meet the demands of 'Byles the butcher', she did not conceal the asperity of her attitude towards Henley's borrowings. She forgot that for years Henley had acted for Stevenson as unpaid literary agent; she forgot such occasions of opportune repayments as 'that hundred quid' on their departure to Davos in the autumn of 1881. For Stevenson's collapse at Nice in the new year of 1884, she blamed Henley as the inspiration of Stevenson's recklessness, and had ever since regarded Henley's boisterous ebullience, exciting such infectious high spirits as delighted her son Lloyd, as 'bad for Louis'. On their return to Skerryvore after Stevenson's hæmorrhage at Exeter, she wrote uncompromisingly to Mrs. Sitwell: 'Henley must not come to him now with either work or business unless he wishes to kill him.'

On his side, Henley regarded Fanny as an unfortunate encumbrance—the inevitable legacy of an irrevocable indiscretion by Stevenson. His own wife, gentle and self-effacing, confined her dominion to the duties of housewifery, encouraging rather than seeking to curb the inclinations of his temperament. With impatience he witnessed, as an impertinence, Fanny's proprietary manner of managing her husband. Measuring her literary pretensions at their obvious worth, he felt a strain upon his fund of tact and politeness in tolerating her presumption when offering counsel and criticism concerning Stevenson's work; memory of Stevenson's activity before marriage suggested that Fanny was inflicting her own hypochondriacal habits upon her husband in insisting on his regimen as an invalid.

His background afforded little experience of the refinements and subtleties of delicate sensibility, and he was accustomed to frank and free expression of opinion with his friend; he readily supplied grounds of provocation upon which Fanny was not slow to seize, and feeling himself attacked, he retorted with such criticism of Fanny as Stevenson could not in loyalty allow to pass unchallenged.

In consequence, during the previous winter, a coolness had developed between them; after explanations on both sides, Stevenson considered that a reconciliation had been effected. But Henley felt an absence of the old affectionate confidence; after reference to the Nixie story and some remarks about his brother Edward's theatrical tour with *Deacon Brodie*, his letter proceeded to describe his feeling of dejection and need of friendship.

'Why the devil do you go and bury yourself in that bloody country of dollars and spew? And you don't even get better. . . . However, I suppose you must be forgiven, for you have loved me much. Let us go on so till the end. You and I and Charles— D'A., and Porthos, and Aramis. 'Twas a blessed hour for all of us, that day 13 years syne, when old Stephen brought you into my back-kitchen, wasn't it?'

'Don't show this to ANYBODY,' he asked, and repeated, '*burn this letter*'.

'Anybody' obviously meant Fanny; if Stevenson refrained from showing her the letter, he communicated the gist of the paragraph about the Nixie story, and Fanny's fury sent him smarting to his writing-table.

'I write with indescribable difficulty; and if not with perfect temper, you are to remember how very rarely a husband is expected to receive such accusations against his wife. I can only direct you to apply to Katherine and ask her to remind you of that part of the business which took place in your presence and which you seem to have forgotten. . . . When you have refreshed your mind as to the facts, you will, I know, withdraw what you have said to me; but I must go further and remind you, if you have spoken of this to others, a proper explanation and retraction of what you shall have said or implied to any person so addressed will be necessary.'

With more in the same strain, he added, 'To have inflicted more distress than you have done would have been difficult', and, concluding, 'You will pardon me if I can find no form of signature; I pray God such a blank will not be of long endurance', he signed simply, 'Robert Louis Stevenson'.[1]

Unluckily, in his dismay on receiving such a seemingly implacable ultimatum, Henley omitted to reply immediately, probably because he wished first to consult Charles Baxter and Katherine de Mattos. When, therefore, Stevenson received from Henley's assistant editor a formal inquiry about an article on Rodin which he was to write for the *Art Journal*, he concluded that Henley, mortally incensed, had decided on the dignity of silence. Tortured in conscience at having been forced into a false position by Fanny, he wrote immediately to Henley: 'I am sorry you took so strong a step, and that you cannot write to me yourself upon a point of business'; having dealt with the matter of the article, he concluded:

'I will say no more on any other matter; indeed I now somewhat regret my last; for if you feel so much disinclined to write, it is perhaps better for you to let it alone. On all this, judge for the best; and believe me still and always, if I never saw your face again, —Yours affectionately, Robert Louis Stevenson.'

Without retracting the position assumed under the prick of Fanny's spur, this letter was a gesture towards reconciliation, hinting as plainly as he dared that the previous letter had been written to appease Fanny, that his own affection for Henley was unchanged, and that he desired an apology only to satisfy Fanny.

Seeking to leave Henley in no doubt of his intended message, he wrote on 23rd March to Charles Baxter, as the only friend of stature sufficient to mediate between himself and Henley:

'In the melancholy that falls upon me, I must break out at least upon paper. I fear I have come to an end with Henley; the Lord knows if I have not tried to be a friend to him, the Lord knows even that I have not altogether failed.'

[1] Copious extracts from the correspondence appear in Mr. John Connell's *W. E. Henley*, London, 1949, but the presentation of Stevenson's undated letters to Baxter as 'consequential' to Henley's letter of 7th May produces an effect prejudicial to a sympathetic understanding of Stevenson's conduct.

Conscience, as usual, demanded self-justification: there was 'not one of that crew . . . in Shepherd's Bush'—meaning, besides Henley, Bob Stevenson and his wife, and Katherine de Mattos, who all lived as near neighbours—whom he had not striven sincerely to help; 'since I left (I could not say it to them —I say it to you) I think not one of them has had anything but money from me'; he referred to the plays, 'which I have gone on writing without hope, because I thought they kept him up' —'I can say he never knew—and never shall know—that I thought these days and months a sacrifice'. 'To get an acknowledgment of the way in which the facts really are is my first purpose,' he stated, 'and whatever you do, pray do nothing that may compromise any hope of getting this.' Having thus written to secure Baxter's intercession, he tortured himself with the notion that Baxter, instead of interceding, might take Henley's side, and he wrote next day to emphasise his reasons for appealing to Baxter:

'I must keep all this from Colvin. Because if Colvin knew he would probably have no more to do with Henley, and that is the last thing I wish. . . . I confess I am glad I wrote you yesterday, and am glad I sent the letter. It has been a huge relief to me; and if it has been pain to you, you must try to forgive me. . . . I feel shame to write "Yours affectionately" to you; it was so I used to sign to Henley, and the dreadful part of a thing like this is that it strikes your confidence in all affection and inspires you with a strange, sick longing to creep back into yourself and care for no one. For all that, I do care for you; and I do care for Henley, too; and all his fine spirit and courage and geniality and loyalty—though to me, of these late days, he has not been loyal—and his rich temperament which was a fund of pleasure to me.'

Then came a letter from Katherine de Mattos, to whom Henley had conveyed news of the complaint:

"As Mr. Henley's very natural but unfortunate letter was written without my wish or knowledge, I have refused to let him go further in the matter. He had a perfect right to be astonished but his having said so has nothing to do with me. If Fanny thinks she has a right to the idea of the story I am far from wishing to reclaim or to

criticise her in any way. . . . It is of course very unfortunate that
my story was written first and read by people and if they express
their astonishment it is a natural consequence and no fault of mine
or any one else. . . . I trust this matter is not making you feel as ill
as all of us.'

This letter made Stevenson 'utterly miserable', since it convicted Fanny and left no room for hope that Henley would save
her face by an apology. To Baxter he once more recapitulated
the circumstances, before accusing Katherine of having
prompted Henley's protest:

'I need not remark how very small a degree of kindness it had
required—supposing me ever in the wrong—to have said nothing of
so small a matter; nor how very little an amount of tact would have
enabled them to understand how much pain they would give. . . .
I feel this business with a keenness that I cannot describe; I get on
during the day well enough; only that whenever I think of it, I have
palpitations. But at night! sleep is quite out of the question; and I
have been obliged to take to opiates. God knows I would rather
have died than have this happen. I am going to write of it no more;
if I get a satisfactory answer—how can it be one?—good and well.
If not, I will simply communicate no more with either; and we must
make some arrangement about an allowance to Henley. I cannot
let the old boy quite go from me. . . . Pray pardon my pouring
out to you. As I have said already you are the only one to whom I
can unbosom. . . . Events keep me quite apart from Simpson; of
all my friends you and Colvin are the only ones that remain.'

Five days later, on 10th April, he wrote again to Baxter, telling
how he had 'lain awake night after night suffering to think of
Henley receiving' his letter, of 'the hash it might make' of the
essay he was writing on Dumas, of 'how it would dash the
pleasure of his verses'. He enclosed a codicil to his will, for,
in view of Fanny's hostility to Henley, he realised 'there may
be war among my heirs'; he felt 'troubled' that Henley was
not mentioned in his will, 'yet I could only leave him a legacy,
which he would throw into the sea at once', and he had already
asked Baxter to devise a means of making Henley an allowance,
which might appear to come from some such patron as Hamil-
ton Bruce, one of the financial backers of *London*, 'or—anybody
but me'.

Baxter did his utmost to reconcile the matter, and having heard from him, Stevenson wrote on 20th April:

'God bless you for your letter; it is impossible to write more kindly to both W.E.H. and me; and God knows I wish I could just write and say I have forgot it all. I will enclose you a copy of Katherine's letter. . . . Suppose that I am insane and have dreamed all that I seem to remember, and that my wife has shamefully stolen a story from my cousin, was this the class of matter that a friend would write to me? God knows, if I heard ill of Henley's wife, I should bottle it up in my heart from him, not write it to him in the midst of fulsome protestations of love. . . . But does one friend write to another accusations against his wife? And such an accusation—a theft of money and of reputation? Either my wife is innocent, and then I suppose even my enemy would hold his peace, or she is guilty, and then, O surely almost my enemy would try to hide it from me! If this be friendship, I am not robust enough to bear it. If it be want of tact, it is strangely like want of heart. . . . You speak of his nerves; the thought of that has been heavy on me; if I knew my soul at all, I would have done anything to have delayed this trouble till his book was out. But friendship—which I am sure he has had for me in his hours, and most sincerely too—friendship has surely some obligation of ordinary kindness; it is not a covert from behind which a man is to fill you with injuries and reproaches and escape safe himself. . . . He has not sent me a word. And whether this be good or evil, I know not. . . . Henley may so write that I shall feel able to pass it over, I do not know; but I shall insist at least that I am to be no longer a pin cushion for his outrageous arrows, but shall be written to, if I am written to at all, with some ordinary consideration for my feelings. It is of course quite true that Katherine's attitude absolves him of three parts of what I had against him, but the fourth part that remains—that willingness to seethe up against me and mine in my absence and that heartless willingness to wound me—was it seems the fact that I most keenly felt. . . . O, a little kindness will go far—and yours was much, my beloved friend. And what you say of him is all true. I know his merits, damn him! The trouble is, he deceives himself; he does not love me any more. It is only a habit with him now to be my friend; it has long been divorced from any regard to my feelings.'[1]

[1] Another letter to Baxter, of 12th April, relates: 'Last winter I was disagreeably affected to remember that a number of works in my hand were in Henley's possession, that he might die any day, and these highly unprofitable exercises might fall into the hands of his brothers. Thereupon I wrote to Henley

After this letter to Baxter, he received from Henley a letter dated 11th April, pointing out that the offending letter from his assistant editor had been written in the course of office routine, and actually before Henley had received Stevenson's complaint. To the complaint Henley referred only obliquely:

'I want this to go tonight, so I will only say again, forgive me, and have faith in me yet. I am not ungrateful nor disloyal. Surely you should have known that much of me by now? And the old affection, the old kinship, the old affinity (*enfin!*) is as living and dear as ever.'

Henley waited nearly another month for Baxter to come from Edinburgh to London. Whatever Baxter advised, Henley could not be persuaded to offer an apology that would be satisfactory to Fanny. He wrote to Stevenson on 7th May:

'My dear Lad,—Your letter is heart-breaking; and I do not know how to reply to it, for it convicts me (I now see) of a piece of real unkindness, unworthy of myself and our old true friendship. You may blame me in the bitterest terms you will for the cruel blunder I made in opening my mind to you; and I shall not complain, for I deserve them all. I should, I know now, have said nothing; and I shall never cease from regretting that I gave you this useless, this unnecessary pain.

'You must not believe, though, that I struck to hurt. I did not, I thought the matter one of little consequence. It seemed right that you should know how it looked to myself. . . . It was surely as well (I reasoned) that you should hear of certain coincidences from me as from another quarter. . . .'

So it went on, generous, affectionate, confessing fault and asking forgiveness, but still asserting the 'coincidences' and without a mention of Fanny's name, much less of any apology satisfactory to her. Stevenson sent the letter to Baxter, with a pencilled endorsement:

(it was in the worst of our estrangement) asking him to destroy them, and explaining it was partly in Lloyd's interest. I am sorry to say he paid no regard to my request.' Asking Baxter to 'find out if they are destroyed; and if they are not, see that they are', he explained further: 'It occurs to me that you may be puzzled (knowing my opinions) at my eagerness about having the verses destroyed. One word will explain it: the lad has had scandals enough about his own father, it would be too bad if there followed one about me.'

'His original position carefully saved throughout; and yet (1) I gave him my word as to certain matters of fact; (2) and yet the letter (in consequence of this) can never be shewn to my wife; (3) and yet, even if he still thinks as he did, I think a kind spirit would have even lied. R.L.S.'

As he had hinted as plainly as possible, he wanted a lie—to save Fanny's face, to save his own face with Fanny. A man more subtle and less sincere than Henley might have lied. As it was, Stevenson had to choose between his wife and his friend. To Baxter, describing his 'frame of mind' as 'hardly human', he wrote: 'The bottom wish of my heart is that I had died at Hyères; the happy part of my life ended there; since then I have never been well enough really to enjoy life except for a day or two at a time; and I fear that my character has suffered; and I know that troubles have grown upon me.'

The part played by Fanny in his life, carefully concealed by Colvin and Balfour, emerges in the ruin of his friendship with Henley. The Bohemian, who had condemned respectability in *Lay Morals*, now wore the burden of respectability's yoke. When Sargent painted his portrait of Stevenson in December 1884, he still saw predominant the lineaments of Hyde—the quick, humorous glance, the quizzical smile, an almost elfin sense of lively alertness; in the St. Gaudens medallion of three years later, of Hyde there is no trace—the demeanour is that of Jekyll, with a head of nobility and dignity, brow and eyes speaking sombre reflection, a jaw-line almost aggressive in grim endurance. In the portrait to be painted by Count Nerli at Samoa in 1892, the face is that of the St. Gaudens medallion grown painfully older, of a man haunted and driven, haggard, stricken, lashed by tragedy, with a look wary, yet weary with a hunted hopelessness, in the eyes. Hyde was now allowed no outlet; Jekyll survived alone by necessity, with no means of escape into his other self.

Risen from her bed of sickness, Fanny departed to visit her relatives in San Francisco, while Stevenson and his stepson, after a fortnight in New York, went at the beginning of May 1888 to the seaside resort of Manasquan in New Jersey. Writing to Fanny of his decision in regard to Henley 'simply to let "silence be the rest"', Stevenson felt 'that this is a dreadful misery, and I am surprised if any good comes of it', and 'I envy you flaming people who rage up so easily with hate; the days go, and this is the more dreadful to me'. Unable to work on *The Master of Ballantrae*, he struggled with two of the essays for *Scribner's* and began re-writing Lloyd's story of *The Finsbury Tontine*, of which he reported to Miss Ferrier, 'the lad wrote a tale this winter, which appeared to me so funny that I have taken it in hand, and some of these days you will receive a copy of a work entitled "*A Game of Bluff*, by Lloyd Osbourne and Robert Louis Stevenson"'.

From the sea voyage across the Atlantic he had derived such benefit that, to his cousin Bob, he had written of his idea of chartering a yacht, in which he would return to England by way of the West Indies, and then 'take a run to Havre, and try the Baltic, or somewhere'. Having no mind to be ship-mates with any of 'the Shepherd's Bush crew', Fanny wrote from San Francisco that a yacht named the *Casco* was available for a Pacific voyage. Thomas Stevenson's fortune of some twenty-six thousand pounds was left to his widow for life, but there was a bequest of three thousand pounds to Stevenson, who now wrote to Baxter for two-thirds of this patrimony. He intended 'going the full pitch for seven months' in the hope that he might 'get my health back (more or less)'; 'if this business fails to set me up, well, £2,000 is gone, and I know I can't get better'.

Early in June, once more he made the journey from New York to San Francisco, this time travelling *de luxe* instead of in an emigrant train; at the end of the month he sailed for the Marquesas. He enjoyed the life on the yacht, and on arrival at the islands, delighted as much in the character of the natives as in the climate and the surroundings. Every day he made copious notes for a travel book to be called *The Cruise of the Silver Ship*; it eventually appeared serially in *Black and White* as *The South Seas* between 6th February and 19th December 1891, but was published in book form only after his death. 'I did not dream there were such places or such races,' he wrote to Colvin in a letter signed exultantly 'The Old Man Virulent':

'My health has stood me splendidly; I am in for hours wading over the knees for shells; I have been five hours on horseback: I have been pretty near all night waiting to see where the *Casco* would go ashore, and with my diary all ready—simply the most entertaining night of my life. Withal I still have colds; I have one now, and feel pretty sick too; but not as at home: instead of being in bed, for instance, I am at this moment sitting snuffling and writing in an undershirt and trousers; and as for colour, hands, arms, feet, legs, and face, I am browner than the berry; only my trunk and the aristocratic spot on which I sit retain the vile whiteness of the north.'

Since its serial course in *Scribner's* began in November, the need for finishing *The Master of Ballantrae* became pressing, and for two months before Christmas the party remained on shore at Tahiti while Stevenson worked. Here he 'almost finished *The Master of Ballantrae*, which contains more human work than anything of mine but *Kidnapped*', and wrote most of the ballad called 'The Song of Rahéro'. On Christmas Day, they sailed from Tahiti for Honolulu, through 'thirty days of calms and squalls, a deplorable passage'. 'My wife is no great shakes,' wrote Stevenson to Baxter; 'she is the one who has suffered most.' His mother was having 'a Huge Old Time; Lloyd is first chop; I so well that I do not know myself—sea-bathing, if you please, and what is far more dangerous, entertaining and being entertained by His Majesty here, who is a very fine intelligent fellow, but O, Charles! what a crop for the drink!' Fanny wrote to Mrs. Sitwell: 'I hate the sea and am afraid of it . . . but I love the tropic weather and the wild people, and to see my two boys so happy.' As she had disliked the cold of the mountains at Saranac as much as at Davos, she was delighted to have reason for stating: 'It has been a mistake about the cold places, warmth and hot sun is what he needs.' She had another reason for emphasising the benefits of a tropical climate, accounting also for the decision to voyage in the Pacific instead of in the Atlantic, as Stevenson had first suggested: her daughter Belle was living with her husband at Honolulu, and when the Stevensons left after a stay of five months, she and her small son, Austin Strong, accompanied them.

In January 1889 Stevenson reported from Honolulu to

Scribner's that, 'as soon as I am through with *The Master*, I shall finish *The Game of Bluff*—now rechristened *The Wrong Box*', which he wished to sell 'cash down'. But *The Wrong Box* was finished before *The Master of Ballantrae*. On 8th March he told Baxter, 'Lloyd and I have finished a story, *The Wrong Box*', which was so 'funny' that he had 'split over writing it'. More than a month later he was 'quite worked out, and this cursed end of *The Master* hangs over me like the arm of the gallows'. For his difficulty, he blamed Burlingame, the editor of *Scribner's*, for imposing a sense of urgency by beginning the serial publication before the story was completed; he blamed also the climate of Honolulu. 'Even here in Honolulu I have withered in the cold,' he wrote to Henry James, and the experience inspired the decision that 'I am not coming home for another year', as 'I have had more fun and pleasure of my life these past months than ever before, and more health than any time in ten long years'. Not till the middle of May was he able to announce: 'I have at length finished *The Master*; it has been a sore cross to me; but now he is buried, his body's under hatches,—his soul, if there is any hell to go to, gone to hell; and I forgive him: it is harder to forgive Burlingame for having induced me to begin the publication, or myself for suffering the induction.'

Stevenson had reason to doubt the quality of the conclusion in *The Master of Ballantrae*, of which he had written to Henry James after beginning the novel over a year before:

'Five parts of it are sound, human tragedy; the last one or two, I regret to say, not so soundly designed; I almost hesitate to write them; they are very picturesque, but they are fantastic; they shame, perhaps degrade, the beginning. I wish I knew; that was how the tale came to me however. . . . The older brother goes out in the '45, the younger stays; the younger, of course, gets the title and estate and marries the bride designate of the elder—a family match, but he (the younger) had always loved her, and she had really loved the elder. Do you see the situation? Then the devil and Saranac suggested this *dénouement*, and I joined the two ends in a day or two of constant feverish thought, and began to write. And now—I wonder if I have not gone too far with the fantastic? The elder brother is an INCUBUS: supposed to be killed at Culloden, he turns up again and bleeds the family of money; on that stopping he comes and lives with them, whence flows the real tragedy, the nocturnal duel of the brothers (very naturally, and indeed, I think, inevitably arising), and second supposed death of the elder. Husband and wife now really make up, and then the cloven hoof appears. For the third supposed death and the manner of the third reappearance is steep; steep, sir. It is even very steep, and I fear it shames the honest stuff so far; but then it is highly pictorial, and it leads up to the death of the elder brother at the hands of the younger in a perfectly cold-blooded murder, of which I wish (and mean) the reader to approve.'

Two-thirds of the story sustain the breathless interest of *Kidnapped*, charged with a deeper emotion; there is a pervading sense of fatality and foreboding, a consciousness of impending tragedy, gathering impressiveness from the finely wrought atmosphere of fateful gloom. But, with the entrance of the Indian, Secundra Dass, the illusion becomes unconvincing, as by an intrusion of the incompatible; a straining for effect supervenes, and the story is forced to a climax of disappointing bathos. In his reviews, Andrew Lang tempered enthusiasm only with the characteristically irrelevant regret that Alan Breck could not have brandished a claymore in mortal combat with the Master. But in his considered estimate of 'Mr. Stevenson's Works', in *Essays in Little*, Lang diagnosed 'the obvious weak point' as Secundra Dass, 'the freakish changeling' who 'brought in an element out of keeping with the steady lurid tragedy of fraternal hatred'; this weakness, he thought, prevented the story from being 'completely successful—a victory all along the line'.

'In *The Master of Ballantrae* Mr. Stevenson makes a gallant effort to enter what I have ventured to call the capital of his kingdom,' wrote Lang; 'he does introduce a woman, and confronts the problems of love as well as of fraternal hatred.' Yet failure to depict the conflict between good and evil in Alison Durie, as in *Markheim* and in *Jekyll and Hyde*, is—apart from the introduction of Secundra Dass—the palpable flaw that deters the story from reaching the heights of emotional tragedy. Stevenson himself recognised his failure with the character of this heroine when he wrote, in 1890, that 'I have never pleased myself with any women of mine' except the two minor characters of the Countess in *Prince Otto* and Madame Desprez in *The Treasure of Franchard*. He felt the need for freedom of expression, already noticed by George Moore; contemporary readers would have been outraged if he had shown the inevitable outcome of Alison Durie's passion for her brother-in-law. Accused of 'immorality' in *The Beach of Falesá*, he wrote to Colvin in January 1892: 'This is a poison bad world for the romancer, this Anglo-Saxon world; I usually get out of it by not having any women in it at all; but when I remember I had *The Treasure of Franchard* refused as unfit for a family magazine, I feel despair weigh upon my wrists.' Fanny's influence was always on the side of the angels, as with *The Travelling Companion* and with *Jekyll and Hyde*; there is no evidence of her interference in *The Master of Ballantrae*, but she would certainly have opposed any such indiscretion as a realistic portrayal of Alison Durie's emotions. Since Henley's withdrawal, she was more than ever securely seated in the saddle of criticism. 'Louis is coming round now to my view of his book of travels,' she wrote at this time to Colvin, referring to Stevenson's intention of writing an historical survey of the islands and their inhabitants, while she wanted an anecdotal account of personal travel, suitable for a popular magazine.

In June 1889, leaving Fanny and the others at Honolulu, Stevenson made a twelve days' excursion to the leper settlement of Molokai, where he witnessed the extent of the welfare work achieved by Father Damien, the priest whose character he defended from slander in Australia the following winter. At this time Fanny wrote to Colvin:

'He never has a sign of hæmorrhage, the air cushion is a thing of the past, and altogether he is a new man. How he will do in the English climate again I do not know, but in these latitudes he is very nearly a well man, nothing seems to do him harm but overwork. That, of course, is sometimes difficult to prevent. Now, however, the *Master* is done, we have enough money to go upon and there is no need to work at all.'

Stevenson now hired a trading schooner called the *Equator*, in which he sailed, towards the end of June, for the Gilbert

Islands. His mother had gone home to England the previous month, but Fanny's daughter Belle and her son were included in the party. During a voyage lasting six months, he made two protracted stays on shore—firstly, at Butaritari, and then at Apemama, described at length in Parts III and IV of *In the South Seas*. This book of travel was now planned, and he began two stories in collaboration with Lloyd; *The Pearl Fisher* was 'part done', but as the manuscript was left behind when they touched at Sydney, they began to write *The Wrecker*. 'My good health does not cease to be wonderful to myself,' he wrote; 'Fanny is better in these warm places; it is the very thing for Lloyd; and in the matter of interest, the spice of life, etc., words cannot depict what fun we have.' On arrival at Samoa in December, he had withstood the rigours of the voyage more successfully than the others: 'My wife suffered badly—it was too rough a business altogether—Lloyd suffered—and, in short, I was the only one of the party who "kept my end up".'

At Samoa he fell so much in love with the island and its natives that he 'decided to settle', and soon informed Baxter:

'I have bought 314½ acres of beautiful land in the bush behind Apia; when we get the house built, the garden laid, and cattle in the place, it will be something to fall back on for shelter and food; and if the island could stumble into political quiet, it is conceivable it might even bring a little income. . . . We range from 600 to 1,500 feet have five streams, waterfalls, precipices, profound ravines, rich tablelands, fifty head of cattle on the ground (if any one could catch them), a great view of forest, sea, mountains, the warships in the haven: really a noble place.'

At the time of purchase, he intended to use the place only as a base for further voyages in search of health. But after a voyage by steamer from Samoa, on arrival at Sydney in February 1890, he fell almost immediately ill, suffering a bout of fever and hæmorrhage such as he had not experienced since leaving England. From the Union Club, where he was staying alone while Fanny and the others were lodged at an hotel, he wrote again to Baxter:

'I am sure I shall never come back home except to die; I may do it, but shall always think of the move as suicidal, unless a great change comes over me, of which as yet I see no symptom. This visit to Sydney has smashed me handsomely; and yet I made myself a prisoner here in the club upon my first arrival. This is not encouraging for further ventures; Sydney winter—or, I might almost say, Sydney spring, for I came when the worst was over —is so small an affair, comparable to our June depression at home in Scotland.'

In April, in the steamer *Janet Nicoll*, he departed on a voyage to recover from his illness, and visited New Caledonia. Returning in August, he stayed a month in Sydney while preparations were made for settlement in Samoa, which he announced in a letter to Henry James:

'I must tell you plainly—I can't tell Colvin—I do not think I shall come to England more than once, and then it'll be to die. Health I enjoy in the tropics; even here, which they call sub- or semi-tropics, I come only to catch cold. I have not been out since my arrival; live here in a nice bedroom by the fireside, and read books and letters from Henry James. . . . But I can't go out! The thermometer was nearly down to 50 the other day—no temperature for me, Mr. James: how should I do in England? I fear not at all. Am I very sorry? I am sorry about seven or eight people in England, and one or two in the States. And outside of that, I simply prefer Samoa. . . . I was never fond of towns, houses, society, or (it seems) civilisation. Nor yet it seems was I ever very fond of (what is technically called) God's green earth. The sea, islands, the islanders, the island life and climate, make and keep me truly happier. These last two years I have been much at sea, and I have *never wearied*; sometimes I have indeed grown impatient for some destination; more often I was sorry that the voyage drew so early to an end; and never once did I lose my fidelity to blue water and a ship. It is plain, then, that for me my exile to the place of schooners and islands can be in no sense regarded as a calamity. . . . Even my wife has weakened about the sea. She wearied, the last time we were ashore, to get afloat again.'

The afterthought about Fanny was hardly accurate; she went to Samoa with resignation rather than rejoicing. On arrival in Samoa after a voyage encountering rough seas and much discomfort, she wrote to Mrs. Sitwell:

'Because I make my sacrifice with flowers on my head and point
out the fine views on the way, do not think that it is no sacrifice and
only for my own pleasure. The Samoan people are picturesque, but
I do not like them. . . . My time must be so arranged as not to clash
with them. I shall be able to get no servants but cannibal black
boys. . . . A great part of the housework I shall have to do myself,
and most of the cooking. The land *must* produce food enough for us
all, or we shall have nothing to eat. I must also manage that. Oh it
makes me tired to speak of it; and I never feel well, then. I don't
want to complain. I am not complaining, really, only telling
you. . . . I do want Louis, and I do want everybody to think I
like going to Samoa—and in some ways I do like it; I don't want
people to think I am making a sacrifice for Louis. In fact I *can't*
make a sacrifice for him; the very fact that I can do the thing in a
way makes a pleasure to do it, and it is no longer a sacrifice, though
if I did it for another person it would be.'

Her letter ended with a remark of cryptic relevance, 'I understand you better than you understand me'. Fanny was one of
those women who always understood others better than they
understood her; Stevenson must have become irritably accustomed to the assertion as inevitable in every marital discussion.
With a feminine instinct for self-dramatisation, she lacked generosity and the delicacy of refinement; she could never bestow
a kindness without emphasising its impulse as a virtue in herself, she could not realise that the kindness seemed grudging
when given under such protest, and if anybody evinced resentment at her manner of giving, she felt aggrieved at their want
of appreciation.

Stevenson was loyal in preserving inviolable the privacy of
his domestic life. Colvin and Balfour subscribed obediently to
Fanny's self-portrait as an uncomplaining wife dedicated in
selfless devotion to an invalid of genius. None of Stevenson's
biographers have drawn attention to the fact that, throughout
the years of her marriage to Stevenson, Fanny rarely, if ever,
confessed to feeling well in health. It was left to her son to
reveal that his mother was a hypochondriac. Passages suppressed by Colvin in Stevenson's letters to Henley afforded
indications of her various ailments. When she was said to be
suffering from 'drain poisoning' at Davos in November 1881,

it was discovered at Berne that she had passed a gallstone, and the doctor, 'very glum', suspected ulceration of the bowels. Reference to 'pain' with 'bloody stool' suggests haemorrhoids. A suppressed passage in a partially published letter to Henley from San Francisco in February 1880 suggests more serious affliction: 'Fanny is so much better, so almost quite well—in spite of another fit; I count these damned fits like coffin nails—that my heart is very light.' If Fanny was an epileptic, her morbid temperament had ample justification, and the obvious reason emerges to explain why Stevenson's own health became so much more infirm after his marriage. Recovery from tubercular tendency would be hopelessly hindered by the nervous strain of anxiously watching for symptoms indicating the imminence of epileptic attacks.

Whatever the justification for her moods, Stevenson's married life was undoubtedly shadowed by his wife's querulous temper and morbid habit of mind. At this time, too, her insistent interference with his work caused acerbity in argument. Some three months after their settlement at Samoa in October 1890, Stevenson went by steamer to Sydney to meet his mother and Lloyd Osbourne, who had travelled out together from England. Fanny remained behind, because 'I was not well enough to stand the knocking about of the ship'; she had 'been very ill since Louis went', though 'of course he doesn't know that', and it had been 'a little alarming to find my head going wrong in the middle of the night, and no one on the premises but an imbecile drunken German man'. Supposing that Lloyd, during his visit to England, had informed Mrs. Sitwell of 'my desperate engagements with the man of genius over the South Sea book', she continued:

'He holds a most vexing theory at present. I plunged into the work of the plantation with so much interest that he says I have the true peasant nature, and lack the artistic temperament; thereupon my advice on artistic matters, such as a book on the South Seas, must be received with extreme caution. He says I do not take the broad view of an artist, but hold the cheap opinions of the general public that a book must be interesting. How I do long for a little wholesome monumental correction to be applied to the Scotch side of Louis's artistic temperament.'

When Stevenson continued to resist her demands for an entertaining book of gossip, she threatened: 'I'll gather together all
my letters, and publish them.'

Presumably Stevenson was undisturbed by this threat, since
he knew that Fanny was incapable of assembling a book without his assistance, but he allowed her arguments to overweigh
his determination of writing a purely historical account of the
islands and their inhabitants, with the result that *In the South
Seas* proved too superficial for acceptance as an authoritative
study, yet too sophisticated for success as a magazine serial.
On the eve of its serial appearance in *Black and White*, Gosse
recorded in January 1891 'a good deal of disappointment
among the few who have read the approaching *South Sea
Letters*'. As he also remarked that 'we are all disappointed here'
with the volume of *Ballads*, published by Chatto and Windus
in 1890, Gosse thought, 'The fact seems to be that it is very
nice to *live* in Samoa, but not healthy to *write* there', inspiring
the complacent conclusion, as Gosse was living in Delamere
Terrace, that 'within a three-mile radius of Charing Cross is the
literary atmosphere, I suspect'. 'Between you and me and
Lake Michigan,' confided Gosse to a receptacle of his great
thoughts, 'the versification is atrocious.' He deplored 'the
effort to become a Polynesian Walter Scott', and when Stevenson invited his opinion on the *Ballads*, he did not reply. He
professed that he had not received Stevenson's letter, though it
duly appeared when Colvin came to edit the correspondence.
Evidently Gosse regarded Stevenson as a waning flame; he was
watching with interest the rising star of another of Henley's
young men, Rudyard Kipling, and felt disinclined to waste
time and paper upon a man he was never likely to meet again.

There was some reason for suspecting that Stevenson was a
spent force, for he had published no fiction since *The Master of
Ballantrae*. In an effort to account for his inactivity, he had
listed in a letter of the previous autumn, as work of which he
was contemplating completion, all the stories he had begun and
laid aside, including, besides *The Wrecker* and *The Pearl Fisher*,
The Great North Road of five years before. 'Since *The Master*
nothing has come to raise any coins,' he noted in December
1890, and oppressed by the need of money to meet the expenses

of his estate, called Vailima, he drove himself to work on *The Wrecker*.

Sydney again proved prejudicial to his health; he suffered 'a smoking hot little malady' there before returning with his mother to Samoa in February 1891. On the boat he planned a new romance, incorporating two ideas of years before; it was 'to be told in the third person, with some of the brevity of history, some of the detail of romance', and to be called *The Shovels of Newton French*. But at the end of April he was 'out of condition still, and can do nothing, and toil to be at my pen'. During the previous year he had completed the first of his South Sea stories, *The Bottle Imp*, published in two numbers of *Black and White* of 28th March and 4th April 1891; he now worked on another, at first called *The High Woods of Ulufanua*, a title changed to *The Beach of Falesá*. The writing of this—the best of his 'novelettes' after *Jekyll and Hyde*—occupied most of the summer months, and the need for finishing *The Wrecker* became imperative when it began as a serial in *Scribner's* of August 1891. In October he was 'trying to write the last four chapters of *The Wrecker*', while announcing that '*David Balfour*, second part of *Kidnapped*, is on the stocks at last'. *The Wrecker*, which he described as 'a violent, dark yarn with interesting, plain turns of human nature', was finally finished in the middle of November; *The Beach of Falesá* had been already dispatched to McClure, and to Colvin's dismay Stevenson announced that he was now writing an account of the Samoan political troubles, published by Cassell's in 1892 as *A Footnote to History*.

To Colvin, Baxter, Henry James, and others, he wrote detailed accounts of his occupations, and the patient Colvin had already ventured a protest against his preoccupations with the parochial interests of the islanders. Stevenson asked Colvin to 'remember that my life passes among my "blacks or chocolates"', and to 'put yourself, perhaps with an effort, into some sort of sympathy with these people, or how am I to write to you?' His situation appealed to his romantic imagination; seeing himself as a Robinson Crusoe—or, rather, as a Fletcher Christian of Pitcairn—he recognised the value of literary talent in such a situation. Books like Captain Cook's *Voyages* and

Bligh's memoirs of the mutiny in the *Bounty* survived by reason of their documentary value; such a work by a professional writer must surely rank as unique in literature. Deciding early in his residence at Vailima 'to send a long letter every month to Colvin', he intended the letters to form a journal and eventually a book for publication. Published after his death as *Vailima Letters*, the book possesses precisely the same curious interest as the journal of any other exile or explorer; it has a documentary value, but none of the attractions of a work of art, such as he might have achieved by writing up his notes with a narrative design.

Conscience compelled an active interest in the wrongs of the natives with whom he lived; his concern with their affairs awakened in him that instinct to legislate and govern which has rendered the British the greatest race of empire-builders since the Romans. As the principal white resident in Samoa, he became virtually the ruler of the island; by sympathy and understanding he acquired such dominance over the islanders that he wielded the authority of a patriarchal chieftain of a Highland clan. Known to the natives as Tusitala, the teller of tales, he was credited with almost supernatural powers, and won love and reverence as their protector and prophet by championing their grievances against the corrupt practices of the governing whites. His friends at home deplored his obsession with local politics as a prodigal waste of his talents, and certainly such a work as *A Footnote to History*—relating the abuses and grievances of the Samoans during recent years as a plea to the great powers for better conditions of administration—might well have been entrusted to a special commissioner of the colonial service. Fanny, indeed, socially ambitious, hoped that her husband might be made consul. In these occupations Stevenson found satisfaction through a sense of achievement active and practical; after finishing the sequel to *Kidnapped*, in the last year of his life he wrote to W. H. Low:

'I think *David Balfour* a nice little book, and very artistic, and just the thing to occupy the leisure of a busy man; but for the top flower of a man's life it seems to me inadequate. Small is the word; it is a small age, and I am of it. I could have wished to be other-

wise busy in this world. I ought to have been able to build lighthouses and write *David Balfours* too. . . . We take all these pains,
and we don't do as well as Michael Angelo or Leonardo, or even
Fielding, who was an active magistrate, or Richardson, who was a
busy bookseller.'

This was the grumble of a man doomed to sedentary occupation and demanding a life of activity. The Bohemian of Barbizon would have desired no such distraction from the pursuit
of art as the business routine of magistrate or bookseller.
Jekyll was still seeking to escape into the character of Hyde,
but, after a sweet taste of freedom in the two years of sea voyages,
Stevenson found himself even more completely sequestered at
Samoa than at Bournemouth. Fanny was not to be tempted
into further cruises, and devoted herself ardently to managing
the estate. In a letter to J. M. Barrie, jocularly listing the
characters of his household, Stevenson described her personality
as 'the weird woman', Tamaitai:

'If you don't get on with her, it's a pity about your visit. She
runs the show. . . . In company manners presents the appearance
of a little timid and precise old maid of the days of prunes and
prism—you look for the reticule. Hellish energy. . . . Can make
anything from a house to a row, all fine and large of their kind. . . .
Doctors everybody, will doctor you, cannot be doctored herself.
. . . A violent friend, a brimstone enemy. . . . Is always either
loathed or slavishly adored.'

While Fanny managed and developed the estate, Stevenson
had to pay for the development; the magnitude of his expenses
provided a constant reminder that he must work. 'Byles the
butcher' knocked on the door as loudly as ever, and with no
such idleness as was enforced by illness at Bournemouth,
Stevenson drove himself to write harder and harder.

Before finishing *A Footnote to History* in May 1892, he was
working on the sequel to *Kidnapped*, *David Balfour*, and planning
another novel called *Sophia Scarlet*, which was to be ' a *regular
novel*; heroine and hero, and false accusation, and love, and
marriage, and all the rest of it—all planted in a big South Sea
plantation run by ex-English officers'. There were 'three

women to handle', and perhaps the difficulty of handling them with decorum decided the laying aside of this novel in favour of a romance of the '45 rebellion called *The Young Chevalier*, an idea suggested by Andrew Lang. Of *The Young Chevalier*, a prologue and part of the first chapter survive; the Master of Ballantrae reappears in the story, which may have been rejected in its turn because Fanny felt disfavour for the emotions of the wine-seller's wife on surveying Ballantrae's handsome companion. With *David Balfour* he persevered; it was finished by the beginning of November 1892.

If Gosse, with the publication in 1890 of *Ballads* and *In the South Seas*, considered Stevenson a spent force, his impression was corrected by the reception of his publications in 1892 and 1893. The *Scribner's* essays of 1888 were published in book form during 1892 by Chatto and Windus as *Across the Plains*; they received uniformly handsome reviews, and Richard Le Gallienne asserted that 'Mr. Stevenson's final fame will be that of an essayist, nearest and dearest fame of the prose writer'. *The Wrecker* followed from Cassell's; it enjoyed equal success as a serial and as a book, for, as Andrew Lang said, 'it is a magnificent yarn' and 'a splendid novel for a magazine, because one was always panting after the secret, as in the old days of Wilkie Collins'. *The Wrecker* appeared over the joint signatures of Robert Louis Stevenson and Lloyd Osbourne; praising it as a successful effort in a new field, the 'blend of the novel of manners and the pure "adventure" romance', Le Gallienne shrewdly suspected that, while his collaborator had worked on the plot and 'thrown in out-of-the-way experience of ships and shipmen', Stevenson had 'done all the writing'. Lloyd Osbourne stated that *The Wrong Box*, which Stevenson entirely rewrote from his stepson's rough draft, 'was more mine as a whole than either *The Wrecker* or *The Ebb-Tide*', and Stevenson informed his cousin Bob of *The Wrecker*, 'as for the manner, it is superficially all mine, in the sense that the last copy is all in my hand. Lloyd did not even put pen to paper in the Paris scenes or the Barbizon scene . . . I had the best service from him on the character of Nares'.

Unlike *The Wrecker*, *David Balfour* was not a success as a serial, and though the title was retained in America, Cassell's published the book in England as *Catriona*. It was one of the successes of the year, for the same reason as Le Gallienne praised *The Wrecker*; by blending the novel of manners with the adventure romance, Stevenson captured the whole fiction-reading public, being 'light' enough to appeal to the masses demanding merely entertainment, while the play on character and skill in construction satisfied the fastidious. Henry James could not 'repress the enthusiasm that has surged within me ever since I read *Catriona*'; 'if it hadn't been for Catriona', he thought, 'we couldn't, this year, have held up our head', for 'we grow systematically vulgarer and baser'. He spoke of 'how rare an achievement I think the whole personality and tone of David and with how supremely happy a hand you have coloured the palpable women'. Lang, too, though he protested that 'more claymores, less psychology suit a simple taste' and 'one wants more of Alan Breck and less of the hero's conflicts in conscience', declared that 'Mr. Stevenson has drawn a good petticoat at last'. Yet, only less than in the case of Alison Durie, Stevenson displays discomfort in observing the demands of decorum with the character of Catriona; in the chapters where David shares lodgings with Catriona; it is only at the expense of causing his hero to come close to seeming a zany that the author succeeds in traversing a tightrope across the chasm of impropriety.

Henry James was also enthusiastic about *The Beach of Falesá*: 'the art of *The Beach of Falesá* seems to me an art brought to a perfection and I delight in the observed truth, the modesty of nature, of the narrator'. Serially *The Beach of Falesá* appeared in the *Illustrated London News* between 2nd July and 6th August 1892 in a truncated form as *Uma*; the editor objected to the fraudulent marriage ceremony by which Uma becomes Wilt-shire's wife, and Stevenson refused to comply with a 'plaintive request' that he should 'make the young folks married properly before "that night"'. With justice he thought highly of this story, and wished it to appear alone in a small volume like *Jekyll and Hyde*; as the publishers considered its length too short, he reluctantly consented to its inclusion with *The Bottle Imp* and *The Isle of Voices* in *Island Nights' Entertainments*, published by Cassell's at six shillings in April 1893. He wanted to include a fourth story, *The Waif Woman*, which he described as 'a cue from a saga', but 'my wife protests against the Waif-woman', he told Colvin; the story was eventually published only after Fanny's death, and it is interesting to speculate on the morbid impulse inspiring Fanny's objection to this moral tale of a wife's possessive avarice punished by fate.

Fanny's criticism undoubtedly reflected faithfully the crude taste of Victorian prudery, but knowing her point of view to be false, Stevenson was increasingly oppressed by a sense of frustration in approaching his work. With Henry James he shared the opinion that the stuff of fiction came from play of character upon character, and fear of offending prim convention prohibited truth in portrayal of women.

In January 1893 he fell a victim to an epidemic of influenza afflicting the islands, and he had a slight bout of 'Bluidy Jack'. But the hæmorrhage, quickly over, did not recur, and his convalescence was brief and unattended by the complications familiar at Bournemouth. As he recovered, he began a new historical romance, *St. Ives*, dictating the story to his stepdaughter, Belle Strong; when he was well, he continued the successful experiment of dictation, as a means of relief from 'scrivener's cramp'. The idea of *St. Ives* was suggested by his reading *A Gentleman of France*, by Stanley J. Weyman, then running serially in *Longman's Magazine*; he waited so eagerly for the magazine instalments that, on one occasion at the Apia post office, he settled in the postmaster's room on collecting his mail, 'had a bottle of beer in', and read with 'the most exquisite pleasure' 'a real chivalrous yarn, like the Dumas' and yet unlike'. The adventures of the escaped prisoner of war in *St. Ives*, hunted by scheming foes, follow swiftly in the same manner as those befalling Weyman's hero; the writing of the story was 'like a school-treat to me' after working on the more ambitious scheme of *The Justice-Clerk*, which he had begun in the previous November after finishing *David Balfour*.

The Justice-Clerk was the beginning of *Weir of Hermiston*, the masterpiece left unfinished at his death. The germ of the story came from this study of 'the hanging judge', Robert Mac-Queen, Lord Braxfield (1722–99), in whose character he became interested years before when writing the essay, 'Some

Portraits by Raeburn'. Already he had made use of the subject by writing, in collaboration with Fanny, a play called *The Hanging Judge*. Fanny shared Henley's faith in plays as a likely medium for profit; from Pitlochry in 1881 she wrote to Henley as 'My dear Friend', 'Do pray keep your eagle eye fixed upon the stage where I am convinced a gold mine shows outcroppings that you and Louis may work to your very great advantage'; after Henley's last collaboration with Stevenson on *Macaire*, she evidently desired to show that she could perform the part of collaborator as well as Henley, and *The Hanging Judge* was completed at Saranac, though neither printed nor performed. Stevenson addressed to Charles Baxter repeated requests for books and documents of legal and political history; he also wanted 'anything about fashions and manners (fashions particularly) for 1814', as 'both the *Justice-Clerk* and *St. Ives* fall in that fated year'. Of *The Justice-Clerk* he told Baxter:

'It is pretty Scotch, the Grand Premier is taken from Braxfield— (Oh, by the by, send me Cockburn's *Memorials*)—and some of the story is—well—queer. The heroine is seduced by one man, and finally disappears with the other man who shot him. . . . Mind you, I expect *The Justice-Clerk* to be my masterpiece. My Braxfield is already a thing of beauty and a joy for ever, and so far as he has gone, *far* my best character.'

To J. M. Barrie, on finishing *David Balfour*, he wrote:

'It is a singular thing that I should live here in the South Seas under conditions so new and so striking, and yet my imagination so continually inhabit that cold old huddle of grey hills from which we come. I have just finished *David Balfour*; I have another book on the stocks, *The Young Chevalier*, which is to be part in France and part in Scotland, and to deal with Prince Charlie about the year 1749; and now what have I done but begun a third which is to be all moorland together, and is to have for a centre-piece a figure that I think you will appreciate—that of the immortal Braxfield.'

Commenting that 'no writer writes best about his background when he is in it'—a statement which seems a corollary for prose fiction on Wordsworth's theory that poetry should be concerned with emotions recollected in tranquillity—Mr.

Compton Mackenzie reflects on 'what a series of South Seas masterpieces we might have had' if Stevenson had lived to return to his native Scotland.

While assimilating the material for the historical background of *The Justice-Clerk* and *St. Ives*, he wrote one more story of the South Seas. Consciousness of the need for earning money turned his attention to a task that could be finished more quickly than the novels involving reading for background, and he took up 'a most grim and gloomy tale', which was 'the butt end of what was once *The Pearl Fisher*'. The beginning of the story seems to have derived from yet another plan, devised at the same time as *The Wrecker* and *The Pearl Fisher*, called *The Beachcombers*; starting to work on it in February 1893, Stevenson called it *The Schooner Farallone*, but the title was changed to *The Ebb-Tide* after he had written in Chapter VIII of the beachcomber Herrick:

'He had complied with the ebb-tide in man's affairs, and the tide had carried him away; he heard already the roaring of the maelstrom that must hurry him under. And in his bedevilled and dishonoured soul there was no thought of self.'

Another reason for working on *The Ebb-Tide* appears in a letter to Baxter, telling him that 'you can prepare to dispose of the serial rights of *The Schooner Farallone*':

'There is a peculiarity about this tale in its new form: it ends with a conversion! . . . It would make a boss tract; the three main characters—and there are only four—are barats, insurance frauds, thieves, and would-be murderers; so the company's good. Devil a woman there, by good luck; so it's "pure".'

The difficulty of writing about women was a continual deterrent to his more ambitious plans; Fanny can have hardly approved of the fate intended for the younger Kirstie in *Weir of Hermiston*.

At the end of April 1893 he was 'grinding singly at *The Ebb-Tide*, as we now call the *Farallone*', and drove himself to the conclusion in a few weeks. He wished it to be published in the *Illustrated London News*, with illustrations by Gordon Browne, who had illustrated *Uma*, but *The Ebb-Tide* eventually appeared

serially in a weekly periodical called *To-Day* between 11th
November 1893 and 3rd February following. *The Ebb-Tide*
ends abruptly, and Stevenson realised it: 'I know I ought to
re-write the end of this bloody *Ebb-Tide*: well, I can't. *C'est
plus fort que moi*; it has to go the way it is, and be jowned to it!'

Finding himself unable to resume *St. Ives* or *Weir of Hermiston*,
he decided to 'take a go at the family history', meaning
Records of a Family of Engineers, another work left unfinished.

'I think that will be wise, as I am so much off work. And then, I
suppose, *Weir of Hermiston*, but it may be anything. I am discontented
with *The Ebb-Tide*, naturally; there seems such a veil of words over
it; and I like more and more naked writing; and yet sometimes
one has a longing for full colour and there comes the veil again.
The Young Chevalier is in very full colour, and I fear it for that
reason.'

In another letter, describing *The Ebb-Tide* as 'a dreadful,
grimy business in the third person, where the strain between
a vilely realistic dialogue and a narrative style pitched about
(in phrase) "four notes higher" than it should have been, has
sown my head with grey hairs,' he wrote: 'The truth is, I have
a little lost my way, and stand bemused at the cross-roads.'

Sorely he needed such encouraging reassurance as he had
been accustomed to receive in the past from Henley. In the
quality of his work there was no cause for despondence; the
description of Herrick's attempted suicide in Chapter X of
The Ebb-Tide might have sufficed alone as evidence of his
mounting powers in portraying the psychology of emotion.
Since 1887 his earnings had been 'at the rate of £4,000 a year
or thereabouts', yet he continued to worry about money as
in the days of 'Byles the butcher'. If his faculty was declining,
if he had worked himself out, if—a possibility of which he was
continually reminded by Fanny's criticism—he lost his public
by striking an unpopular vein, his income might rapidly
dwindle or disappear. News of his popularity in England and
America was heartening; when he paid a visit to Sydney, he
found his fame 'much grown', and felt it 'very queer' how
'people all looked at me in the streets'. But such encouraging

signs afforded no solace for his inward misgivings; he needed an assurance that he might dare to write as he felt impelled.

In his ever enormously increasing correspondence, he received congratulatory letters from many writers of distinction, and with many he encouraged an exchange of opinions, in the evident hope of deriving some consolatory stimulus from fellow-artists. He corresponded with Kipling ('by far the most promising young man who has appeared since—ahem—I appeared'), with Conan Doyle, S. R. Crockett, W. B. Yeats, and—though Barrie had written a disparaging article on his work in *An Edinburgh Eleven*—with J. M. Barrie. Hopefully he invited Doyle and Barrie to make a voyage to Samoa; he hungered for visitors, and only occasionally some came—the historian and autobiographer, Henry Adams, with the American artist, John Lafarge, in 1890; Graham Balfour (his biographer) and Lady Jersey in 1892, as well as Count Nerli, who painted his portrait; a young Irish writer, Sidney Lysaght, in the winter months of 1893–94. John Galsworthy and his friend, E. L. Sanderson, started out to visit Samoa in 1893, but, recalled to England, returned from Australia on the boat carrying Joseph Conrad as its mate. One of Stevenson's few intimates among the white population of the islands was the land commissioner, Bazett Haggard, a brother of the novelist, Rider Haggard.

Further distraction from work was caused by an outbreak of strife among the Samoans, such as Stevenson had vainly striven to avoid. Much occupied with native affairs during the summer months, when he resumed work in the autumn, he resorted to desultory dictation of *St. Ives*. Still unable to concentrate on *Weir of Hermiston*, he planned yet another new novel in December, *Heathercat*, which he described to his cousin Bob as 'an attempt at a real historical novel, to present a whole field of time; the race—our own race—the west land and Clydesdale blue bonnets, under the influence of their last trial, when they got to a pitch of organisation in madness that no other peasantry has ever made an offer at'. Nearly three chapters of *Heathercat* survive, revealing a level of writing comparable with *Weir of Hermiston*, but doubtless Fanny disapproved the 'daffing' and 'meddling' with the 'big lass',

Janet M'Clour, and the three chapters went into a drawer with *The Young Chevalier*.

An apprentice before the mast of a clipper on the run to Australia, A. Safroni-Middleton, discovered evidence that 'there were *two* Robert Louis Stevensons, one a soberside prematurely ageing man writing books, the other a lank-haired, boyish haggard being, who seemed to be ever wandering by night like a lost soul seeking to find its real self'. He found that Stevenson 'loved to play truant by night, and entering Apia's saloon bar, listen to the wild and wonderful reminiscences of the sunburnt bluffers'. Wearing 'dirty white shoes, and a threadbare peaked cap', with 'his lank hair, face longish, and the absurd moustache', he had the look of 'a disillusioned schoolmaster "gone native".' Discovering that the ship's apprentice was an accomplished violinist, Stevenson invited him to Vailima, but the visit 'was not bright and cheery'.

'R.L.S. at home and subjected to the domestic restraint of his faithful guardian wife, and surrounded by Samoan servants, seemed a strangely humbled man. His expressive eyes seemed to hold the light of tragedy. Notwithstanding the spacious comfort of his apartments, well furnished, good wine, and assiduous attention of those he loved, an atmosphere of gloom prevailed.'[1]

When, at Stevenson's request, he played on his violin 'several Scotch melodies', Safroni-Middleton realised that 'both he and his wife suffered from homesickness', and 'it was even something of a relief when the pretty native maids smiled'.

In health he was little troubled by the old disease. His lungs were 'pretty right', but his 'stomach nowhere'; he despised himself as 'a white-livered puppy' for giving up drinking and smoking, and did 'not like to think of a life without the red wine on the table and the tobacco with its lovely little coal of fire'. When he again resumed work on *St. Ives*—which was completed after his death by Sir Arthur Quiller-Couch—he despised it as 'in no style in particular, a tissue of adventures, the central character not very well done, no philosophic pith

[1] From A. Safroni-Middleton's autobiography, *In the Green Leaf*, quoted in a paper, 'With R.L.S. in Old Samoa', included in the *Journal of the Robert Louis Stevenson Club (London)*, May 1950.

under the yarn'. He felt that he would 'never do a better book than *Catriona*'; that was his 'high-water mark'.

'I begin to grow old; I have given my top note, I fancy;—and I have written too many books. The world begins to grow weary of the old booth; and if not weary, familiar with the familiarity that breeds contempt. . . . The little, artificial popularity of style in England tends, I think, to die out; the British pig returns to his true love, the love of the styleless, of the shapeless, of the slapdash and the disorderly. There is trouble coming, I think. . . .'

When Charles Baxter proposed the project of the Edinburgh Edition of his collected works, Stevenson was at first 'particularly pleased . . . because I am come to a dead stop'. Having drafted a preface for *The Master of Ballantrae*, he promised to do so for other volumes, but '*Prince Otto* I don't think I could say anything about, and *Black Arrow* don't want to'. If he had known how completely the edition was to succeed, he might have felt less depression at his inability to work. Like Thackeray, he was haunted by the urge to work, in order to secure a competence for his dependants. In September, 'trying hard to get along with *St. Ives*', he told Colvin:

'I should now lay it aside for a year and I daresay I should make something of it after all. Instead of that, I have to kick against the pricks, and break myself, and spoil the book, if there were anything to spoil.'

Colvin emphasised that he vented his depression only in correspondence; to Fanny he confided none of his worries about his work, and 'to those about him, whether visitors or inmates, he remained the impersonation of life and spirit, maintaining to the last the same gaiety as ever, the same happy eagerness in all pursuits and interests'.

The suddenness of his end was thus the more shocking to his household. In October 1894 he laid aside the unsatisfactory *St. Ives*, and attacked *Weir of Hermiston* in a burst of creative energy. Throughout November he worked exultantly, enjoying 'a consciousness of perfect command over his subject and his means'. On Monday 3rd December he wrote hard at *Hermiston* all the morning; during the afternoon he wrote letters; in one he wrote: 'I am at present engaged in treating a severe case of middle age in one of my stories, *The Justice-Clerk*. The case is that of a woman, and I think that I am doing her justice.' At sunset he came down, full of spirits, to help Fanny in preparing supper:

'he was helping his wife on the verandah, and gaily talking, when suddenly he put both hands to his head and cried out, "What's that?" Then he asked quickly, "Do I look strange?" Even as he did so he fell on his knees beside her'.

He never spoke again, and died the same evening. The medical verdict was apoplexy, followed by paralysis of the lungs. After twenty years in dread of tubercular disease, it was ironical that he should have died from the strain of overwork.

INDEX

Index

Index